Visual Sociology

Visual sociology has been part of the sociological vocabulary since the 1970s, but until now there has not been a comprehensive text that introduces this area. Written by one of the founding fathers in the field, *Visual Sociology* explores how the world that is seen, photographed, drawn or otherwise represented visually is different from the world that is represented through words and numbers.

Douglas Harper's exceptional photography and engaging, lively writing style will introduce:

- visual sociology as embodied observation;
- visual sociology as semiotics;
- visual sociology as an approach to data: empirical, narrative, phenomenological and reflexive;
- visual sociology as an aspect of photo documentary;
- visual sociology and multimedia.

This definitive textbook is made up of eleven chapters on the key topics in visual sociology. With teaching and learning guidance, as well as clear, accessible explanations of current thinking in the field, this book will be an invaluable resource to all those with an interest in visual sociology, research methods, cultural geography, cultural theory or visual anthropology.

Douglas Harper is Professor of Sociology at Duquesne University. He has published five books with the University of Chicago Press, which include innovative uses of photography as well as other qualitative methods. Harper has also edited or co-edited four books on visual sociology. He is the founding editor of *Visual Studies*, the official journal of the International Visual Sociology Association. He has published more than fifty chapters, articles and photo essays, and has been invited by more than 100 universities and academic societies in the US and abroad to lecture on qualitative methods and visual sociology.

"The discipline of sociology owes (and will continue to owe for years to come) an immense debt to (the work of) Douglas Harper whose contributions to visual sociology have culminated in the (kind of) guide and guidance that this book provides. He has always been interested in the power of visual representation, not only in what is seen and less seen but also in who sees and who needs to see more. As a world-class ethnographer, Harper understands by intellect and experience how sociology (has been and) can be further enriched by the act of seeing. It does require at least one eye to see, but it should never be underestimated how much Harper's commitment to improving the sociological vision arises from his heartfelt dedication to truth, beauty, and human dignity."
—*Jonathan B. Imber, Wellesley College; Editor-in-Chief of* Society

"Harper's book—comprehensive, imaginative, interesting—contains everything someone who wants to use visual imagery to understand society could want. Its clear, penetrating prose, carefully chosen photographs and profound understanding of the issues involved, show readers how to understand visual sociology and how to do it themselves."
—*Howard S. Becker*

"With a deep knowledge of the documentary tradition and a passion for the visual, Doug Harper's *Visual Sociology* beautifully demonstrates how photography and film provide a distinctive way of understanding and representing the many changing cultures of the everyday. Many talk and write about the relevance of the visual in understanding the human condition, but Doug Harper takes the most comprehensive and deep approach yet, giving us what will clearly become the defining text on the distinctive power of visual representations of culture, the opportunities of the visual in teaching and learning, and the profound lessons embedded in photographs. Harper's eloquence and wisdom grows out of his own work as a photographer, fieldworker, and scholar. *Visual Sociology* is the result of years of looking, thinking, and careful study. For years to come Harper's work will resonate with readers and teachers in many disciplines, and will be used by many with diverse interests and perspectives. It's a brilliant work."
—*Thomas S. Rankin, Director of the Center for Documentary Studies, Duke University*

Visual Sociology

Douglas Harper

Routledge
Taylor & Francis Group

LONDON AND NEW YORK

First published 2012
by Routledge
2 Park Square, Milton Park, Abingdon, Oxon OX14 4RN

Simultaneously published in the USA and Canada
by Routledge
711 Third Avenue, New York, NY 10017

Routledge is an imprint of the Taylor & Francis Group, an informa business

British Library Cataloguing in Publication Data
A catalogue record for this book is available from the British Library

Library of Congress Cataloging in Publication Data
Harper, Douglas A.
  Visual sociology/Douglas Harper.
  p. cm.
  Includes bibliographical references and index.
  1. Visual sociology.   I. Title.
  HM500.H37 2012
  301 – dc23   2012000150

ISBN: 978-0-415-77895-4 (hbk)
ISBN: 978-0-415-77896-1 (pbk)
ISBN: 978-0-203-87267-3 (ebk)

Typeset in Univers by
Florence Production Ltd, Stoodleigh, Devon

Printed and bound in Great Britain by
TJ International Ltd, Padstow, Cornwall

For Colter Jesse Harper, who sees interesting things

Contents

Figures

Tables

Acknowledgments

My deep thanks to the IVSA, my intellectual family for my whole career. Their collective work is the basis of the book, as will be easy to see. Strong thanks to my mentors, Howie Becker and Bruce Jackson. My thanks to my wife, Suzan, who has been a big part of many of these projects. Her drawings of Willie's shop were important to that study and are important also to this one. G. Igor Schaffner produced an intensive, comprehensive and savagely useful edit of the nearly completed manuscript, as he has done for most of my books. Thanks Igor! At times like this, publishing a book that draws on my whole career, I'm drawn to remember great teachers, friends and mentors who helped me develop the visual approach and who have passed on. They are Tim Asch, Everett Hughes, Jim Spradley and Tom Lyson.

I've had the opportunity to work on these ideas with friends and colleagues in many corners of the globe. In Holland they include Rob Boonzajer Flaes, Ton Guiking, Marije van Mierlo, Jasimijn Antonisse, Patricia Van der Does, Sonja Edelaar and Imke Gooskens. In Italy they include Patrizia Faccioli, Pino Losacco, Marina Ciampi, Francesco Mattioli, Alick McLean and Piergiorgio Degli Esposti. In the UK, important colleagues have been Caroline Knowles, Elizabeth Chaplin and Jon Prosser. Yannis Scarpolis has had that role in Greece, as have several others in Germany, Iceland, Sweden, Russia and France.

For thirteen years I edited the journal *Visual Sociology*, and I could not have done that without Jon Rieger, who singlehandedly managed the business of the IVSA for almost two decades. Now that the IVSA is all grown up, these precarious times seem like ancient history, but they are history none-the-less.

Special thanks to Jon Imber at Wellesley, Les Black at Goldsmiths, Elijah Anderson at Yale, Francesco Erspamer at Harvard, Francesco Mattioli at the University of Rome, Gil Gillespie at Cornell, Hubert Knoblach at the Technical University in Berlin, Mitch Duneier at NYU, Ricabeth Steiger of the Swiss National Museum in Zurich, Michael Schwalbe at North Carolina State, Linda Burton at Duke, Heather Sullivan-Caitlin at SUNY Potsdam, Greg Scott at DePaul, Oleg Pachenkov, Lilia Voron and Oksana Zaporozhets at several universities in Russia, and others who have invited me to lecture, teach workshops, meet with graduate students and in general to spread the message of visual sociology.

I have always learned from my students and there have been many over the decades I've taught visual sociology at SUNY Potsdam, the University of South Florida, Duquesne University, the University of Bologna, the University of Amsterdam and at workshops at many of the IVSA meetings. My current collaboration with Maggie Patterson at Duquesne has led to our student-based film collective, and our first documentary is underway. My current teacher, John Cantine at Pittsburgh Filmmakers, has guided me gently back into studenthood and John Caldwell has steered me though the labyrinths of digital processing.

There have been photographers who have inspired throughout my career. They include Ricabeth Steiger, Bruce Jackson, Mark Maio, Dianne Hagaman, Chuck Suchar, Steve Gold, Russ Chabot, Colter Harper and several others of those listed above.

A small number of inspired editors have been critical for visual sociology, committing to projects that were outside the mainstream, and often had very little precedent. Those editors have been Doug Mitchell at Chicago, a magnificent seer, editor and friend; Janet Francendese at Temple, who sponsored a series on visual studies of society and culture and continues to publish excellent visual studies, Fran Gamwell at Cornell, who publishes one creatively visual project after another. At Routledge I thank Gerhard Boomgaarden for his interest when we first discussed this project several years ago and his extraordinary patience and support throughout its long gestation. Editorial assistants Jennifer Dodd and Emily Briggs have been a joy to work with; patient, competent and efficient.

Finally, Dean Jim Swindal and Provost Ralph Pearson at Duquesne University, my intellectual home for the past nearly twenty years, supported this project in concrete and meaningful ways. I thank them deeply. In my own department, my colleague and friend Chuck Hanna has read parts of the book, encouraged me, and always been a source of good ideas.

It's clearly impossible to thank everyone, so I'll just draw this to a close. It's been a good ride; a million images later, and it's not over yet.

Introduction

When I was twenty years old, at the height of the Vietnam War, I traveled to India to study philosophy. It only took a few hours in the chaos of Bombay to realize that just getting through the next seven months would take everything I could muster. I was overwhelmed by it all: the sounds, smells, the crowded universe of touch, but most of all by the world pouring into my eyes. Philosophy would have to wait.

My father had lent me his treasured World War Two vintage Argus C3, but it met an unhappy end on my second day in Bombay. After a few weeks of being camera-less I implored my parents to empty the family coffers so I could buy a Nikon F from two travelers I'd met who needed cash to get home. The money was wired, the camera purchased, and I still remember holding the camera in my hands for the first time, bringing it to my eye and releasing the shutter. There was a feeling of seeing being made concrete; having something left over from the reality passing by. Maybe in this way I could manage India.

I returned to the States with a new interest—photography—and a new major in anthropology, which eventually led to a Ph.D. in sociology. During that period Howie Becker wrote what became the seminal article on sociology and photography[1] and, like many, I was inspired by his call to make sociology visual. In his article Becker suggested that the meaning of *reliability* (will the research produce the same results over and over?) and *validity* (is it "true"?) may shift when we talk about photography, but the concepts were still useful and relevant. He also suggested that documentary photographers might gain something from sociological literature on the various subjects they photographed, and that sociologists might have something to learn by studying how documentary photographers work. Becker's article was inspiring to many of us who had perhaps been too cautious to make this argument ourselves.

Sociology was very different in those times, being at center stage of politics big and small. It was not enough to keep one's distance and to regard the world as a laboratory. Sociology was an invitation to unmask inequalities, to inspire change, to involve oneself in social movements and to experiment with new ways of living. Many of us thought that making sociology visual was a parallel to making society

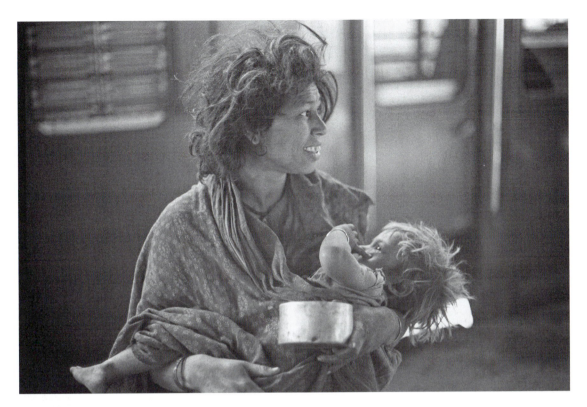

Figure I.2
Homeless woman and child.
Through images I tried to
imagine the previously
unimaginable extremes of
Indian society.

Figure I.1 (opposite)
Women washing clothes near
the caves of Adjunta and
Ellora. I remember seeing the
women and the sculptures as
a pattern combining the
ancient and modern.

(Unless otherwise noted, all
photographs were taken by
Douglas Harper.)

visible, and that led to seeing into social realities via engaged field work, merging theory with observation and practice.

Becker was then studying the sociology of art, assigning photo projects in research methods classes and writing on photography, art and other issues that became part of visual sociology. He also taught workshops for several summers at the Visual Studies Workshop in Rochester, and many people who became active in the visual sociology movement were trained in those classes.

Becker was not, of course, the only sociologist to think visually, but he was probably the most well known. In the meantime, by the mid-1980s, visual sociologists organized as the International Visual Sociology Association (IVSA),[2] after failing by a vote or two to become a section of the American Sociological Association. Looking back these were fortunate events, because the organization that came into being was truly international, not just a North American organization with the adjective affixed, and as an independent organization we have sponsored yearly conferences and workshops in which the discipline evolved. In the meantime visual sociology has flourished in the UK and continental Europe, and is beginning to take root in India, the Middle East, Russia and several locations in Asia and South America. It has become a truly global movement and is even beginning to be accepted as a normal part of sociology in the US, which has proved to be more conservative than many of us would have imagined.

A small number of journals have directly served the growing movement. The *International Journal of Visual Sociology*, published between 1984 and 1985 in Germany and edited by the Dutch sociologist Leonard Henny, was followed by the *Visual Sociology Review*, a newsletter, which in 1991 became the journal *Visual Sociology*.[3] In 2002 Taylor & Francis adopted the previously self-published journal and renamed it as *Visual Studies*. The current journal has a multi-disciplinary approach, and has become an important venue for visual anthropology, communications and other fields in addition to sociology. While the large format of the journal, and the attention to design and high quality production, has made it an appealing outlet for visual material, it is also true that more and more journals now routinely publish articles that include visual data; clearly there are no longer barriers to building an academic movement or having our work published and seen by others.

The book is based on the premise that the world that is seen, photographed, drawn or otherwise represented visually is different than the world that is represented through words and numbers. As a result, visual sociology leads to new understandings and insights because it connects to different realities than do conventional empirical research methods. The world behind statistical data exists (all those people did put marks on a questionnaire at some moment in their lives) but indeed the world behind the numbers is a very abstract reality, and one that is normally taken for granted in social science research. The world that is seen, photographed, painted, graphed, virtually reproduced or otherwise encountered visually also exists in a complex and problematical way, but it is no less suitable for sociological study than is the world behind the numbers.

Many of us believe that a visual approach can invigorate a discipline that is increasingly abstract and distant from the world it seeks to understand. It is often said that very few sociologists ever speak to a human in the course of their research, but most are very good at statistics. Visual sociology is an invitation to open the eyes of the discipline to a wider and infinitely more interesting perceptual world than a computer screen filled with numbers.

The book is also premised on the idea that seeing is very complicated in and of itself. What we see depends on the physical position of the viewer and, if we record it, the limitations of the technology used. Seeing also depends on the *social* position of the viewer: personal histories, gender, age, ethnicity and other factors that lead a person to see one message from an infinite number possible in a given visual universe. The construction of meaning does not stop there; images gain successive meanings as they are interpreted by one audience after another.

The idea of seeing as socially constructed is at the core of visual sociology. In one small example, when I was studying the history of dairy farming I discovered that female and male photographers who worked for the same organization saw and photographed the same social worlds in very different ways.[4] I suggested that it was this "gendered lens" that led women to see the work performed by farm women and children (male photographers mostly didn't), and even to photograph activities on the farm in a way that highlighted the cooperation of those involved, while men tended to see male farmers as individuals, doing individual tasks. The photographers saw, and thus photographed, in a way they had been taught by their moments in history, their social location and their skill and temperament.

There are several excellent texts on visual methods, but this is the first to be titled "visual sociology." What is the difference? The previous books have been primarily written by anthropologists, communications experts or researchers from disciplines such as cultural geography or cultural studies. The authors review debates in the visual studies movement and position themselves as positivist, constructivist, feminist or postmodernist, and much of the energy of these books is spent defining one's position relative to others.

This book has a different focus. It intends to speak first to sociology, addressing durable themes such as social construction of reality, social change, community studies, social identity, material culture, urban public life and institutional analysis, to name a few. I hope to appeal to sociologists who have never thought of a visual approach as well as to those already committed. To do so I've written chapters that cover some but certainly not all of contemporary visual sociology. The chapters can be read separately although the book is most effective if the sequence is followed. Strategies for teaching visual sociology are continually evolving and the IVSA website should be consulted for ongoing discussions of ideas and approaches to complement those offered here.

I also hope to build a better bridge between visual sociology and anthropology. Visual anthropology has its great heroes, including the nineteenth-century photographer, Edward Curtis, early twentieth-century filmmaker Robert Flaherty, anthropologists Gregory Bateson and Margaret Mead, whose photographic work, discussed in this volume, was the real beginning of visual ethnography, and Claude Lévi-Strauss, who photographed in the field as he was inventing structuralism. John Marshall filmed the San of the Kalahari Desert in the 1950s; Jean Rouch made nearly 120 films in Africa in the 1950s and 1960s; more recently John Gardner, Timothy Asch, Jay Ruby and David and Judith MacDougall, and many others, have continued to redefine (seldom with agreement!) anthropological filmmaking. Anthropology is home to a new generation of filmmakers, photographers, theorists and ethnographers who come to visual anthropology from several locations worldwide and who engage in exciting and often contentious debates about representation, ethics and epistemology. Visual anthropology journals are flourishing and ethnographic film festivals are common around the world. Visual anthropologists are positioned in the mainstream of the discipline, and are well represented in national and regional meetings, though they often ask for more legitimacy and power. Consumed as they are by their well-earned success few probably even realize there is a parallel movement toward the visual in sociology.

Visual sociology also has its strong voices—photographers, theorists and filmmakers—though these have not been as recognized as those of visual anthropology. Sociologists who have made careers doing visually based work include Jon Wagner, who has written extensively on the theory of visual sociology; Jon Rieger, who has spent decades studying the visual dimensions of social change; Steve Gold, who has applied the visual to his extensive studies of immigration; and Jon Prosser and Eric Margolis, who have used imagery to understand the sociology of schooling. John Grady has made documentary films as well as writing theory that connects visual sociology to pragmatism and other theoretical traditions; Chuck Suchar has studied gentrification and urban change in many countries; Jerry Krase has done extensive visual studies of urban ethnic communities and Luc Pauwels has studied the semiotics of vernacular landscapes and the impact of the web on home photography while contributing sociological bent to the street photography tradition. Sociologist Barbara Norfleet has curated photo collections at Harvard and has written several books that were based on her own photos of the upper class, or on collections she discovered off the beaten track. Michael Schwalbe has developed a sociology of photographic portraiture and Steve Papson and Robert Goldman have spent their careers analyzing advertising, and innovating multimedia as a part of the process. Patrizia Faccioli and several others have developed visual sociology in the Italian university, where it is currently flourishing, as it is in sociology departments in Greece, Scandinavia and Russia. French sociologist Bruno Latour's influential work on the city can be called "visual ethnomethodology." Caroline Knowles and her colleagues at Goldsmiths in London have created programs in urban visual ethnography and Elizabeth Chaplin has skillfully woven the themes of cultural studies into visual sociology. Some of the most important visual sociologists have worked outside the university. For example, sociologist/photographer Camilo José Vergara, who has never had an academic appointment, won the Robert E. Park award for his photographic work on the American ghetto and the visual sociology of the religions of the American poor.

This list just scratches the surface (and apologies to those excluded) but the point is clear: a large number of sociologists from all around the world have made successful careers focusing on the visual. We are scattered across the discipline, teaching courses in visual sociology, developing new research techniques, publishing visually based articles in typical sociology journals as well as our own, earning tenure on the basis of our visual research, and occasionally publishing books that connect our movement to the discipline and to wider audiences. We resemble the long but very thin root systems of a fungus; we have a worldwide network, but we are only beginning to become visible.

I also hope that this material will be useful for the growing number of applied social scientists and other researchers who are using visual methods in their own intellectual communities. For example in the past months I have uncovered over 150 research articles and papers on public health advocacy, leisure and tourism research, disability research, child development, environmental management and other related topics that use collaborative visual methods. Because the papers are published in specialized journals, they are seldom read by visual sociologists, and a look at their citations shows that few of their authors read our work. Communication across these parallel universes will move us all ahead.

Last words

I end this introduction by admitting to a strong predilection for photography: the "thing itself," often filleted by postmodernists and critical theorists. Mine is an affection, such as one has for pastel paintings or bebop, that I first discovered as an art student and that has only grown in the decades since. I like to take photos because I never am sure what the camera is going to teach me about seeing, and I take great pleasure in looking at photos, whether printed, reproduced in books or on computer screens. I have found that photography is about self-discovery as well as the discovery of society, which explains its presence in liberation movements and participatory research as well as the fine arts. So I approach the field with this in the background, but I also recognize that an interest in photography is neither required nor even expected in the visual sociology community; many visual sociologists never touch a camera.

Our students are now very good at recording the world visually and spreading these statements around the world, with nary a nod to an f-stop. Cameras used to be tools for professionals; now they are part of the cell phones most people carry. Perhaps being skilled at using a camera has become less important than being skilled at software that allows images to be made into YouTube videos, documentary films or multimedia projects. But in any case the world has never been more visually aware and visually engaged, and this means that the time for visual sociology has most certainly arrived.

Chapter 1

Visual ethnography

Near the end of the first text on visual anthropology, John Collier and his son Malcolm describe the work of their student, Naomi Togashi, who studied acculturation among Japanese immigrants. Togashi photographed seven homes in Japan and sixteen homes of first, second and third generation immigrants in San Francisco.[1] She photographed every room in each house and then coded the photos for 108 variables that included room purpose and function, styles and content of decoration (including family shrines and the display of Japanese artifacts), and the proxemics, or human use, of the space. In her final project the photos were presented in "ascending order of evolution and acculturation" and were accompanied by a statistical analysis of how the variables played out in the photos. She concluded that acculturation was a visual process for the Japanese immigrants; becoming American was something you could see from the outside looking in.

Togashi was concerned with the same questions that any researcher faces, namely validity (do the data mean what the researcher says they mean?) and reliability (do the data retain their meaning from case to case?). The only difference in her case was that the data were visual. She took advantage of the camera's ability to record a version of what existed in front of the lens, as she decided on focus, aperture, shutter speed and framing. Assuming she didn't manipulate the images by adding, subtracting or changing elements in the photos they show what they are asked to; they are pretty much preserved sight, editorialized by all of the choices that lay behind the creation of an image.

But if Togashi's photos are useful as empirical evidence, does that mean that they are true? That they represent *what* was there, *only* what was there, and *all* that was there? If this is not the case, can they still be thought of as empirical data?

These questions are not only relevant to visual data and they remind us that all data, visual or otherwise, are constructed. Numerical data are, in fact, shorthand ways of summarizing material that is often far from hard-edged. We categorize reactions to an idea or experience as equally spaced attitudes ("strongly agree," "agree," "no opinion," "disagree," "strongly disagree") when in fact they are reactions that are not equally spaced nor even similar in intensity. Or we draw arbitrary lines across income levels and call one group "higher class," another "middle class" and the third "lower class," which places people who make one dollar difference in income into different class groups (not to mention the varieties of meaning that a similar income level has in different settings within the area being studied). Sociologists are so used to empirical shorthand that it is seldom questioned.

When photography was invented in the nineteenth century it was thought that finally there was a means by which the world could be depicted without editorializing, but that did not turn out to be the case. As soon as there were cameras there were choices of lenses, apertures, points of focus, ISO ratings for film or digital sensors, and there is always the issue of how to frame the world through a given lens. Indeed, the photographic image is as constructed as a cave painting, but maybe less transparently. With the advent of digital photography (and with it the ease with which photos can be altered) it seemed that the photographic image suddenly lost all correspondence with truth, but since photos had always been socially constructed this was not big news, either. That does not necessarily make them less useful! In fact, it makes photographs more like other kinds of data, not less like them. The beauty of photography is how transparent the process of interpretation can be. We'll introduce the idea with an example.

Many years ago Howard Becker suggested that sociologists learn to analyze photographs by first concentrating on the act of looking itself. Rather than glancing and moving on, Becker suggests, give yourself five minutes. In the case of Figure 1.1, look beyond the quirky, almost humorous construction of the image (at least to our eyes in 2012). See that behind Herbert Underwood is a small barn and a silo large enough for the corn grown on a 10-acre field. Who filled the silo and what animals did it feed? Behind the farmer are two more apple trees. These suggest the family's self-sufficiency, otherwise the farmer would not be spending a February afternoon preparing them for spring. The farmer works alone on a winter day; we know from other research that his small herd of milking cows is resting—dried off—until they give birth in the spring and so he has time for such chores.

Following Becker's suggestion, we scratch the surface of the visual evidence in the image. We imagine Herbert Underwood working at his own pace on a job that will bring him a nice crop of apples six months later. We examine the material environment and confirm information about farming practices and his relationships with his neighbors that we've gained from other forms of research. We are provided with a visual gestalt that suggests a pace of life, skill, even a personality of Herbert the farmer, and all the farmers he's an example of. In fact from this single image we understand a great deal about a culture; we are on the way toward visual ethnography.

Figure 1.1
Reading a photo: Herbert
Underwood, a farmer, pruning
trees in his apple orchard.
Wallingford, Vermont,
February, 1946. (Photograph
by Charlotte Brooks.)

Visual ethnography

Traditionally, ethnography referred to the study of a whole culture; tools, houses
and other forms of material life; and dances, rituals, socialization practices and other
patterns of shared social life. That perspective, fundamental to anthropology during
its formative years, is less common and often critiqued, but ethnography as the study
of local or specific cultures is ever more prevalent in anthropology, sociology and
several related disciplines.

Visual ethnography is an effort to understand culture by making it visible, and the frame of reference is usually much smaller than a whole culture. Togashi's study of immigrant rooms is a good example. She uses visual information, first as seen and then as photographed, in a focused study. Togashi assumes that by studying the rooms and the objects within them she is studying the motivations, traditions or habits that lie behind organizing the space. The rooms are the result of human action that is part of a shared world-view.

There is visual evidence of culture in most forms of human behavior, whether it is the things people do together or alone: putting on clothes, making gestures or expressions, or occupying space. A photo of a jazz group may show how the group occupies a stage, looks at sheet music (or does not), communicates within itself and responds to audiences. The audience members interact with each other and engage the music in ways that reflect values and sentiments, and these can be read from photos.[2] Any time people "do things together" (to use Howard Becker's phrase) they do so according to cultural scripts, and most of these can be studied and read through photos. Visual studies of culture in this more limited frame of reference have been done on work or occupations,[3] deviant identities,[4] ethnic or racial identity and politics[5] or community and social class,[6] to name a very few, as we will see in the succeeding analyses.

I'll start with a project that most of us continue to respect and many of us hold in a kind of awe. It is Mead and Bateson's study of Balinese character.[7]

The project began in the 1930s, and was published in 1942, the year the US entered World War Two and the world was debating, with terrible consequences, whether or not race was a biological reality, and whether culture emerged from genes or circumstances.[8] Anthropologists had used photography before Mead and Bateson's study, and as summarized by Elizabeth Edwards,[9] photography provided the data that supported racist theorizing of early anthropology. Specifically, photos recorded body measurements and physical characteristics that were used to classify cultures and societies. Mead and Bateson changed the direction of visual anthropology because they used photos to make new arguments about culture. Few if any subsequent visual ethnographies approach their study's depth or reach, and their book has achieved a sort of canonical status, both praised and criticized.

I approach the book by asking: what did it do well, and what not so well? Was it a convincing argument for visual ethnography? Why, given its importance, did it not revolutionize anthropology and begin a simultaneous movement toward visual sociology?

Balinese Character came from a discipline that believed it was a science. The authors both had an extensive background in Pacific Islands anthropology; Mead had already published important books on adolescent adjustment among young women in Samoa, and Bateson had written an ethnography situated in New Guinea. Mead's orientation was to the level of the specific (her Samoan research led her to question whether adolescent crises of adjustment typical in the US were our own cultural invention), while Bateson had begun to search for universals in human and animal culture and behavior. Bateson later left anthropology to study cybernetics, schizophrenia and animal behavior.

Mead often expressed her frustration over using words to express the reality of one culture in the words of another. Perhaps photographs could partially help. She wrote in her application for funding to the SSRC (Social Science Research Council) that "the camera will neither be naive at the start nor experienced at the end of the research;"[10] it was a tool that recorded what was there, no less, no more, and balanced the inherent bias of words.

No one had attempted a photo project on the scale they imagined, and they underestimated what it would involve. Writing in her autobiography several decades later, Mead observed:

> When we planned our field work, we decided that we would make extensive use of movie film and stills. Gregory had bought seventy-five rolls of Leica film to carry us through the two years. Then one afternoon when we had observed parents and children for an ordinary forty-five minute period, we found that Gregory had taken three whole rolls. We looked at each other, we looked at the notes, and we looked at the pictures that Gregory had taken so far and that had been developed and printed by a Chinese in the town and were carefully mounted and catalogued on large pieces of cardboard.
>
> Clearly we had come to a threshold—to cross it would be a momentous commitment in money, of which we did not have much, and in work as well. But we made the decision. Gregory wrote home for the newly invented rapid winder, which made it possible to take pictures in very rapid succession. He also ordered bulk film, which he would have to cut and put in cassettes himself as we could not possibly afford to buy commercially the amount of film we now proposed to use. As a further economizing measure we bought a developing tank that would hold ten rolls at once and, in the end, we were able to develop some 1,600 exposures in an evening.
>
> The decision we made does not sound very momentous today. Daylight loaders have been available for years, amateur photographers have long since adopted sequence photography, and field budgets for work with film have enormously increased. But it was momentous then. Whereas we had planned to take 2,000 photographs, we took 25,000. It meant that the notes I took were similarly multiplied by a factor of ten . . . and the volume of our work was changed in tremendously significant ways.[11]

When they returned to the States they printed several thousand of their most important images on film stock, which they projected, studied and coded on individual cards. All images had been dated, and were coded to field notes written by Mead. Eventually 759 of the 25,000 were published in their well-printed and elegantly designed book that commemorated the 125th anniversary of the New York Academy of Sciences. It is unlikely that anthropology had or has ever looked as good!

The large format of the book made it possible to print five to twelve images on a page that appeared across from long captions. Some photos required longer captions than others, and some topics used more photos than others. Mead wrote a fifty-page introduction on the photos and the book concludes with an essay on the history and the then current situation in Bali, but it is the images that carry the argument.

The photos first portray Balinese material culture, including the layout of the villages and details of agriculture including irrigation and tool use. This leads to the study of proxemics and body language (kinesics), trance, mother–child interaction, sibling interaction, stages of child development and rites of passage. The visual logic moves from the material world to culture, family interaction and development. Photos of rites of passage emphasize social integration. Some sequences show unfolding events over a few minutes and are more like film excerpts; others combine photos from different events and times. Bateson sometimes photographed close up; in other instances his photos are overviews. He primarily worked with 50 mm and 200 mm lenses on his 35 mm Leica, and seldom if ever used his 35 mm wide angle.[12] His framing was tight when he photographed social interaction; centering his subjects and excluding extraneous information. The telephoto lens, hard to use on his rangefinder Leica, allowed him to photograph details from a short distance. While the authors describe Mead as directing Bateson's photography, Bateson also wrote that

> We recorded as fully as possible what happened while we were in the houseyard, and it is so hard to predict behavior that it was scarcely possible to select particular postures or gestures for photographic recording. In general, we found that any attempt to select for special details was fatal, and that the best results were obtained when the photography was most rapid and almost random.[13]

Bateson made photos with his mind and eye working in an unconscious discovery mode. Seeing through the camera and releasing the shutter became a matter of instinct, guided by knowledge.

Mead and Bateson concentrate on how culture adapts people to each other. We see the simultaneous tendency of people to place themselves into groups, and then to seek to separate from each other in "awayness" or trance. The study emphasizes how Balinese define, touch and categorize their bodies and the food that goes in and the excreta that comes out. We learn a great deal about rituals that move the Balinese from one stage of life to another. We learn hardly anything about how Balinese meet, court and marry each other, or how young adults interact with their parents. There is some but not much attention paid to material culture, especially housing and agriculture. The plates often integrate images of Balinese art with photos of people mimicking the postures and poses portrayed. Like all ethnographies *Balinese Character* tells some stories of the culture but not all, and Mead introduces the book by saying that there was great variation from one part of Bali to another, and that their story is incomplete.

Their method works better for some topics than others. Bateson's photos record details of trance and parent–child relationships particularly well but they are less successful at depicting the details of burial rituals. The authors write

> . . . when a new corpse which has been kept in the house about ten days is to be carried to the graveyard for cremation, all the repulsion toward the fact of death crops up. Men overcompensate, plunge their arms into the rotting corpse and boast that their skin has crawled with maggots . . .[14]

The photos don't show much of this; it is nearly impossible to understand how the rituals unfold from the photos alone. Likewise, a topic that should take well to photos, the positioning of hands in daily life (Plate 21) is limited to eight photos, and several are more descriptive than anthropological. Plate 29 (Eating meals) shows how the Balinese regard eating with shame (their backs are to each other; they look down when they eat in crowds; they quickly shove food into their mouths off the backs of their hands) but other sequences such as Plate 36 (Eating snacks) shows actions without much context or explanation. Throughout the book some photo sequences have greater clarity, power and significance than others.

This points to a larger problem with visual ethnography, which is that it is easier to create an argument with words than with photos. We are used to linking meanings together from words, but less used to doing this with photos. I've come to think of photo sequences in a project like *Balinese Character* as a series of windows on a large building, and through those windows are unfolding aspects of culture. But there are many spaces on the wall between the windows that the viewer must fill in. The view is always incomplete.

Balinese Character remains a strong argument for a visual ethnography. It is artful science; a vision of what the discipline could become. Why then, did it fail to revolutionize anthropology and, perhaps, social science in general?

There are, I think, four answers. First, the project came to represent visual ethnography per se, but impressive as it was, a single book is simply not powerful enough to revolutionize an entire discipline. This may be an unfair criticism because Mead and Bateson had modest goals for the book, as reflected in their introductory statement:

> This volume is in no sense a complete account of Balinese culture, even in its most general outlines. It is an attempt to present . . . those aspects of our results and those methods of research which we have judged most likely to be of immediate use to other students . . .[15]

A second explanation is slightly ironic in the context of the first: the book set the bar higher than could be reasonably reached by others. Few ethnographers have the skill or energy to do a project of similar scale, and few academic publishers were likely to be willing to publish what looked more like art than anthropology.

Even when anthropologists subsequently used a great deal of photography in ethnographic research, they seldom used the photos imaginatively and rigorously. Consider a project completed several decades ago as described by the Colliers in their text on visual anthropology. Bernard and Shirley Planalp did field research for eighteen months in an East Indian village, exposing 1,000 rolls of 120 mm film and producing more than 1,000 medium-format images. The Colliers say this was a great success; the "technical and visual content of their study," printed by a professional lab, "could match any professional study made in India."[16] It was undoubtedly a great achievement to have made the photos, but to my knowledge the photos did not lead to an academic publication, and their impact on the discipline was minimal. Like most photos made during field work, they took a lot of work to make and they were studied when the author wrote her or his ethnography, and then they were left in a file cabinet to age and yellow. In the end, *Balinese Character* has had few real imitators, even when field workers were skilled photographers. As a result most ethnography has remained word-based, and when images are used, they are used to add descriptive detail.

The third reason the project can be said to have failed is that many contemporaries felt the book lacked scientific rigor, which was at that time anthropology's holy grail. For example, Lois Barclay Murphy and Gardner Murphy, who reviewed the book in 1943 for the *American Anthropologist*, found that the photographs were not up to hypothesis testing. The Murphys cite Mead and Bateson's assertion that deflection of emotion among children leads to withdrawal among adults, but the reviewers point out that the authors do not use their photos to test this hypothesis. The photos show that some children seem to deflect emotion and that adults are withdrawn, but the photos are limited to demonstrating the assertion. The reviewers suggest that Mead and Bateson should have chosen children at random and photographed them over time, allowing for systematic comparison. It would be possible to do this, but it would require a vast effort with a large research staff. In any case, the reviewers assert that testing a hypothesis is very different than showing a handful of cases where a cultural phenomenon exists.

The reviewers also question whether the authors are guilty of sampling error. Do the photos show typical situations, people and circumstances? There are some ways to crosscheck the photos by looking for common elements in their backgrounds, but more written information would help. They write:

> What can be photographed, and what gets left out because it is hard
> to photograph? How should such gaps be filled in? How universal are
> the specific situations which are photographed, or which provide the
> most usable pictures from the point of view of visual clarity rather than

documentary completeness? . . . In our culture, and presumably in others, one tends to photograph those who are photogenic, those who do not move around too fast.[17]

The reviewers want to know much more about the people and circumstances shown in the photos. They call this "checking the indirect evidence" from photos, and this would involve the analysis of full demographic and sociological information on all people who are in the frame. But they acknowledge:

Obtaining adequate records of all the essential kinds of people defined in age, sex, class terms, as well as other terms important to the specific culture . . . catching the sequence of life through the seasons and through the individual life history, all this may well be regarded as a frightening undertaking.[18]

Thus they are caught in the same conundrum that scientific critiques of ethnography usually come to: it cannot measure up as science, and basing ethnography on images makes this more, not less, obvious.

The final perspective from which to assess the effect of *Balinese Character* is more recent. The postmodern critique of anthropology, coinciding with intellectual movements in other social sciences, has questioned whether anthropology and sociology can or should mimic science and Bateson and Mead's project, hailed as a seminal ethnography, is an easy target. Thus we are left with the irony that reviewers in the 1940s rejected Bateson and Mead's work because it was not scientific enough; modern reviewers see it as a naïve attempt to create a science of human studies. In other words, it fails for both audiences for opposite reasons.

It is also likely that *Balinese Character* did not force a paradigm shift in anthropology because soon after it was published film rather than photography became the dominant form of visual ethnography. This was partly due to technological breakthroughs. Coincident to the development of the 35 mm Leica camera, which made quality photo work in the field possible, portable 16 mm film cameras were developed. Mead and Bateson exposed several thousand feet of movie film during their research that became important ethnographic films, and Mead devoted considerable energy to anthropological filmmaking throughout her career. It may be that film (and, eventually, video) is a better way to do visual ethnography than still photography. Whole events can be shown; human action can be seen in context; and the subjectivity of a culture can arguably be communicated more successfully in moving images, with or without sound (and the early cameras could not coincidentally record sound) than still photos. These arguments are taken up in the many histories of anthropological filmmaking[19] and lie outside the purview of this book.

We are left to ponder the fate of visual ethnography as represented by Bateson and Mead's project. It began a tradition that continues to this day, despite the waxing and waning of ethnography per se. It continues to show the potential of analysis drawn from imagery, and it reminds us of the effort that in-depth projects require. The imperfections and failings are easy to see, but the work never seems to be diminished by the critical attention it continues to receive.

From *Balinese Character* we leap three decades to John Collier's text on visual anthropology,[20] first published in 1967 and currently in its fourth edition. The Collier text is a bit creaky (much of the discussion of film photography has little relevance in a digital world, and the positivist bent does not anticipate or address its postmodern critique) but it remains a useful demonstration of the scientific or realist paradigm in visual ethnography. While photo-based visual ethnography did not become the centerpiece of visual anthropology, it has continued to develop, though now feebly. Notable examples include Richard Sorenson's visual and ethnographic study of child development in New Guinea,[21] anthropologist Danforth and photographer Tsiaras's photo study of death rituals in rural Greece,[22] Franck Cancian's photographic study of central American peasant culture[23] and Charles and Angeliki Keil and photographer Dick Blau's study of the role of music in Romani lives.[24] The list is rather short, and while there is no simple explanation for this trend, the answers may not be so different from our musings on the inability of *Balinese Character* to revolutionize the discipline seventy years ago. Anthropologists interested in visual ethnography are drawn to film and video because it communicates more directly and vividly than does a book. While many anthropologists still believe in, and do, traditional ethnographies of whole cultures, there is an active critique that says such a goal is impossible, aside from whether or not it is visually based. Thus visual ethnography is something of an odd bird in the visual sociology movement. We continue to evaluate the old accomplishments and a few of us produce our own versions of visual ethnography, but we do so in the context of the well-known postmodern critique of ethnography, and the even more fundamental question regarding whether culture can be conceptualized and studied. The tenuous status of visual ethnography, however, has pushed it toward more experimental forms, as I hope the next chapters will show.

Chapter 2

Documentary photography

In this chapter I describe documentary photography as natural kin to visual sociology. Documentary photography is, however, a rapidly moving target; always hard to define. It is closely related to, and sometimes overlaps photojournalism, which is also transforming in the face of the decline and probable end of print journalism. Some might even question spending time on documentary photography in a book on visual sociology, but I do so for three reasons. First, many great documentarians worked very much like visual sociologists and studying their work helps us do ours. Second, studying documentary photography allows us a kind of access to the worlds that they described. Third, studying documentary allows us to see how photos create meaning in historical, sociological and political circumstances that are themselves in motion. This view implicitly critiques the idea that either documentary photography or writing produces a truth about the past; rather, like all texts, their meanings are created, changing and often at odds with their claims.

There are two fundamental approaches to documentary photography and we will use them both. The first is to assume that classifying photos as *documentary* identifies a quality that some photos have and others do not, just as beauty, from this view, indicates a quality that some objects have and others do not. This approach, which we might call an essentialist view, is more typical of aesthetics, art history, theology or ethics than it is of sociology. But while an uncommon perspective in sociology, and not my primary orientation, it is still useful. For example, looking at documentary in this way reveals commonly agreed upon definitions and conventions in documentary practice, including:

- Verisimilitude: Documentary shows what existed at a given point of time and location.
- Sympathy: Documentary is expected to engage the viewer. This may be due to the topic, how the photos are composed and presented, or a combination of the two. Photo historian Naomi Rosenblum commented ". . . that while the social documentary photographer is neither a mere recorder nor an 'artist for

art's sake, his reports are often brilliant technically and highly artistic'—that is, documentary images involve imagination and art in that they imbue fact with feeling."[1]

- Relevance: A documentary image addresses a political or social issue. This can be as specific as a social movement of fishermen fighting a corporation that has dumped mercury into their fishing grounds (W. Eugene and Aileen Smith's *Minimata*),[2] or as broad as an interpretation of an entire culture (Robert Frank's *The Americans*).[3] In other words, documentary argues. Again we turn to Rosenblum: ". . . images in the documentary style combine lucid pictorial organization with an often passionate commitment to humanistic values—to ideals of dignity, the right to decent conditions of living and work, to truthfulness."[4] This perspective continues to define documentary; turning to a magazine published by the Center for Documentary Studies at Duke University we read: "CDS promotes documentary work that cultivates progressive change by amplifying voices, advancing human dignity, engendering respect among individuals, breaking down barriers to understanding, and illuminating social injustices . . ."[5]

This view of documentary is consistent with critical sociology (dating at least to Marx and Engels); muckraking sociology of the Chicago School; the sociology of social protest during the 1960s; and the contemporary concept of public sociology. In other words, whether or not it accurately describes documentary photography, it certainly describes how a lot of people see sociology.

It is also a lightning rod for critical comment from theorists including Abigail Solomon-Godeau, Martha Rosler, Sally Stein and Susan Sontag.[6] The postmodern critique of what I've called the essentialist documentary includes the idea that all photos are documentary in the sense that they have an indexical relationship with what was in front of the lens when the image was made; there is nothing in the essence of a photo that makes it documentary, and nothing in the essence of a photographer that makes her or him a documentarian. Rather than types of photos, the postmodern critic has helped us see different uses for photographs, and from this point of view these uses in one way or another promote the interests of the social class that dominates the ideological apparatus of the society. The photographer Dorothea Lange, whose images from the American Depression have great standing in communities that define documentary from the essentialist perspective, is often singled out because her photos appear to offer compassion to those in the middle of the economic crisis, but in creating ragged heroes and heroines Lange actually deflects the true cause of their plight; the structural failure of capitalism. Martha Rosler writes:

> In the liberal documentary, poverty and oppression are almost invariably equated with misfortunes caused by natural disasters: causality is vague, blame is not assigned, fate cannot be overcome . . . Like photos of

children in pleas for donations to international charity organizations,
liberal documentary implores us to look in the face of deprivation and
to weep (and maybe to send money . . .

The critique further suggests that documentarians advance their own privileged
positions as they document misery and suffering, even to the point of turning the
people and objects in their photos into beautiful canvases.

These are important critiques, and they often include examples of new photo
documentary projects that incorporate the critical view. Many of these projects
appropriate the work of well-known photographers and reassemble them into
collages that try to raise unasked questions. In other words, the critique is much
more than a rejection of previous practices; it is the basis of work that creatively
reimagines photography itself. Generally these critical voices and the new
experiments are taking place in departments of art or cultural studies, and rarely in
sociology, but it is clearly a direction visual sociology must explore.

The second view of documentary avoids the argument about whether or not
the practice and its products can be defined by an essential ingredient or essence.
This view, which we may call a *constructionist* view, asks how documentary has
been created and developed in the practical activities of individuals, groups and
institutions. From this perspective documentary produces objects (photographs, texts
and movies, for example) that were made in the context of institutional practices
and historical events or eras, which both reflect and sometimes challenge them.

When we look at the institutional arrangements that surround documentary
work we ask such questions as: Is it paid work? If so, who pays and under what
circumstances? Does it lead to a career? A profession? Who certifies it as such;
who are the gatekeepers? Who are the audiences for documentary, and how do
they consume the work? What is its relationship to other careers or professions,
such as photojournalism or academic sociology? And, what messages is documentary allowed to generate? What is its relationship to the state? (It may suppress
documentary, or it may use documentary as propaganda, for example.)

Documentary expression depends on technologies to make and distribute
information, and these technologies and the expertise they require are continually
evolving. For example, with the invention of very inexpensive digital cameras and
the vast increase in the size and influence of the Web (especially YouTube videos),
documentary photography and film have become democratized far beyond what
anyone's imagination would have predicted even a few years ago.

For documentary to succeed, there has to be an audience, and audiences
depend on many factors, including something as simple as whether there is a way
to reproduce the information and make it available to potential viewers. At one point
or another in the process, a cultural product gains the approval of cultural
gatekeepers. For example, folklorist Tom Rankin oversaw the publication of the family
photos of Maggie Lee Sayre, who spent fifty-one years on a houseboat on rivers in
Ohio and Kentucky as a member of a family of commercial fishermen.[8] Sayre's

photos are worth preserving, Rankin suggests, because she interpreted her world in the context of her inability to hear or speak, in addition to the unusual world she inhabited on the rivers of mid-America. Left to itself, the album would have never gone beyond Sayre's small family circle. It was Rankin, director of the Center for Documentary Studies, who was a gatekeeper with sufficient influence to define it otherwise.

This perspective is well developed in Howard Becker's 1982 book *Art Worlds*,[9] but Becker also discussed this approach in relation to our topic in his recent article on documentary, photojournalism and visual sociology,[10] to which this analysis is indebted.

No matter how one approaches it, it is clear that documentary is an in-between category, having never become a strong cultural tradition in its own right. Very few people define and support themselves as documentary photographers; most occupy the nooks and crannies of several occupations and practices. Some are former photojournalists who want to explore a topic in more depth, and they may get support from agency funding; others are art photographers who explore subjects usually reserved for journalists. Some documentary writers, photographers and filmmakers are academics who integrate documentary into related disciplines like English or folklore. Psychiatrist Robert Coles has worked with photographers including Alex Harris to produce some of the most respected documentary projects of recent decades.[11] The Center for Documentary Studies at Duke University, which published the documentary journal *Doubletake* (now sadly defunct) is a rare example of documentary expression as a program in a university. The career of Bruce Jackson, an English professor whose work includes documentary writing, photography and filmmaking,[12] demonstrates that a traditional discipline (English) can make room for a scholar doing (a considerable amount of excellent) documentary. There may be a very few documentarians who eke out a living from royalties, but they are rare.

There is a relationship between visual sociology and documentary, but they are not the same. In his 1974 article, Becker argued that the topics studied by documentary photographers and sociologists overlapped, and that they often worked in similar ways. But the products were often different; documentary in the end depended on compelling images or texts. Sociology is also an exploration, Becker suggested, but it is reasoned through social theory. I think Becker meant theory in a broad way: not just the ideas of the few who make their way into theory textbooks, but rather the general practice of analytical thinking. But even with this proviso, the nod to theory marks a real difference between the two forms.[13]

In the following I will describe documentary projects that have a particular resonance with visual sociology. I am interested in the organization of documentary as a job or a career; how it generated a public, how it found a topic, and how it connected to history, economy and social change. But I am also drawn to these projects because they communicate strongly and effectively. They are excerpts from a long list, and every sociologist who develops an interest in documentary would have their own.

P.H. Emerson[14]

I begin with the work of a nineteenth-century medical doctor, P.H. Emerson, who abandoned his medical career for photography in order to photograph East Anglia in the 1880s.[15] The central question for photography at the time was not whether it was sociology, but whether it was a fine art, and I may be the first to claim him as a visual sociologist. Certainly the story of the social construction of photography at that moment in history is intriguing.

The movement for photography as a fine art in the latter nineteenth century—the world that P.H. Emerson contributed to—was part of the emergence of the rising middle class; managers, bureaucrats, officials and salaried workers riding the rising tide of industrial capitalism. With their new wealth they sought cultural legitimacy; suddenly art found an audience beyond the old elite. The rising middle classes consumed the mechanically produced art of the camera in family portraits and decorative photos, and they became amateurs who purchased cameras, joined camera clubs, entered their photos into competitions and made photography into a mass phenomenon. In this era, which dates to the 1860s, a style known as pictorialism came to dominate fine arts photography. The leader of this school was Henry Peach Robinson, who made staged photos with costumed models playing allegorical roles, posed in elaborate still lifes. They were the rage for the new middle classes; to today's eye they are sentimental and strange.

Photographs made in the pictorial tradition were expected to resemble paintings; they were constructed in studios with props, artificial lighting and background sets. If photographers worked outdoors they modified negatives to improve the look of an image, even painting on negative surfaces or combining negatives to fix contrast problems. Robinson's 1886 book, *Pictorial Effect in Photography*, "provided the serious amateur with a guide to the beautiful in art based on respected principles dating from the Renaissance to Ruskin."[16] Because photography was to mimic painting, the ability of the camera to record sight accurately (for example, the sharpness of the camera lens) was seen as a problem rather than a solution.

Pictorialism produced a reactionary movement called naturalism; the new view held that the camera should be a conduit between the world and the photographic negative. The artist should embrace photography's possibilities to make something new in the art worlds of a new age. The photos made by naturalists such as P.H. Emerson were compared to impressionist paintings; a product of an artist mediating nature in a self-conscious way.

I regard Emerson as a visual ethnographer because through his photography he observed and classified nature, including the people who inhabited the places he studied. It is likely he would have been drawn to either visual anthropology or sociology had they existed.

Emerson's subjects were peasant farmers and fringe people who lived by legal or illegal means in the lagoons, swamps, long tidal flats and rivers of coastal east England. In the several years he and his collaborator T.F. Goodall spent in their company they observed how people fished, farmed, poached, managed the seas and inland waters and maintained their old beliefs and superstitions. They made photographs that won the respect of the international art world and that delight the modern eye. We see how people managed their environments, and how they were defined by their expressions, gestures and clothes. They are graceful images that show people comfortable in their places and spaces; the water is tranquil and the light is muted. Portraits show people surrounded by their tools and gear, and marked by lives of hard labor.

Emerson's photos were made with a view camera on a tripod, carefully composed, correctly exposed and printed and reproduced with an eye to craft and quality.

What was the sociological context of this work? How did it fit into art worlds, and how did it gain sponsorship and audiences?

Between 1884 and 1888 Emerson published four books on the cultures of East Anglian people, that combined photography and text.[17] They were produced in editions of a few hundred copies, and they included original platinotype (platinum) prints. Emerson was learning the then esoteric secrets of engraving and printing; halftone printing had yet to become common, and he oversaw the printing of the originals that became the pages of his books. He made limited editions of the photographic albums and books, and afterwards destroyed both negatives and printing plates. The books were expensive at a price of £5, which would pay for about six weeks in a luxury hotel in the UK at the time. These have now become precious commodities in the art collection world; searching in 2010 I found an Emerson original title listed for $84,000.

Emerson's photography could be called "art approaching ethnography." The art worlds of that time and place rewarded Emerson with an influential career that he only enjoyed for a brief time because of his own indecision over what he was trying to accomplish. His audience was the rising middle class, who consumed the rather idealistic image of England with one foot in the pre-industrial past. His books were precursors to visual ethnography, though he recorded observations and stories without the pretence of social theory. His work is regarded as the beginning of what came to be known as "straight" photography, clearing the path for figures including Alfred Stieglitz, Frederick H. Evans, Edward Steichen, Paul Strand, Edward Weston, Ansel Adams, Eliot Porter, Henri Cartier-Bresson, Brassaï, André Kertész, Walker Evans, Dorothea Lange, Imogen Cunningham, W. Eugene Smith, Minor White, Harry Callahan and Aaron Siskind:[18] though, of course, he was not alone in regarding photography as a way to show how common people lived in their normal circumstances. Because his subjects were rural people living in old ways his work took on a romantic, evocative quality, even though it was simultaneously regarded as a record of a different aspect of rapidly changing British life.

Emerson may be an unusual place to start. His books were briefly the rage of a new art world that otherwise focused its attention on salons, galleries or international expositions. But he also understood how photos and writing could tell a story of a little-understood culture. He examined a way of life at the geographical fringes of England during a time of rapid social change, and created a sympathy for the people he found there. From some points of view this is quite consistent with visual sociology.

Jacob Riis

Regarding the origins of social documentary, Naomi Rosenblum writes:

> Because social images were meant to persuade, photographers felt it necessary to communicate a belief that slum dwellers were capable of human emotions and that they were being kept from fully realizing their human qualities by their surroundings ... By selecting sympathetic types and contrasting the individual's expression and gesture with the shabbiness of the physical surroundings, the photographer frequently was able to transform a mundane record of what exists into a fervent plea for what might be. This idealism became a basic tenet of the social documentary concept.[19]

She was referring to the work of Jacob Riis, a Danish photographer and writer contemporary of P.H. Emerson, whose work has been of interest to sociologists for several decades.

Riis was an immigrant who spent three hard years in his early twenties (1870–73) in New York City, often spending his nights in police lodging houses on cots or hammocks suspended several high in a shabby room. These hard times developed a social consciousness that guided his next forty years as a journalist, a freelance writer and one of the first documentary photographers to take his camera into the dark sides of industrializing cities.[20] His view that poverty created social problems stood at odds with prevailing sentiment, usually religious or social Darwinist, that saw the poor as responsible for their misery.

He was first a police reporter and later a newspaper and magazine journalist and photographer. He was among the first to use a flash to make photos at night; this involved setting off a small magnesium explosion that created a harsh brilliance that showed dirt, raw wood grain and filthy skin and clothes in more detail than a human eye would have seen. Riis' flash photography placed night-time people in a surreal visual universe. The experience of being photographed this way also probably left the subjects, often crammed into beds with whole families, wondering what had happened. Riis' flash photos reinforce the point that the camera sees in a way the eye cannot; that photos are records editorialized through technology.

Rosenblum argues that documentary has a humanitarian purpose, showing good humans surviving bad conditions. The circumstances Riis photographed included people sleeping in small cubicles made from rough-cut lumber, stacked from floor to ceiling, or buried en masse in cheap pine boxes; children sleeping in stairwells or mobsters congregating in back alleys. Photos of police lodging houses show twenty or more sleepers jammed together on ledges, awakened for a photo, looking disconcerted. Riis not only photographed homelessness and the living conditions of the very poor; he also depicted piecework such as sewing taking place in people's crowded apartments.

Riis showed a side of urban life that by and large had not been seen in the US, though there were photographers working in the UK who had been photographing slums for several years.[21] He explored the meaning of his images with sociological logic; showing how tenements had developed, how people had migrated from one region or city to others, and what had happened as a result. He was interested in the effects of mixing the cultures of different immigrants from Europe and the American South in the rapidly changing cities of the North. The prejudice that sometimes marks his writing is startling, but it may tell us about the casual way in which people were categorized in these times:

> Cleanliness is the characteristic of the Negro in his new surroundings, as it was his virtue in the old. In this respect he is immensely the superior of the lowest of the whites, the Italians and the Polish Jews, below whom he has been classed in the past in the tenant scale. This was shown by an inquiry made last year by the Real Estate Record. It proved agents to be practically unanimous in the endorsement of the Negro as a clean, orderly, and profitable tenant.[22]

His approach was to connect images to concepts and ideas, and to explain what he had found in terms of economics, history and sociology. In particular, Riis identified economic variables that coincided with social characteristics or patterns of behavior for which he found visual referents. Riis found an audience because the liberal public had begun to question whether variables such as income, racial or ethnic identity or employment status influenced dependent variables such as crime rates and other indicators of social dysfunction. He was a part of what is now known as public sociology long before it was defined as such and subsequently influenced social policies (the police lodging houses were closed, for example, after his exposé, which raises the question of where the homeless were to find shelter!).

Halftone printing was being developed just as Riis came on the scene; his most important book, *How the Other Half Lives*, bridged overlapping printing technologies. Images in books or newspapers had been done via wood engravings; in Riis' book there were forty plates, of which seventeen were halftones and the rest were wood engravings. The wood engravings did not reproduce the tonality or detail of a photograph, and because the engraver usually only drew the person or event in the center of the frame they tended to highlight individuals and de-emphasize backgrounds, which were the sociological contexts of the images. By the time Riis wrote his later books the halftone process was common, and his halftone printed books were the first photo documentary projects. Others, such as Lewis Hine, soon followed.

Riis gave hundreds of lectures illustrated with lantern slides, a technology that had been used in one form or another for hundreds of years. The lantern slide system projects a transparency by means of a lamp and a lens. Transparencies were first painted on to glass, but by the end of the nineteenth century photographic slides had been developed, and so began the "slide show" that for several decades was the boon and bane of middle-class family entertainment. In Riis' day slide shows were public entertainment, showing faraway lands and famous people. Riis, however, offered a visual sociology of tenements, urban poverty, homelessness and sweat shops to audiences of activists preoccupied with the ills of industrial capitalism. Riis' importance is often connected to the perfection of the halftone printing process, which made his work inexpensive to reproduce, and to his lantern slide projection shows, which encouraged an audience of reformers who sought images to reinforce their arguments. Because Riis worked before the movies became common, his presentations were among the first image shows for the masses.

Riis' most well-known images include the "bandit's roost," which has a foreboding quality because of the postures and poses of the shady cast of characters it portrays, and a photo of three crumpled youngsters who are perched sleeping on a fire escape ledge (though one of the kids has a slight smile; maybe Riis posed them!). Other memorable images include a photo of an empty police lodging house where people were given a sloping piece of canvas on which to sleep—these strips of canvas were several high and many deep in such a human warehouse—or a photo of officials burying the unknown dead by stacking pine boxes in a mass grave. Riis focused on visual scars, but in a way that stressed the role of the social conditions rather than the actions of individuals. He showed people what was happening just around their corners, and demonstrated that images could amplify the meanings of statistical charts and tables. His work demonstrated how documentary and visual sociology overlapped and reinforced each other.

The 1930s

I next examine the role of documentary in an era of tumultuous social change: world economic depression (1929–42 in the US); the rise of fascism in Italy (1923–45) and Nazism in Germany (1933–45). In the Soviet Union the revolution of Lenin in the early 1920s had given way to the totalitarian dictatorship of Stalin.[23] Photo documentary is a seam running through these events, in each culture done differently and serving different ends. Still photography and documentary film in the form of newsreels overlapped as significant ways in which the societies told their stories, and I will discuss them both.

We left P.H. Emerson investigating hidden cultures behind British industrialization and Jacob Riis revealing social problems during a period of rapid industrialization in the US. Industrialization altered all things, including how war was waged, first in the Boer War in Africa, where the machine gun mechanized face-to-face killing, and then in World War One, which introduced the widespread use of mustard gas, aerial bombing and trench warfare, where troops rose from muddy gullies to charge across a narrow no-man's land into the fire of machine guns. World War One was photographed, but the visual stories did not find a mass audience. It was in the 1930s that documentary captured the public imagination, in part because there were suddenly several ways to view the images.

We begin with Italy and the formal beginning of fascism in 1923. Prior to his rise to power Mussolini had been a journalist and had understood the importance of controlling what people saw and read. Until the war for colonial conquest in Ethiopia nearly bankrupted Italy, the fascist dictatorship rebuilt much of the Italian infrastructure. The material progress was accompanied by the suppression of democracy and dissent. Newspapers were put under state control by 1926 and non-fascist newspapers were shut down. Libraries were controlled by the state; Italian history books were rewritten, and teachers and professors were required to belong to the fascist party and teach in party uniforms. How did Mussolini create public support for a totalitarian dictatorship in a society that had long identified itself as the cradle of Western civilization? One way was by mobilizing a kind of documentary photography, in this case in the form of newsreels.

The popular cinema industry in Italy operated mostly without censorship through much of the fascist era, and large numbers of American movies were shown during the 1920s and 1930s. Rather than control feature films, the government concentrated its propaganda efforts on an extensive newsreel industry. Beginning in 1925 the state-owned film industry LUCE (which means light in Italian) produced a steady stream of newsreels that were to precede every commercial film. LUCE made between 100 and 200 newsreels per year, covering world events and trends, and even topics such as clothing fashion in the ever-popular US, but the main focus was on fascist programs, including "public works projects, highway and railway construction, colonial expansion in Albania and Ethiopia, the Battle for Grain . . ."[24] Because the Italian population had limited access to radios and there was a low rate of literacy in Italy, and because cinema was popular throughout Italy, newsreels were a powerful way to build and maintain support for the regime. Here was social documentary organized by the state that left out the suppression of democracy and dissent, increasing poverty, ill-fated wars of conquest in Africa, anti-Semitic laws and the implications of the "pact of steel" which Mussolini signed with Hitler in 1939. The newsreel system was a carefully orchestrated documentary tradition that contributed to consensus in a dictatorship.

In 1932, on the ten-year anniversary of the fascist rise to power, the LUCE newsreels were edited into a feature-length documentary, *Mussolini Speaks*.[25]

It was intended to create a favorable image of Mussolini abroad, and it was successful, particularly among Italian immigrants in America.

The Italian example shows the power of documentary in a closed system. The state needed to maintain consensus at home and make friends with the capitalist democracies. For the regime to succeed, it had to convince its population that only fascism had the strength to confront Soviet communism, that the social progress in Italy was real, the wars of conquest in Africa were legitimate, and that Mussolini was a capable leader. The newsreel system was an effective means to these ends.

The Italian example, though extreme, was not unique. In the UK the newsreel dates to 1910 and became a powerful form of propaganda during World War One. One newsreel company was run by the British War Office, but several companies produced them simultaneously, seeking market share by emphasizing popular news stories and avoiding controversy.

Newsreels were also an important part of mass culture in the US. American newsreels during the 1930s focused on world history (titles included "The march toward war" and "Hitler comes to power in Germany") but more typically focused on fashion; sensational national news such as the death of gangster John Dillinger; Congressional bills passed; Olympic competitions and other national sports events such as the World Series; popular culture such as national parades; and the stories of heroes such as Amelia Earhart. The introductory music was rousing and patriotic, and the montages that preceded the movies were meant to inspire, but until World War Two approached their ideological messages were mild.[26]

The left also communicated through documentary during the 1920s and 1930s. The most well-known example was the German magazine *AIZ* (*Arbeiter Illustrierte Zeitung*), which was created in 1921 to express solidarity with the Russian revolution. *AIZ*, which at the height of its popularity was distributed to over a half million readers in Germany alone, focused on the socialist worker movement in Germany and elsewhere in Europe, and featured photos submitted by amateur photographers, reporting from the world of work and politics. This worker photography (*Arbeiterphotographen*) depicted political rallies, collectivist organizations, political meetings and the social problems of a German society in severe economic crisis. In addition to the worker-produced photography, *AIZ* featured the photo montages of John Heartfield (a German who anglicized his name to protest the demonization of Britain in Germany following World War One), which vilified Hitler, National Socialism, militarism, war profiteering and the connection of capitalism to war. Heartfield used photographs to create visual metaphors, for example depicting a stack of coins as Hitler's throat, or a stack of artillery shells as a cathedral. They were a vivid visual protest against National Socialism, speaking the language of metaphor.

With the ascendency of National Socialism in 1933, all critical German documentary, including *AIZ*, was repressed. The success of Nazism is measured in part by its domination of the ideological machinery in Germany from 1933 until the end of World War Two. Aside from newsreels resembling those made in Italy, there was no critical documentary record of German Nazism. The fate of photographer August Sander tells this story: In the early 1930s Sander made formal portraits of a wide range of Germans, listing them by occupation, social class, ethnic background and regional location, but this portrait of contemporary Germany was not consistent with the German concept of Germany as an Aryan race, and Sander's work was surpressed. His photo work during the Nazi era was limited to industrial settings and state projects like the autobahn. Both projects were documentary, but only one fitted the mission of the state.

In the UK, documentary and photojournalism appeared in magazines and newspapers such as *Picture Post* and *Harper's Bazaar*. Perhaps the most sociological of the photojournalists was Bill Brandt, who is sometimes referred to as the most important British photographer of the twentieth century. While he became most well known after World War Two for his surreal nudes, his original notoriety came from two books published during the 1930s, *The English at Home* and *A Night in London*.[27] These books relied on the juxtaposition of opposites to comment on social class and on poverty and wealth in Britain. For example, facing photos in *A Night in London* depict an apparently condescending upper-class couple being waited upon from a sumptuous serving table at an upscale restaurant. The facing photo, showing the street outside the restaurant, features a homeless man searching a garbage can for food. The photo of the homeless man has been reversed, so the shape of his bent-over body matches that of the waiter in the facing photo; they bend toward each other and complete a circle. The reversing of the photo is apparent due to the words "wood" and "new" which appear backwards on the boxes of garbage. Both images have a strong message, but their juxtaposition increases their power. Brandt, writing in 1970, described this work:

> The extreme social contrast, during those years before the war, was visually, very inspiring for me. I started by photographing in London, the West End, the suburbs, the slums. I photographed everything that went on inside the large houses of wealthy families, the servants in the kitchen, formidable parlourmaids laying elaborate dinner-tables, and preparing baths for the family; cocktail-parties in the garden and guests talking and playing bridge in the drawing rooms: a working-class family's home, with several children asleep in one bed, and the mother knitting in the corner of the room. I photographed pubs, common lodging-houses at night, theatres, Turkish baths, prisons and people in their bedrooms . . . After several years of working in London, I went to the north of England and photographed the coal-miners during the industrial depression. My most successful picture of the series, probably because it was symbolical of this time of mass unemployment, was a loose-coal searcher in East Durham, going home in the evening. He was pushing his bicycle along a footpath through a desolate waste-land between Hebburn and Jarrow. Loaded on the crossbar was a sack of

small coal, all that he had found after a day's search on the slag-heaps. I also photographed the Northern towns and interiors of miners' cottages, with families having their evening meal, or the miners washing themselves in tin-baths, in front of their kitchen fires.[28]

Brandt is often thought of as a purist, but he often arranged and manipulated his images. He used models when necessary (his brother and his parents' maid appear in several of his images); he altered prints with paint, ink and pencil, and he even scratched lines in his negatives when he wanted to stress a particular message in the photo. For example, a photo of a dirty child, shoeless, in a London street, contains a white smiling face on the background wall that appears to be chalk graffiti, but was added by Brandt by etching the negative with a knife.[29] He printed skies from one negative and foreground from another to alter the mood of the image. Midway through his career he decided that he liked stark contrast and thus reprinted his most important images on #4 paper contrast, which eliminated much of their shadow and highlight detail. As a result he became known for a contrasty look that only appeared decades after he had made his well-known documentary images.

His alterations were crude by today's standards, and you sense that he would have enjoyed working with modern digital methods. By the war's end he became disenchanted with documentary, and purchased an old Kodak wide-angle camera designed for police work, to make surreal landscapes. Brandt wrote that he was inspired by Edward Weston's comment that "The camera sees more than the eye, so why not make use of it?" and thus he used the wide-angle lens of the Kodak camera because it "created a great illusion of space, an unrealistically steep perspective, and it distorted." He had been interested in surrealism early in his life and he used the old camera to photograph nudes, often outdoors, taking advantage of the peculiar focus, lack of sharpness and remarkable perspective of the lens to explore dreams, visions and the human form. Brandt summed it up:

> When I began to photograph nudes, I let myself be guided by this camera, and instead of photographing what I saw, I photographed what the camera was seeing . . . the lens produced anatomical images and shapes which my eyes had never observed.[30]

Brandt documented social class in Britain by breaking some of the rules of the method, and he later left the genre. He was a photographer first, and followed the camera to several interesting topics and methods.

The final look at the 1930s focuses on the use of documentary by the American government to make a case for its programs and actions. The Farm Security Administration (FSA) photo documentary project is probably the most well known in the history of documentary. It was directed by Roy Stryker, who had been an economics professor before joining the government. Stryker directed twenty-two photographers[31] from 1935 until 1944 (FSA was only marginally active after the US joined the war), who collectively made more than 250,000 images. Stryker's mission, purely and simply, was to show how the New Deal agricultural programs were both necessary and successful. This was an abstract goal for the photographers Stryker hired, who needed to make decisions about where to point the camera. What was their topic and how was it to be photographed?

Stryker was a close friend of Robert Lynd, co-author with his wife Helen, of the community study *Middletown* (1924) and its follow-up ten years later, *Middletown in Transition* (1936). In 1936 Stryker met with Lynd to peruse early examples of the FSA work. According to stories that surround this meeting[32] it was there that sociological photography was first discussed, as Stryker and Lynd thought about directing photographers to record themes, subjects and ideas that would be natural topics to a sociologist. The results were called "shooting scripts;" practical guides for photographing social conditions.

Shooting scripts encouraged photographers to think comparatively, asking, for example: How do people of different social classes spend time at home, attend church, do activities outside work or spend leisure time? The shooting script asked the photographers to visualize the answer to specific questions: for example, speaking of the neighborhoods of different social classes, "What do you see out of the kitchen window?" The photographers were instructed to make images that would examine the relationship between density of population and pressed clothes, polished shoes and other indicators of self-esteem; they photographed newspaper headlines in various locations to see how local, national and international news was being disseminated. They were to photograph agricultural and industrial production: how food was grown, how animals were raised, how farming was being mechanized and how factories, shops and other modes of production were in operation. Stryker asked his photographers to record government projects no matter how mundane; he also instructed them to photograph what the government wanted the country to look like as it fought its way out of a ten-year economic depression. Stryker wrote:

> We must have at once: Pictures of men, women and children who appear as if they really believed in the U.S. Get people with a little spirit. Too many in our file now paint the U.S. as an old person's home and that just about everyone is too old to work and too malnourished to care much what happens.[33]

The shooting scripts were intended to provide a mental grid for photographers entering a new town, region or event, but it is not at all clear that they paid a great deal of attention to the scripts beyond that. There was no systematic comparison in the FSA archives between how social classes worked, lived in separate neighborhoods, spent leisure time or raised children, as Stryker and Lynd envisioned when they created the shooting script idea. The shooting script was a potentially powerful strategy, but it became largely background music for what took place. In the meantime, shooting scripts have been revived by modern visual sociologists for course assignments and other projects.[34]

The FSA has been studied in depth; several years ago I found a several hundred page catalogue listing books, articles and shorter references specifically on the topic. In the meantime more books have been written and more academic theses prepared. In other words, there is a literature awaiting those who wish to study this further.

These examples of documentary during the 1930s, both as still images and film scripts, show how a world in economic turmoil turned to photography and film to explore social problems, to argue for change and to bolster governments, both democratic and totalitarian. To go more deeply into this topic, one would examine socialist realism in the Soviet Union,[35] and the propaganda machine in Germany that included newsreel, film and still photography. The newsreel tradition in Italy was not so different from the newsreel tradition in the US, which lasted until the 1960s. Given that there was yet to be a mass media in the modern sense of the term, the examples discussed above show how photography—still and moving—could be controlled by the state, or could question its legitimacy.

The 1950s and 1960s

In the 1950s in the US two documentary projects are interesting in their extreme contrast. One was Edward Steichen's 1955 photo exhibit "The Family of Man," first exhibited at the Museum of Modern Art in New York, and eventually in nearly forty countries, and published as a book which sold more than four million copies worldwide. Steichen intended to find a common thread in the human experience and to use photography to document it. The exhibit of slightly more than 500 images is guardedly hopeful, emphasizing rituals of birth, marriage and death.

The other documentary bookend of the 1950s (at least in the US) was Robert Frank's *The Americans*,[36] drawing from 30,000 photos Frank made over two years as he drove across the US. Frank, a Swiss photographer, photographed American materialism, class and racial difference, political expression, how Americans meld into and use architecture, and a kind of overriding cultural malaise. The book was first published in Paris because Frank was unable to find an American publisher. When the book was eventually published in the US it was panned by reviews in the popular photography press; one review that became widely quoted assailed Frank for the "meaningless blur, grain, muddy exposures, drunken horizons and general sloppiness"[37] of his images. The American printing was introduced by Jack Kerouac and became a pre-countercultural statement about America. The importance of this work has only increased; in 2009 the book was reprinted and the collection toured major galleries in the US and Europe.

I was an undergraduate in 1968, becoming interested in photography and sociology, when Aperture published an oversized edition of *The Americans*. For me, and many others, the book was a revelation. Frank's photos said that the problem in America was not the war in Vietnam or gender or racial oppression; it was American culture itself. Frank's photos were a visual confirmation of sociology written during the era by the likes of David Riesman, C. Wright Mills, Jules Henry and Christopher Lasch. They were, however, more than that; they created a general sense of the times that continues to be seen as a viable interpretation of a culture at a moment in its history.

The placid 1950s led to the social turmoil of the 1960s, an era that produced a flood of photographic documentary. The range and quality was astonishing. Among the highlights is Bruce Davidson's photo study of Harlem, in which he used a tripod-mounted large-negative camera to photograph the residents and street people of E100 Street.[38] The photos appear to bridge the differences in class and ethnicity that separated Davidson from his subjects, though the book has been criticized, like many similar projects, for transforming poverty into art. The long exposures in the dark settings encouraged stern, serious expressions and formal poses. But the photos were also ethnographic: Davidson showed families in their spaces inside and outside their apartments, doing what they normally did. The book showed how African-Americans and Puerto Ricans cohabited a densely populated urban space, not just the fact that they did.

Davidson's focus had been common ground for documentary photography: East Coast; urban; the poor. During the 1960s, however, documentary expanded to cover a wide range of sociological topics. At about the same time Bruce Davidson photographed Harlem (the early 1970s), Bill Owens, a photojournalist, took a course from visual anthropologist John Collier, who assigned him the task of photographing his own community. His work resulted in the book *Suburbia*,[39] which shows the middle class in one of the many communities that were sprouting in flimsy abandon from the fertile fields of California. Owens photographed houses with thin walls and fake Italian decoration; refrigerators stuffed with huge apples and oranges, large loaves of white bread, beer and pop. People were (often) chunky and softly muscled but they were having fun; they appear satisfied with their lives. In one photo a family turned toward the camera, disturbed from a Sunday afternoon football game, with mildly annoyed expressions that seemed to say: "Get on with it so we can go back to our game!" A portrait of Owens and his wife is included in the gallery at the end of the book and he photographed his fifteen-member extended family in their suburban living room. Most photos have brief captions: for example, a couple is pictured in front of their open garage filled with motorcycles, cars and a speedboat and the caption reads: "We enjoy having these things." A photo shows a teenage son climbing in a very small tree, his father below, sweeping leaves toward the street. The caption expresses the son's perspective: "My dad thinks it's a good idea to take all the leaves off the tree and rake up the yard. I think he's crazy." There are no bookshelves in any of the homes; the furniture and decorations are inexpensive and the dwellings look insubstantial; for my European students they confirmed stereotypes of America. The project showed that photo documentary could highlight one's own place and the rhythms of life that sustained it. Owens' sequel[40] had more detail but less of a sense of discovery, and he subsequently produced few projects that caught the public's eye. In the meantime several documentary photographers photographed their communities; their photos were also studies of social class. They include Mary Lloyd Estrin's album of her family and their neighbors in the manor-like homes of a Chicago gated community;[41] Norman Sanders' photographs of his family and neighbors in upscale Rockland County, New York;[42] Larry Clark's photographs of his friends, whose lives circled around hard drugs, sex, violence and guns;[43] Peter Simon, who photographed life on a rural commune,[44] and Eugene Richards, who photographed his working-class community in Boston, caught in the politics of school desegregation.[45] These were visual ethnographies in the form of visual community studies; records by insiders of ways of life across a broad swath of society. Some, like Eugene Richards' visual poem on his desperate neighborhood, have been sufficiently important to be reprinted by Phaidon, one of the finest photo publishers in the world. Nothing has equaled this vast documentation of the range of communities in a society.

The war in Vietnam appeared in vivid color each week in the pages of *Life* and other then ubiquitous news magazines, and the constant barrage of photojournalist news imagery affected the growing anti-war sentiment. Many visual sociologists, myself included, were of draft age and trying to figure a way through the moral and political issues that the war represented. Several books of documentary photography helped us understand the war, the Vietnamese and the experience of the American soldier.

The most influential of these projects was Magnum photographer Marc Riboud's extended photo essay on North Vietnam, published in 1970.[46] As a French photojournalist Riboud was able to travel extensively in North Vietnam (as he had traveled and photographed in China in the 1950s, well before the country was open to the West). Riboud and writer Philippe Devillers showed a North Vietnam that appeared to be collective, organized and heroic in the face of the rain of bombs falling from American planes. It was a bicycle society in which war production took place in underground factories. The population was disciplined and devoted to leader Ho Chi Minh, who had fought against the French, the Japanese occupiers during World War Two and now the Americans. The book told a different story than had been told by the popular press; the enemy had a face and it was an appealing one.

The other great documentary book on the war was Philip Jones Griffiths' *Vietnam Inc.*,[47] a result of three years in the country. Griffiths' war was a manifestation of American imperialism, and the power of Griffiths' visual argument was his juxtaposition of the mechanized war machine (and the corporations who produced its components) and the determined peasantry it was unable to defeat.

Discussion of photo documentary and the war would be incomplete without mention of *Life* photographer Larry Burrows, whose work was published in book form thirty-one years after his death in combat in Vietnam.[48] Burrows was a photojournalist who spent several years in Vietnam before and during the American military buildup, and his photographs were compelling because he seemed to understand the war in a more complex way than did photojournalists whose cameras showed the carnage alone.

His first *Life* magazine essay was published in 1963 and it contains an image David Halberstam (who wrote the text for the posthumous publication) says captured the essence of the war:

> a photo of about a dozen bodies sprawled in the Delta muck, the Vietcong flag along side them, another group of Vietcong prisoners huddled down, and the background, two American chopper pilots, ever so casually surveying the dead . . . The essential truth of that photo would take some time to dawn on the architects of the war and the general public—that if in the end it took Americans and American technology to kill Vietnamese, then the war could not be won, because the politics of it would inevitably favor the North Vietnamese.[49]

Life let Burrows choose his stories and the war in Vietnam allowed photojournalists a degree of freedom they have not possessed previously or since. Photojournalists were able to move through the country at will; in one essay Burrows looks over the shoulder of a helicopter machine gunner and down 500 feet at soldiers slogging their way through rice paddies. The next photos take the viewer to the ground level, moving through the rice paddies, about to engage in battle. The dead are everywhere and North Vietnamese or Viet Cong prisoners are sullen, resigned or terrified; threatened and bullied by American soldiers or soldiers from the South Vietnamese army. Wounded American soldiers cry out in anguish or hug each other as they lay dying, as they suffer through battles at Khe Sanh or Mutter Ridge.

Burrows looked beyond the facts of the war to understand it. For example, he photographed ten-year-old Nguyen Lau, who had been paralyzed from a mortar fragment, as he spent two years in treatment in the US and returned to Vietnam as a cultural outsider. He photographed a hospital that manufactured and fitted artificial limbs for children. *Life*, which had long been identified with the political right, ran stories week after week in which grisly spreads of wounded or dead American soldiers bled across two-page spreads. It is often said that these news stories had a powerful effect on the declining support for the war.

Much of the 1960s documentary photography focused on social movements. An example is W. Eugene and Aileen Smith's previously cited photo study of a fishing village's response to the poisoning of their fishing grounds. The Smiths became involved with the movement in addition to recording it; during a protest at the trial, Smith, then elderly, was beaten by goons from the corporation that the villagers were suing, which led to the temporary loss of his eyesight. Other photo studies of countercultures showed the civil rights movement, the student movement for democratic action and other manifestations of the 1960s. Among the most important are Alan Copeland's 1969 *People's Park*,[50] which shows Berkeley hippies turning a trashed-out parking lot into a countercultural park, at which point the police tore it up and beat people up in the process. Lorraine Hansberry's 1964 documentary[51] shows social conditions preceding voting rights and the civil rights movement, including lynchings, police violence and a shocking image of a black man burned on a cross. Danny Lyon's photographs of the civil rights movement were published after the fact by the Center for Documentary Studies at Duke University, and present a visual record of the Student Nonviolent Coordinating Committee (SNCC) from 1962 to 1964.[52] It is a visual history of protests, police violence, solidarity and, in one photo, Bob Dylan singing on the back steps of a community center. David Fenton reproduced images from the Liberation News Service, which briefly served as an alternative source of images and information.[53] Finally, the 1973 battle for Wounded Knee, which became a military standoff between Native American activists and the FBI that led to bloodshed, was documented from the inside out, and forever changed how Native American struggles were viewed.[54]

Documentary photographers also told the story of countercultures—hippies in communes[55] and outlaw motorcycle gangs,[56] prisons,[57] deviant lifestyles, including prostitution[58] and traveling carnival strippers.[59] Garry Winogrand documented high society, political culture, public demonstrations, art openings and other manifestations of how the cultural elite weathered the storm of the 1960s.[60] Chauncey Hare photographed the routines of life in corporate America before leaving his engineering job; his visual ethnography of bureaucracy shows the ordinariness of cubicles, files in boxes and workers dwarfed by their habitat.[61]

Because of these and other similar books, there was a growing idea that culture—whether found in suburbia, corporate cubicles, hippie communes or biker bars—is visual and that it can be photographed. For many young sociologists (myself included) this became the critical backdrop for a visual sociology that laid the groundwork for what we hoped would be progressive change. This view seems naïve several decades later.

And what has happened to documentary in the meantime? It would be hard to know the number of titles published per year, but the range of subjects and the complexity of images and themes seem to have grown while the classical book form has itself been challenged by multimedia and other forms of documentary expression.[62]

But documentary projects continue in the spirit and form of those discussed here. What are some highlights? Eugene Richards[63] is among those who continue to document social problems. Lauren Greenfield[64] and Nick Waplington[65] brought color to photo documentary; Waplington's essay on working-class life in the UK communicates the informality and modesty of the community with photos that are blurred, haphazard in composition, and show typical activities and events, and Greenfield's study of female gender identity, especially among teens, depends on color to tell its story. Dale Maharidge and photographer Michael Williamson[66] document changes in central Iowa when newly arrived Hispanic migrants take over jobs in the local hog butchering economy. Peter Menzel photographed statistically representative families in twenty-some countries and their possessions (the families emptied their houses and stood in the middle of these collections and Menzel photographed them with a view camera from a small platform),[67] systematically comparing lives and circumstances. Menzel used a similar approach to photograph how and what twenty-eight families from around the world eat on a weekly basis. Bruce Jackson[68] uses about a hundred prison identification portraits given to him in 1975 to investigate prisons, portraiture and American social history. The Center for Documentary Studies continues to publish photo documentaries of exceptional quality in conjunction with Duke University Press. The recent publication of Danny Wilcox Frazier's photos of Iowa show the seedy side of the verdant Midwest: despair, drugs, social decline.[69] Frazier's book, which won the Honickman First Book Prize in Photography, is introduced by Robert Frank, now an elderly chronicler of the Americans.

It appears that photo documentary in book form is surviving. Modern cameras and software make it much easier to make photos and design books at a time when the public is overwhelmed with choices of how to view the world. The genre, however, remains largely unused by sociologists aside from the minority in the visual sociology community, and that's a lost opportunity. Frazier's photographic statement about rural sociology belongs in rural sociology courses, challenging theories of rural social change. And so on and so forth.

It is clear that documentary continues to provide models for visual ethnographers. Often documentarians gain access to communities that few sociologists can find their way into, or they have a photographic vision that makes them able to see what most people do not. That is the case of Frazier's vision of Iowa; a tawdry world beyond the pastoral myth is revealed. Menzel's comparative projects are sociological but because they are unconventional and creative they would probably not, sadly, be done by sociologists. Having used Menzel and D'Aluisio's book *Hungry Planet* as a required text in a global sociology course for several semesters, however, I can attest to the excitement of sociology students at having the opportunity to see what they otherwise are only able to read about in sociological textbooks.

As a way of summing up, there are several reasons sociologists should study the history of documentary photography. Documentary photography shows us how the world looked in a particular time and place. Interested in France between 1900 and 1936? Louis Clergeau's photos[70] of small town France, its community rituals and events, and the organization of family life, work and leisure shows it incredibly well. Would you like to confront the visual history of Kurdistan? Susan Meiselas' 400-page "family album" summarizes 100 years of Kurdish life.[71]

Sociologists should study documentary to gain a greater understanding of how visual statements are made; studying documentary is no different than studying television news, literary best-sellers, or any other cultural products. Finally, sociologists should study documentary photographers to remind themselves that sociology begins with the observation of social life.

As a final comment, I cited many sources in this chapter, but included no images. There are practical reasons for this that can be boiled down to expense and space. To do a meaningful visual analysis of any of the photographers I've mentioned would require many images. Rather than to offer a single visual referent to these large bodies of work, I refer readers to the extensive Web resources on most of these photographers, in addition to the books themselves.

Chapter 3

Reflexivity

Visual ethnography has recently developed an acute interest in telling the story of the research process as part of the research results, which is now referred to as reflexivity. In this chapter I describe how reflexivity in visual sociology has worked in three projects based on texts and photos, and briefly review what reflexivity has come to mean in ethnographic films.

Rail tramps and homelessness

Like several early visual sociologists, I was inspired by documentary photography and interested in a new sociology as part of the cultural revolution of the times. I was introduced to anthropology by Jim Spradley, then championing a method called ethnoscience. Spradley's study of the skid row homeless[1] was one of the first studies of an American subculture that showed the limitations of the then standard sociological tool kit of questionnaires, statistical analysis and assumptions of scientific objectivity. He was interested in photography and invited me to work with him on a project that became my dissertation and first book. While people were not then talking about "reflexivity" it was the combination of photography, field work immersion and first-person narrative that allowed the story of the research process to be integrated with the story of the culture, which I hope this overview will show.

I had moved to Boston after graduating from college in order to work on the project Spradley had proposed: a more humanistic and "artful" ethnography of homelessness. For several months I photographed Boston's Skid Row as I imagined a photojournalist would, prowling the tough inner city laden with two Nikon camera bodies and several lenses. Boston was a much tougher city than it is now, and it took some effort to be comfortable on the streets with all my photographic paraphernalia. At first I framed people from a distance with telephoto lenses because I was afraid to approach them directly. After a few weeks I ramped up my courage and began to talk to the people I wanted to photograph; explaining my intentions and asking for their help. I asked about the problems they faced and how they solved them, more than the nature of their culture. I often photographed, but just as often I did not. I had begun to think of photography as a means rather than an end, and it became important to fit in; to show respect and to learn from the people I met on the streets. This was an important transition.

After a few months I met a man, Jesse, who had been a junkie and a pusher for several years, who moved into our small urban commune and became a very good friend. Jesse also became an informal partner in my photo project; accompanying me on several forays into the darker parts of the city. For Jesse homelessness was a normal part of an urban scene with decrepit housing, drug trade, prostitution and other social problems, and his tutoring on the sociology of poverty brought our research and normal life closer. After several months Jesse became addicted again, got in trouble and disappeared. It was a terrible loss for me, and undoubtedly a much worse loss for Jesse, whom I never saw again. I certainly learned that research that takes you in as a whole person also can have huge emotional costs.

Knowing Jesse had spurred me to get more deeply involved and to think of my photography as exploring ideas visually rather than making gripping photos. I had diminished interest, however, in East Coast urban homelessness, which had already been studied extensively, and growing interest in versions of homelessness

Figure 3.1
A bottle gang in Boston. The tramps described the hours they had spent getting the 70 cents for the pint of white port, which they drank fast to get a brief high.

that perhaps still persisted in the American West. The homeless men Spradley had studied in Seattle often talked about jumping freights; I had read many books about the Depression, where the tramp was an American icon. In the early 1970s older men on the road might have known Woody Guthrie personally, amazing as that sounds these decades later. I had no idea if tramps who were part of that tradition still existed, but exploring the idea seemed like a natural extension of the project I had begun in Boston.

The great days of the early 1970s! Taking a temporary leave from my job, I hitched from Boston to Wyoming, where I met an old college friend, and we made our way to Seattle, where I photographed the streets and missions Spradley had described. One rough morning an old tramp pulled a rusty switchblade from his pocket and flashed it against my friend's throat. He'd been rolled one time too many and was determined to protect himself. The Seattle Skid Row was an edgy scene and after a few weeks we drove east in an old van, looking for freight yards, tramps and the culture we'd heard about on the Seattle streets. We paralleled the tracks of the old Great Northern in Idaho, Montana and the Dakotas, hanging around freight yards and camping in nearby lots. Most of the tramps we met wanted little to do with us, but some were willing to share enough information that I began to imagine joining them on the trains.

Figure 3.2
Havre, Montana. The tramps were heading toward the fruit and vegetable harvests in the far west and carried all their gear on a hot afternoon.

That fall I began graduate school and enrolled in a one-year course on field work. After reading several field-work classics and some literature that my sage professor led me to (including George Orwell's *Down and Out in Paris and London*, which had a huge impact), I decided on a project that would consist of a two-week stay on Boston's Skid Row in mid-winter (like many universities, Brandeis closed for a month in mid-winter due to the energy crisis), wearing old dirty clothes and carrying only pocket change. Thus I took the subway late one frigid afternoon in February to Boston's Skid Row and walked for several hours before finding my way to a mission. I was startled by how I was treated in my new clothes; I was suddenly either invisible or an object of disdain.

The Pine Street Inn, the mission where I found a bed, remains a vivid image: more than 200 beds on two floors, 18 inches apart and nearly touching end to end. The beds held a straw-filled mattress covered with a hospital sheet, and a single green army blanket. Turned one way I looked directly into the eyes of a tramp; turned the other I'd stare into the eyes of another. We were dispatched to the street at 5:30 and I learned to pass the twelve hours until we were let back into the mission as the other men did. There was a diner that catered to the homeless and for a quarter I could buy a cup of coffee and a donut. I looked for subway grates in out-of-the-way sidewalks where underground hot air would circulate up; I stood in line for watery soup at a police station where I would also get my chit for the night's stay in the mission. I tried to get hired for daily labor at the temporary labor office but was never successful. I would venture into public libraries until I was asked to leave. I searched public phones for change and felt elated when I found coins in several. How remarkably wonderful those nickels and dimes seemed! The experience became a series of routines to fill up time and to look for resources and I was surprised at how soon it seemed natural to be a bum on the streets.

On the last days of the two-week venture I asked my boss, whom I met every fourth day to check on my safety, to fetch my Leica (a quiet, small and unobtrusive camera I'd begun to use). I wanted photos of what I was now regarding as commonplace. I snuck the camera into the shelter, feeling very compromised doing so, and took a handful of photos by holding the camera on my lap, and setting aperture, shutter speed and focus without viewing through the viewfinder. At night I cradled it in a small bag on the cot where I slept; others had precious possessions with them so this was not in and of itself unusual. I took it with me during the day and likewise recorded my new view of the street; particularly the diner in the early hours of the day; the line at the police station and other normal events I had not seen before.

I also spent several hours each day writing descriptions of what I saw; people I met and conversations we had, and what I was feeling. In this way I had begun to integrate photography and a personal kind of writing that my Brandeis professors felt was a legitimate path for ethnography. From these experiences I had begun to find my voice as a narrative field worker.

After this experience I found myself more interested in developing the study
I had begun the summer before, and so over the next three summers I rode freights
through the American West, always photographing and writing.

I made the second trip with a tramp named Carl, a World War Two combat
vet who had spent most of his adult life on the road. We left late one afternoon
from the Minneapolis freight yards in separate boxcars after a fairly hostile encounter
(he wanted no company for the last night of his three-week drunk) and a day later
we met again in Montana, having been directed to the wrong train by a brakeman

Figure 3.4 (opposite top)
The diner was the only place in the city center open at 5:30 a.m., and it was packed with men just let out of the mission. A quarter would buy a cup of coffee and a donut.

Figure 3.5 (opposite bottom)
At noon we lined up for a chit to enter the mission at 5 p.m. and a free bowl of chicken noodle soup.

who wanted us out of his yard. I offered some food I had brought along and as a result "buddied up" (as tramps described their momentary relationships) and headed to the apple harvest in Washington State on the freights. It was not unusual for an older tramp to have a young companion, so tramps we met accepted my presence as Carl's sidekick. I told Carl I was a Ph.D. student doing research for my dissertation and for a time he became interested in my project, and shared his personal history; his reflections on our experience, and his interpretations of what we saw. He was articulate, well read and intelligent, though more than a little hardened by his years on the road.

I learned that Carl's life consisted of episodic drunks, often weeks long, followed by rough traveling, abstinence from alcohol and hard physical work. Tramps picked fruit and other crops from Washington to Florida, and did other work connected to agriculture such as cleaning grain spills in freight yards or herding sheep. Tramps were often cheated by labor contractors and exploited by employers, so many of them (Carl included) felt a connection to the hobos of the past and even the radical labor unions of the homeless like the IWW (Industrial Workers of the World).

It was natural to explore the culture, as Spradley had taught me, by asking people to break it down into categories and plans for action. For example, there were many different kinds of tramps defined from the inside and using terms only a tramp would understand. Some examples were bindlestiffs, homeguards, jackrollers and mission stiffs. There were informal rules about getting drunk, riding trains, sharing food and appearing in public. There were self-rationalizations that all ways of life produce: tramps saw themselves as more authentically American than the middle-class vacationers that we saw driving along the highways alongside our freights. Tramps idealized themselves as independent, tough, individualistic, living in the moment, and escapees from the materialistic trap of the middle class.

I became interested in the various stations of tramp life: the drunk, trips across the whole breadth of the US and intensive periods of work. Identities were threads between various versions of self, and many tramps understood the contradictions between what they said and what they did. I worked at making these categories and the transitions between them visual in the photos I made.

The project became my dissertation and eventually a book,[2] published as the new crisis of homelessness emerged from the Reagan era recession and the final de-industrialization of the northeast. I was often called upon to comment upon this new homelessness, which comprised families in search of work, moving from the northeast to other regions of the country. Nothing I had studied had anything to do with this new phenomenon, but journalist Dale Maharidge and photographer Michael Williamson had just completed a documentary project[3] that explained the role of homelessness in the new social crisis. The two projects—one documentary; one sociology—were similar in method and delivery, both were reflexive in the modern use of the term, and I found their similarity encouraging for both the future of documentary and visual ethnography.

Figure 3.8
As we approached the harvest area, Carl shaved and washed up and made it clear that I was expected to do so as well.

Figure 3.6 (opposite top)
Freight yard with brakeman. A brakeman was often willing to tell a tramp which trains would take us toward our destination if we asked the questions correctly!

Figure 3.7 (opposite bottom)
Carl inside boxcar. For two days Carl said little as he worked through a hangover from a three-week drunk.

During this period both photo documentary and ethnography had assumed a defensive posture; declining in popularity and attacked from the emerging postmodern criticism of science and art in documentary[4], which curiously came together in visual ethnography. The flood of documentary books that examined American social issues had receded; the society in the 1960s that had been so interested in critical self-examination was suddenly less so. Photo documentary became rare even in the professional associations such as the Society for Photographic Education, while the popularity of cultural studies soared.[5] A minority of sociologists used qualitative methods and only a handful were interested in visual approaches. Finally, there were only a few publishers willing to publish books that were partly artful and partly sociological, books that looked and read like nothing in the market at that time. For a while those of us who were interested in visual ethnography and new documentary forms were a very small group, indeed.

Part of the resuscitation of this approach has been due to the sudden popularity of what has been called reflexivity. It was not a new idea, but with a new label it suddenly made ethnography viable again.

How exactly is the term defined? Charles Goodwin calls reflexivity the "reflective awareness of representational practice."[6] Simply said, this means that an ethnography includes the account of its creation. This rejects the idea that

Figure 3.9
After several days of traveling without time or place to make a fire we relaxed in a jungle in Wenatchee. "What's breakfast without toast?" I kidded Carl. He fashioned a bread holder out of a green branch and toasted our last pieces of stale bread.

Figure 3.10 (opposite top)
We boarded a bull local for the ride up the Okanagan River, to the towns where the apple harvests awaited us. At one point there were thirty-eight men in the boxcar and a train conductor, who I'd never seen speaking to a tramp, leaned in the door and detailed where he'd be stopping or slowing. Clearly the freight train had become a passenger train for the agricultural workforce.

Figure 3.11 (opposite bottom)
Jungle in late afternoon. We waited for several days by the employment trailer and then, after all hiring had taken place in late afternoon, we trudged back to a camp—a jungle—where we cooked up what food we'd found or procured. Mostly the same tramps met each day at the jungle; a few left or were hired out, and others joined the group. There would be a fire, shared food and stories. After the day darkened, tramps would walk into the night to find a tree in the orchard to sleep under. There was strict protocol: one did not follow a tramp into the orchard for several minutes; it was assumed you expected to be alone.

Figure 3.12
The employment office for temporary agricultural workers, Brewster, Washington. We waited with other tramps for several days before being hired by a local orchard owner. With a brief handshake we became workers, trading our rough camping for a small cabin in the orchard.

Figure 3.13
Apples, which I became adept at picking. In fact, it is a delicate fruit to be handled with care. A full day's work paid a very reasonable wage, well over minimum wage rates, and our cabin was free.

Figure 3.14
The freight back. After several weeks of work, the season began to taper off and I headed back to graduate school in Boston on the other side of America. I'd been warned not to ride freights after the harvest because thieves—jackrollers—would have their sights on tramps who they imagined would have their harvest wages. Indeed, an hour after taking this photo two jackrollers in Whitefish, Montana, tried to rob me. Only idiots' luck kept my notes, tapes, film and camera (and wages) from disappearing into the abyss of bad field-work judgments.

ethnography can or should be objective or scientific or that the ethnography represents expert knowledge that clearly distinguishes the author from those depicted. As Gillian Rose describes it:

> reflexivity is a crucial aspect of work that participates in the so-called cultural turn. There reflexivity is an attempt to resist the universalizing claims of academic knowledge and to insist that academic knowledge, like all other knowledges, is situated and partial . . . Frequently now, it is assumed that before the results of a piece of research can be presented, the author must explain how their social position has affected what they found, a kind of autobiography often precedes the research results.[7]

Sarah Pink links reflexivity with the ethics of representation when she states that "In some cases this almost resembles a race to be the *most reflective*—a race that has inspired some to define visual anthropology as an unreflexive, unethical and objectifying practice."[8]

Reflexivity in visual ethnography is likely a spin-off of what had been a revolution in filmmaking, which began in the 1960s (and is partly the result of the development of small sound-sync cameras). Peter Loizos suggests that to be reflexive filmmakers identify themselves usually visually, early in the film, as the filmmakers, so that a film is seen to be made by persons, and not by impersonal, godlike forces. A second means has been to leave various bits of material in the film which indicate the nuts-and-bolts of filming: clapper-boards with shot and take numbers, mike-taps, Academy leaders, are now common . . . Thirdly, and more significantly, films often contain elements by the subjects about the filmmaking process, and what they think about it, and indeed, discussions with the filmmakers about their intentions, or the disruptiveness of filming.[9]

The first well-known reflexive film was *Chronicle of a Summer* (*Chronique d'un été*), made in 1960 by French sociologist Edgar Morin and anthropological filmmaker Jean Rouch. The film explores as its central theme how much "truth" it can produce, as it follows several working-class people through Paris and Saint-Tropez. They are interviewed about current events in France and their own state of happiness. The film concludes with the subjects watching completed parts of the film, adding their commentary about how and why the filmmakers were able to record something they could agree was real. In part because of the importance of filmmaker Jean Rouch, the film had a huge impact, and it continues to be studied. Many of the reflexive aspects of the film have become, in the meantime, commonplace.

Everyone has their favorite example of reflexive ethnographic films; mine is Alfred Guzzetti's 1975 *Family Portrait Sittings*. Guzzetti used reflexive methods to explore his own identity and the relationship between his parents by integrating old home movie footage, interviews with his parents, footage his father made with his 8 mm camera, as he filmed Alfred's filming of family gatherings, and Alfred's own filming of family events. At one point his father pointedly asks him on camera how and why he can justify working on such a dubious project as the film in which he's a star.

It is hard to turn on one's television without facing a reality documentary that one can say draws upon a reflexive strategy, yet if anything the popularized fare shows how much more the concept means than identifying the filmmaking as part of the film; more interesting are art films such as the 1967 Swedish film *I am Curious* (*Yellow*) that seemed to operate at several levels simultaneously. Visual ethnographers seldom discuss assumptions about reflexivity, such as the notion that telling one's story as part of the research process is even possible to do.

It may be that in the written and still image form reflexivity is developed in the most satisfying way. One cannot simply film oneself to include one's own presence as a reminder of the process of construction as you can with film, which demands more creative and hopefully insightful approaches. Sarah Pink argues that

> . . . reflexivity should be integrated fully into processes of fieldwork
> and visual or written representation in ways that do not simply explain

the researcher's approach but reveal the very processes by which the positioning of researcher and informant were constituted and through which knowledge was produced during the fieldwork.[10]

Cited examples are sometimes banal; including accounts of tricky field settings, or including images that show the field worker making videos. Finding a truly new form for ethnographic expression is much more difficult.

It is also true that the separation between non-reflexive and reflexive visual ethnography may not be so firm as critics assume. For example, *Balinese Character*, created at a time when anthropology emulated science, does not include the critique of science implied in reflexivity. However, wider reading of both authors suggests their reflexive frame. These include their grant applications, Mead's autobiography, and other papers in which a fuller portrait of the project emerges. It is clear that they both knew that social science knowledge did not come about in a vacuum, and that visual data helped tell the story of the knowledge being made. Indeed Marcus Banks and Howard Morphy suggest that a close reading of the book reveals its reflexive posture:

> There was . . . a strong element of reflexivity built into the method that they developed, since they contextualized their more subjective statements by associating them in their documentation with photographs and other recordings which helped locate their thoughts in time and place. In effect they provided the evidence for the deconstruction of their representations of Balinese society.[11]

In the case of *Good Company*, I felt that my photography had become more reflexive as I had become more and more a part of the life I was photographing. It was not just that I was photographing from an insider's point of view; I was trying to find a way to capture what I learned analytically. It is a matter, in the end, of where to point the camera.

I also struggled with how to tell the story in a time when first-person narrative was not an acceptable form of sociological or anthropological writing. And after two tries at an objectified, scientific prose I finally returned to the first person, and included my own feelings and reactions as part of my report. When I did this reflexivity was not in the vocabulary, and I committed to that form because it seemed the best way to tell the story of the culture.

I turn to two recent visual ethnographies that are excellent demonstrations of reflexive visual research. The first is a ten-year project by anthropologist Philippe Bourgois and photographer Jeff Schonberg, *Righteous Dopefiend*,[12] that explored the lives of homeless drug addicts in San Francisco. Bourgois describes the role of the photos:

> The composition of the images recognizes the politics within aesthetics; they are closely linked to contextual and theoretical analysis. Some

photographs provide detailed documentation of material life and the environment. Others were selected primarily to convey mood or to evoke the pains and pleasures of life on the street. Most refer to specific moments described in the surrounding pages, but at times they stand in tension with the text to reveal the messiness of real life and the complexity of analytical generalizations.[13]

There is occasional tension between images and text precisely because of the success of the photos to describe the field work experience. The photos take the viewer to the street, and they depict the strategies used by homeless addicts to survive, negotiate their relationships, and interact with the institutions that both use and service them, such as police, welfare agencies and hospitals. They also show the affection, friendship and love that connects addicted street people, as well as the abuse, exploitation and deceit that sometimes characterized their relationships. They are intense close-up images that portray disease, filth, violence, disorder and death. They show the conditions that the field workers shared, often sleeping in the open with them, while fighting their battles or serving as intermediaries between the homeless and the institutions that, for better or worse, intersect with their lives.

A tension between text and image develops as Bourgois theorizes about predatory institutions that further weaken the vulnerable (even as they claim to take care of them). The photos suggest different relationships between addicts and hospitals, social workers and others, who appear devoted to their survival. This leaves the reader and viewer with the interesting question of which interpretive direction to follow. Perhaps the theory best describes the reality of the addicts' worlds and this cannot be visualized; perhaps the theorist and photographer experienced a different social world; or perhaps the essence of the culture is a partly contradictory combination of the two.

The best recent example of reflexive visual ethnography is Mitch Duneier's *Sidewalk*,[14] which combines Duneier's text with photographs by journalist Ovie Carter. The book documents the lives of the homeless and the precariously housed in Greenwich Village, who make their livings by scavenging, stealing and selling used books and magazines, and sometimes panhandling. Duneier's involvement was several years long and his knowledge was based on participating in the life as well as observing it. Duneier bridged difficult social barriers to do the research; he was white and young and the people he worked with were African-American and several years older.

The photographs provide a way to explain the culture Duneier discovered on the street. For example, Carter's initial photo shows three used book and magazine tables from almost directly above. The photo would have been made by bending out of a window from a few stories up, shooting with a telephoto lens (the space is compressed). The photo shows how people are distributed through the space, examining books and talking to each other. The tables are orderly and packed with merchandize, and they are set back from the pedestrian traffic, which flows along the bottom of the frame. The single image takes in much of the social scene and suggests in important ways how it is organized and how it operates.

We then see a social map of the relevant streets, spread across two pages. Imposed on this map of streets and sidewalks are thumbnail portraits of the twenty-four African-American street vendors who played a role in the study, and three Caucasian administrator/politicians who first defended and then opposed street vendors. The thumbnails are captioned with names and brief identifiers; Howard is "a comic book vendor who takes no shit from anyone," Hakim, the central figure in the ethnography, is "a book vendor who for years held court on Sixth Avenue." We are thus introduced to the cast of characters whose lives compose an orderly social topography, which is also the main theme of the book: this social world is driven by norms and other longstanding social understandings.

The photos are otherwise uncaptioned, and they cover at least four aspects of the life: the work of scavenging and selling; the places homeless people spend time when they are not working the tables; the interaction between panhandlers and the public; and the interaction between street vendors and the police. A handful of photos also show the politicians (white, well-dressed) in their efforts to rid the streets of the vendors. While there is a great deal of discussion about whether it is ethical or legal to reveal the identity of research subjects, and many university IRBs (Institutional Review Boards) specifically specify that the identity of all research subjects be hidden, Duneier and Carter not only name and picture them, but their book gives them voice. The main informant, Hakim Hasan, joined Duneier in university seminars, and he wrote the afterword to the book. The book is generally considered a model for contemporary ethnography because it demonstrates how reflexivity actually can make cultural description much stronger.

Trying to tell a complete story of culture always fails, but adding a visual dimension makes the inevitable shortcomings much more interesting. The end of scientific assumptions in ethnography liberated people from straitjackets that limited what could be studied and expressed. Visual ethnography (filmic and photographic) is interesting precisely because of the experiments it encourages and supports. I suggested many years ago that reflexivity was a natural part of the postmodern reform of ethnography and the success of some of the admittedly small number of truly innovative visual ethnographies argues this point well. The best examples of visual ethnography are modest and self-aware, yet creative and deeply informing.

Chapter 4

The visual sociology of space from above, inside and around

I now turn to areas in sociology where the visual approach has worked particularly well. The next chapters introduce the current state of visual sociology and the examples show how thinking visually leads to new discoveries and insights. Not every topic in sociology has a potential visual dimension, but the exceptions are few. On the other hand, the visual approach makes it possible to study subjects, themes and areas that can be studied in no other way.

As I begin this overview it is important to note the contribution of an early collection of essays by Jon Wagner[1] that helped define visual sociology. The contributors to the volume included three sociologists, two anthropologists, two architects, a documentary photographer and others from fine arts and natural resources. The essays made arguments that traditional sociologists would find compelling, showing how imagery (mostly but not exclusively photographs) allowed researchers to study old topics in new and creative ways. Clarice Stasz dug into the history of sociology and noted that photography was commonplace in the early decades of the twentieth century but was abandoned when sociology adopted a "numbers-only" orientation in the early 1930s. My essay discussed ethics in a photographic research project, as I questioned whether sociologists had the ethical right to make photographs in field research just because we were there. Photojournalists and documentarians tended to work with the assumed right to photograph everything, and at all times; did we operate under different ethical guidelines? Jon Wagner's contribution showed how photographs could be used in the research process rather than only as a means of communicating what had been learned. Like Becker's essay, Wagner's collection had a huge impact and was largely read and cited.

My overview of contemporary visual sociology begins with the sociological study of space and I refer to the classic text, *Visual Anthropology*, previously cited, by John and Malcolm Collier. John Collier (the father, who wrote the first edition) worked as a photographer with anthropologists in the 1950s who primarily studied non-industrial, face-to-face societies, where the technologies were mostly hand powered and where rituals were mostly public. Social classes lived close to each other and their material distinctions were easily observed. In other words, Collier had a great deal of subject matter to photograph.

Collier also used aerial photography to study agricultural practices and this seemed quite original and interesting to me, especially because I was then studying an agricultural community.[2] Collier was seeing social practices from a different vantage point and understanding them in a new way. I subsequently discovered that archeologists used aerial photography to study the past; the gently undulating changes in the landscape that are invisible to the surface-level eye hold clues of prior land use, fortifications and other aspects of social life.

As I sought to understand both the history of farming and the types of farm systems that had developed in the neighborhood, it seemed that the aerial perspective might yield new information and a new basis for interpreting what I was discovering by other means.

The rural settlement in my neighborhood consisted of quarter section farms (240 acres of woods, pastures and fields) and they all used the same human-powered or horse-drawn tools and machines in the nineteenth-century settlement era. Innovations in the late nineteenth century included the internal combustion engine, which powered tractors that eventually replaced horses; threshers that replaced hand-powered techniques to remove the germ from the wheat or oat stalk; corn choppers that replaced hand cutting, and so forth. When I studied the farm neighborhood in the 1980s, a two-tier system had evolved that anticipated a full transformation of family dairy farming in New York and elsewhere. There was an old system that had developed during the first stages of industrialization around World War Two, and a new industrial model that represented a considerable leap into the future. The new system included freestall barns, milking parlors and manure pits, and it was larger than a family-sized operation could manage. The prior system, where cows were allowed to pasture, and where they would often be kept for more than a decade (grazing on bucolic pastures, watched over by a farmer who knew them individually and took an active interest in their health and wellbeing) was giving way to a system where the cows were packed into freestall barns, milked hard for a year or two, and then rotated into hamburger in a continual effort to improve per cow milk production through rapid genetic change. The old system, which I called a craft system, maxed out at about eighty cows, which the original barns could accommodate, and a family, with a bit of hired help, could manage. Technology consisted of a small tractor or two, and machines that were developed in the decades before and immediately after World War Two. The more modern system, which I referred to as industrial, required new barns and milking systems, and they could be huge. At the time I did my study one farmer in the neighborhood milked 300 cows and now, twenty years hence, there are several farms that milk 1,000 cows. These new farms required a great deal of hired labor, a source of cow feed far beyond what their land could grow, and a way to deal with the massive amounts of manure produced by the huge herds. On the craft farms manure was mixed with straw, and spread daily on fields through the winter, replenishing nutrients and organic matter on the land that grew their cows' food. On the industrial farms the manure was collected in pits or lagoons and spread only a few times a year, and this system is capable of polluting local water sources (especially the many small streams in the region) and stinking up the neighborhood when spread on the fields.

I interviewed farmers on forty-eight contiguous farms that provided information on farm practices and farmers' plans for the future. I also interviewed with photos made about fifty years earlier which provided the core of the eventual book. Some of the data—in this case the aerial photos—were not fully developed in the book although I did publish an essay on these images[3] that I draw from in these comments.

Visual triangulation

Triangulation in sociology refers to collecting data on a single research question with different methods, usually both qualitative and quantitative. It is thought of as a way to overcome personal or methodological bias. In the following I show how visual information—in this case aerial photos—can be used as triangulated data with the data I collected in surveys, ground-level photographs and in-depth interviews. They added complexity to the two-part model described above.

I suggested above that the craft–industrial dichotomy could be represented by the technology used on different farms: craft farms had stanchion barns and solid manure systems; industrial farms had freestall barns and liquid manure systems. Behind these technologies were deep differences between how farmers treated animals and the land, and how they made sense of their lives and planned for the future. The farm system can be summarized below.

These data suggest that the dichotomy makes sense; craft and industrial farms were distinctive because they had different technologies, numbers of workers and different-sized herds which they treated differently. Very often the farms had contrasting overall strategies and plans. But, was this the total picture?

When I looked at these farms from the air,[4] the model was more complicated. There were several variations of craft and industrial farms, and there were several

Table 4.1 Craft and industrial farms

	Craft (N=35)	*Industrial* (N=13)
Number of cows	14–106	55–268
Mean number of cows	46	108
Mean tillable cropland	205 acres	412 acres
Liquid manure storage	11%	54%
3 x a day milking	6%	38%
Horsepower of farm equipment	192	502
Full-time hired labor	0.37 (1 per 125 cows)	1.7 (1 per 63 cows)
Possibility of expansion in 5 yrs	16%	42%

farms with features of both. The aerial photos helped me tell this story about the neighborhood. I will illustrate that with a small number of examples from more than twenty farms I studied with aerial photos.

Figure 4.1 is a quintessential craft farm. The barn houses about forty milking cows and a small number of dry cows and calves. In front of the barn is a manure spreader pulled by a ten-year-old, 40 h.p. tractor, small by the standards of the day. The original home is in the foreground and adjacent is an attached garage/shop. The family auto is parked outside. There are no buildings of consequence in addition to the original barn and shed. A small silo built in the 1940s or 1950s held the corn grown on a 10-acre field.

The farm keeps its expenses low by using World War Two-era technologies. The farmers make breeding decisions cow by cow, often keeping an animal for a decade or more. As a result, their breeding decisions include the temperament of the animals as well as their milk production.

The son's home is a house trailer across the street from the farmstead. It has a covered entrance to store barn clothes in, and to keep the frigid winter air out. The son's family car is also parked outside. Next to the road is a small shed for equipment and a livestock trailer the farmer uses for a side business of hauling livestock to breed or to auction. Both the nature of the housing—a modest trailer— and its proximity to the main house suggest important issues about the family's plans for the future (the son will move to the main house when his father retires) and their immediate working relationship (the son is close at hand for all duties and responsibilities).

The craft farm looks more like the public image of a family dairy farm than do industrial farms. These visual stereotypes include a hip roof barn (usually red), a two-story home with a porch, a separation of living spaces from work spaces, and a sense of order and control represented in the open spaces between living and working areas, and having buildings laid out in a rectangular pattern. The farm pictured in Figure 4.1 is a working operation without a lot of niceties; there is equipment parked outside, including the tractor/manure spreader, but it confirms the visual stereotypes. The barn is red!

The aerial photo summarizes a great deal of information that is partially visible from ground level. Seeing it from the air allows the viewer to see spatial arrangements that imply farming strategies, both short and long term. Seeing the placement and condition of housing, outbuildings, autos, implements and other miscellaneous material fills in editorial nuances about what it is like to be a craft farmer.

The typology of craft and industrial implies that farms belong to one or the other of two types. Figure 4.2, however, shows how some farms are a hybrid that combines elements of both systems. The farm has the look of a craft farm, with a well-preserved original (red) barn, with trimmed shrubs between the symmetrically positioned windows. The farm exudes a sense of order that is associated with a craft farm operation; additional buildings are placed at a parallel or 90-degree

Figure 4.1 (opposite top)
Craft farm.

Figure 4.2 (opposite bottom)
Hybrid craft/industrial farm.

relationship to the original barn, which was the typical form of the original settlements. The original house is well preserved, with a new shingle roof and a porch. It is surrounded by the original maple trees and several new plantings that will eventually replace dying trees.

But the farm has adopted several industrial features. The barn has been transformed to a freestall operation and the cows are milked in a milking parlor rather than in stanchions. These functions have been integrated into the new farm building adjacent to the original barn. It is, however, impossible to read this information from the aerial photo; we cannot see through the roof of the barn to the organization within!

Equipment is kept in a Quonset hut perpendicular to the new barn and the modern, powerful tractor is parked near the country road.

While the herd is typical of a craft farm (about eighty milking cows at the time of the study), the farmer has a liquid manure system, a defining attribute of the industrial model.

The photo shows that the change from craft to industrial farms is often evolutionary, with overlapping systems, operations and implied strategies. While this information would be understood from the data gathered from surveys, the photo explains what an example of the hybrid—in this example a craft farm with industrial features—looks like. The appearance belies an interesting logic, as the farm maintains an appearance that is not consistent with its functioning reality.

There are several versions of the industrial model evident in the photos but hidden in the data. Figure 4.3 is a farm that milks about 200 cows at the date of the study, uses a manure pit (front left of photo) and inexpensive Quonset-style buildings for a freestall barn and equipment shed. The original silo that stored the chopped corn from a field measuring about 10 acres has been supplemented by several modern silos designed to ferment chopped grasses. The original house is surrounded by machinery and vehicles, and perpendicular to the house is a trailer that houses the hired man.

This is an example of the industrial farm boiled down to its essence; a large enclosed space where animals walk about ankle deep in their manure, which is collected daily by a worker driving through the building on a small tractor fitted with a blade, pushing the manure to a pumping station where it is transferred to a huge holding tank. The farm felt like an industrial workspace with its various machines stored in the open, while animals that produced the milk were not allowed to pasture but were left in their rather dreary space.

The farm includes no visual niceties; buildings are inexpensive and utilitarian. The manure pit, one of the first in the neighborhood, is not visible from the road since the top is above eye level. There was a qualitative change in the life in the neighborhood, however, when the manure pit was built, that resulted from the stench created when the manure was spread.

Describing the industrial model only in terms of numbers of cows or workers, horsepower of equipment and other quantitative measures leaves out information that shows variations of the model. For example, Figure 4.4 is an overview of an industrial farm that is constructed on a different logic than the industrial farm shown in Figure 4.3. This farm, then the largest in the neighborhood, increased in size by adding building after building, leading to a complex and less efficient overall operation than is achieved in an operation built or rebuilt from the ground up. New farm buildings in Figure 4.4 encroach on the green space around the house, seen on the upper right hand corner. There are now several freestall barns, making animal management complex. From the aerial perspective one can see how the original barn (center of photo) was engulfed by a modern freestall barn. In the middle right are new bunker style silos (the scale of the ground level construction is made apparent by the tractors that are moving the feed to and from the feeding stations). The ground silo replaces some or all of the horizontal silos, a prior technology that may no longer be relevant to an industrial farm that purchases increasing amounts of feed. In other words, the aerial perspective shows how technologies evolve and overlap. Finally, the manure pit, a defining feature of the industrial model is out of the frame, reminding us that each choice by a photographer makes some things visible and others not.

The two-part typology does not include those farms that evolved into different forms altogether. Figure 4.5 shows a prior farm operation that symbolizes a gracious and elegant past. This farm, a showpiece of local architecture, was part of the original 1830s Scottish settlement and for several generations had been a leading farm in the neighborhood. When the last farming generation retired in the 1980s, the homestead and barns were restored by a son who was not a farmer and the elderly farmer and his wife moved to the ranch house built for them on the adjoining lot (middle frame, right). The farmer and his aging farm truck are visible behind the new house. The swimming hole, used for decades by family and neighbors, is in the foreground of the image. While the image suggests the resolution of a life of farming into retirement, it does not, of course, communicate the emotional costs of the retirement process for the elderly farmer and his wife and the end of a long and successful history of farming. A year after this photo was taken the barns burned down, severing the farmstead completely from its agricultural past.

In this case the aerial photo provides a history of social and material transition. Some of these elements are visible from ground level, but in a different, more fragmented way. The tiny elements seen in the aerial photo—for example, the retired farmer is still doing some farm work in the context of the gentrification of his previous abode—add a poignant sociological aside.

Figure 4.6 documents another version of the post-farm transition; the deterioration of the original farmstead; its use by adjoining farms, and the transformation of an original housing site to housing for a family of the rural poor.

The photograph documents the deterioration of the original buildings. As is visible in the image, the original barn was a "J" shape, with the sections on the left and front almost completely collapsed. The section on the right was roofed with

Figure 4.5 (opposite top)
Retired farm, Jim and Emily
Fisher.

Figure 4.6 (opposite bottom)
Abandoned farm.

metal but the job was not finished and the remaining roof has rotted, making further repair impossible. The farmhouse (lower left in the frame) burned, but not completely; the owner installed a metal roof over the burned shell to keep it from deteriorating further. The photo shows how haphazard strategies for building restoration lead to irrational decisions (insufficient investment to fix the problem, thus money wasted) and uncompleted tasks. The neighboring farmer purchased the farm, where he stores his round hay bales (visible in the upper left of the image) and keeps his cows not currently being milked pastured (upper right).

Next to the house (foreground right) is a dilapidated house trailer that is now rented for a very modest amount to a family of the rural poor. The trailer uses the electrical hookup and well of the original farmstead and provides a small income for the new owners. In this instance the aerial perspective does not provide all the relevant information on the status of the farm, but it reveals patterns, relationships and stages of several social processes. For example, the metal roof of the house hides the deterioration that is the only thing you see from the front.

It is also interesting to compare the aerial photos with eye-level views.

First we ask, who are the people who inhabit the contrasting farm systems? Figure 4.7 shows Buck and Carmen, father and son, who collectively manage a craft farm (Figure 4.1). It is what has been called an "environmental portrait," that is, the image consists of people in an environment that both defines them and that they define with their presence. They stand in front of the barn and we can see that it has metal siding; they are making money. They are big men, accustomed to large meals and twelve or more hours of physical labor, seven days a week. Their work includes maintaining and using machines such as the tractor and front end loader they stand in front of (they asked to be photographed in front of the tractor) as well as managing animals and the business end of the farm. Finally their expressions are welcoming, as they were for the two days we spent together. It is telling that none of the owners of the industrial farms agreed to be photographed. They were inside people, managing finances, schedules and labor. They had the look of harried office workers, completely different than Buck and Carmen. I was struck at the time by how the physical types of farmers matched their farm operations.

We can extend the eye-level view to the interior of the barns, passing into spaces that are covered with roofs and walls. It is interesting that craft farmers welcomed me to photograph in their barns, because they were orderly and typically shared by both cows and humans, but the free stalls of the industrial barns were difficult to gain access to. I think this was primarily because few humans entered the freestall barns on foot (they drove small tractors through the barns to move manure into the pit) and the space is dominated by several-hundred-pound animals which appear to the eye to be trapped in an environment that is certainly not bucolic.

There are also surprises in the interior views. The craft barn is rationalized in the sense that each animal has an assigned place in the barn, and is held in place

Figure 4.7
Buck and Carmen.

with an apparatus. This appears to be constraining, even cruel. Yet cows walk to their stanchions on their own, as they associate their position with feed and milking. They appear to be at ease in their assigned spots; it is clean, there is straw to lie on and their manure is deposited into a small trench behind their place, and later moved outside, mixed with the leftover straw. The freestall barns, with more cows per square foot, allow cows the freedom to wander but create the problem of unrestricted urine and manure. These issues are visible in the images; the stanchion barn is orderly and the freestall barn is crowded and always dirty.

The aerial and eye-level views can be seen as metaphors for theories that identify overall patterns of social life (functionalism; conflict theory) and those that examine the same reality from the inside (symbolic interaction; ethnography). In the aerial photos we see structure that implies human agency and action. The eye-level view shows the presentation of self and the organization of action within a specific setting. Of course these examples are limited but they do show how visual exploration can contribute to sociological theory.

Figure 4.8 (opposite top)
Freestall barn, industrial farm.

Figure 4.9 (opposite bottom)
Stanchion barn interior, craft farm.

Why aerial photos? Why photos?

The essay on this project caught the critical eye of Emmison and Smith, authors of a text on visual methods in the social sciences. An overriding point of their book is that visual sociology should be centered on the act of seeing rather than photography,[5] and to support this perspective they write:

> ... although these [my aerial photos] are helpful additions to his written text, they are not essential for the completion of his research. Harper could just as easily have observed the differences in the farm spatial layouts as he flew over them, noting pertinent features on a code-sheet and so on. The data which are essential for his research are the observed arrangements in the farm buildings, not the representation of these arrangements in a photographic image. The photographs are cosmetic ...[6]

Emmison and Smith's comments point to an interesting aspect of photographic imagery. Elements in the photos could only become data as I learned to understand their significance by comparing them to data gathered in other ways. I would not, for example, have thought about the significance of a rotting round bale of hay or a broken fence, visible from the air, prior to doing the research. Or, it was not necessarily the number of buildings, or the amount of horsepower that defined one farm type against another, but often how the buildings were placed that suggested their role in the farm, and hence their meaning. These spatial relationships were visible from the air, but not visible at ground level. Often I found new technologies were integrated with the technologies they were replacing. In these ways the photos led to an appreciation of small elements seen in their context.

The images led to a fuller understanding of the typology I had created with observations and surveys, and led to theories of how farms had evolved from one form to the other. The in-between cases told as much as or more than those farms that represented the fully developed examples of craft or industrial.

In reference to criticism by Emmison and Smith, even if I had known what to look for, it would have been impossible to skip the photography and get the same information by marking a code-sheet as I flew over the neighborhood. I doubt if the authors had tried to collect visual data from a tiny airplane, but that is not really the point; the meanings of the photos were in their details and the perspective from which I saw them.

The aerial photos are an interesting example of being true because they contain information that I could verify with other data, and they are constructed in the sense of their unusual point of view. It is interesting to realize that it took airplanes or balloons to make that perspective available; a perspective we now take for granted.

Using aerial photography to do a community study brings up an interesting point about privacy. Photography in the public space is, in the US, a first amendment right. Airspace in most parts of the United States is considered public space (there are exceptions primarily for security reasons), so photography from these spaces toward the ground is legal. Is it ethical? I found myself thinking about this as I showed these photos to farmers; I had photographed practices that were ecologically compromised (deep rutting from overly large tractors in wet fall harvests; the positioning of some manure pits; spreading manure at times of the year when runoff would endanger adjoining water sources) and the photos showed what was often invisible on the level. I also observed illegal activity that was much harder to see at ground level. Since marijuana matures after most other plants have died, and they are often seven or more feet tall when harvested, green marijuana crops nestled into the brown background of surrounding crops in back fields were easy to see. Was I not but another element in the increasingly ubiquitous surveillance systems that oversee much of our lives? Practically speaking, could I even assume that the farmer knew about the marijuana plants growing on the edge of a distant field?

The ever-improving mapping system of Google Earth means the top view of the reality we inhabit is being recorded with ever increasing accuracy, and it is available to anyone with access to the Internet. It is possible in Google Earth to move from a top view to a street view in many places; to literally fly to ground and look around. I examined the farms I photographed twenty years ago in the satellite view of Google Earth to see what I could learn and, as it happens, I learned a great deal. One of the farmers I studied in detail is out of business; his barn is leveled (but his manure pit remains); new industrial farms, several times larger than the biggest I photographed, have sprouted where no farm existed before. But I also learned that the Google Earth data are rough and incomplete; part of the landscape is obscured in clouds and the images were made in late afternoon (long shadows) in August (as determined by the state of green and the crops that were harvested) and foliage obscured many of the details that were needed to complete my analysis. New farm operations are also hard to identify from the air; a ground-up design of an industrial farm looks like several large buildings. My aerial research was craft-based; I took photos in specific seasons and under particular conditions to maximize certain qualities in the photos (for example, I photographed in early or late day to maximize shadows); Google Earth is an automated, industrial system that creates a crude overview.

The aerial project shows the potential of freezing a view of social reality from a distance; from the odd perspective of looking straight down. Humans make patterns as they organize their social lives: these might be buildings on a farmstead, suburban housing on sidewalk-less streets or block patterns in cities. As noted previously, archeologists use aerial photos to study the shapes of prior communities which remain as gentle hills, ridges and gullies hundreds of years after all evidence visible from ground level has disappeared. Even where archeological evidence is still vivid at ground level, the aerial perspective offers new insights. If you doubt me, just ask Google to search "Hadrian's Wall aerial photographs." The social organization of the Roman frontier settlements and fortifications will be revealed in the wall constructions, the castle forts at each Roman mile and the larger fortified settlements here and there along the 100-mile barrier that was the northernmost border of the Roman Empire. For nearly 2,000 years, since the wall and adjoining fortifications were built, but before there was an aerial perspective, people understood how shapes seen at ground level reflected patterns of social life. They are understood in a fuller and better way, however, from an aerial perspective (for example, the social organization of defecation in the public latrines—it was not a private experience—can be seen in Google Earth photos). The aerial overviews communicate new aspects of the social organization of a small piece of the Roman Empire, from the minutia of social life to the bureaucratic organization of an occupying military force.

The aerial perspective also shows the disastrous and contradictory effects of human action on the land. There are many examples, but I'm thinking in particular of Emmet Gowin's aerial photos[7] of nuclear bomb test sites, bomb disposal craters, offroad traffic patterns on the Great Salt Lake, weapons disposal trenches, copper mining and ore processing facilities, labyrinths of trenches left behind from uranium exploration, pivot irrigation and drainage ditches, aeration ponds in toxic water treatment facilities and abandoned Minuteman missile silos through the American West. In Czechoslovakia Gowin photographed what he called the effects of Soviet Cold War bureaucracy: 30-kilometer-long strip mines several hundred feet deep, surely some of the most profound environmental havoc ever created; razed agricultural villages replaced by high-rise "micro-cities" for workers in a newly created industrial landscape, that show the draconian character of decision-making in totalitarian societies. The aerial photos make social policies visible but only from one perspective: American agricultural subsidies create pivot irrigation systems for the production of largely unneeded crops, but the photos do not show the depletion of ground water these irrigation systems produce, which will introduce new environmental crises. They will be shown in the next generation of aerial photos. Taken as a whole Gowin's photos show the ominous background of the preparation for nuclear war, the aftermath of conventional war and the costs expressed in erosion and water depletion of agricultural policies.

The aerial perspective may be most interesting because it reminds us that what we see is a matter of how we look at it. Our knowledge, our values and our data are a product of seeing. When we radically change it, we come to new conclusions. Galileo's view through the telescope forced him to abandon the Christian view of a universe created by God and inhabited by his favorite creatures, us. He didn't want the new knowledge because it challenged his religion as well as everybody else's (not to mention getting him into a lot of hot water), but he could not deny it, either.

Understanding space in the city

So much for looking down at social existence. I now approach the material world at eye level, with the same devotion to making headway on rather conventional questions in sociology. In this case my example is William H. Whyte, a journalist in the 1950s who wrote one of the classics of sociology, *The Organization Man*. Whyte was not a professional sociologist, but he worked on the margins of the discipline and did some of the most interesting work of his era. In 1969 he joined the New York Planning Commission and began sixteen years of research that led to his book, *The City*, and other publications. Though he never used the term, he was a visual sociologist and showed in practical terms how to study the city with images.

He directed research teams in New York made up of graduate students who observed and interviewed, and photographed with still and movie cameras, often mounted on construction scaffolds or positioned in rooms of deserted hotels across from research sites. They used time-lapse photography and film to record the street from above, and hand-held cameras to photograph at street level. They attempted to remain unobserved, hoping not to influence the behavior of the mass of humanity that was their subject.

Their observations were data; there was nothing artful about the images. The images recorded behavior to answer questions about urban life. The book contains 102 photos that are largely without captions, and they have no artistic pretensions. They represent a small percentage of the images made and we don't know how the visual data were coded or analyzed. My guess is that it was very straightforward: a problem was identified for study and images were made to evaluate it. With new digital technology the coding of visual material would be simpler, and probably more effective.

The research teams began with questions such as how many people used an urban space, and what seemed to influence the rate of use? Did people in public appear to accomplish what they intended to? There were also implied questions: Were people having a good time? Did the city provide a positive, safe experience? Did it integrate people; entertain them; enlarge their sense of the possible? What policies created the opposite, that is, alienation of people from each other; boredom, or fearfulness and disgust?

The teams counted pedestrians in different neighborhoods at different times of the day, week and season. They measured sidewalk widths, mapped social interaction in plazas and parks and hypothesized what shapes and sizes of spaces encouraged certain kinds of interactions. They categorized people and watched how they interacted. Some of this is outrageously politically incorrect thirty years later: for example, Whyte observed different types of "girl watchers;" both their behavior and the responses they received from women. They experimented by having the same female researcher dress "beautifully" and "unattractively" (their terms) at different times and noted that it appeared to be the clothes rather than the particular person who wore them that brought the reaction from males.

Most of Whyte's research examined practical questions: how many people could use a 14-foot sidewalk? How could a city encourage the use of its expensive and extensive public spaces? Did street commerce (buying and selling on crowded sidewalks) encourage or discourage people from entering shops? Did restrictive policies keep "undesirables" (which Whyte defined as dope peddlers, muggers and others who preyed upon a public; not the homeless or the eccentric) out of a public space? His answer was that it did not; if you restricted the use of a public space it would attract more of what they termed "undesirables," not fewer. The way to discourage the destructive deviants was to make the space welcoming to all, and a high population density would tend to drive the deviants to other urban regions.

In his obituary, he was quoted as saying that the city "has always been a mess and always be something of a mess," but that was its charm. Clearly he favored urban spaces where extremes met and interacted. He favored an urban block made up of many small shops and enterprises on the street level, on second floors, and in small storefronts, and he noted that when they were replaced by an office tower or, worse, a wall, the city lost a part of its vitality and strength. He believed that density and mixture created the best urban spaces, and that many American cities were being redesigned for low-density use and the elimination of people from the urban scene. Cities such as Dallas, designed for cars rather than people, were singled out as the worst examples. The model Whyte saw emerging has indeed become the typical American city, largely with the outcomes he had predicted.

He had enormous influence as editor of New York's Master Plan, as redesign consultant of Bryant Park and as a frequent consultant in the urban redevelopment process in New York and other cities. Rarely has a sociologist had as much impact on the subject he studied. His use of visual images to study public life in the city, however, has yet to be emulated on a wide scale.

Piazza Maggiore: The sociology of a small urban space

Whyte's efforts inspired an ongoing study of the social life of an Italian piazza I have been working on for several years. I first visited Bologna, an ancient university city in northeastern Italy, in 1988. I spent much of my five days there wandering the streets photographing and I sporadically attended a conference that met far from the city's core. In the city center I was struck by the contrast between the warren-like streets and their covered sidewalks—porticoes—and the piazzas they led to. Some porticoes were more than 1,000 years old and they created spectacular urban spaces; sidewalks covered from the rain or direct sun that funneled pedestrians past fashionable shops and stores. The columns that formed the outer walls separated the pedestrians from the street traffic and created playful patterns of shadow and sun.

The overall urban design was, however, compromised by auto traffic; many piazzas had become parking lots and the cacophony of car and scooter traffic on the narrow streets was amplified in the covered porticoes. But on my first Sunday in Bologna I was startled to walk from my hotel to the central piazza, Piazza Maggiore, to an eerie and enticing soundtrack: no cars; no scooters, just the murmur of thousands of conversations. I discovered that the leftist city government had closed

Figure 4.10
Bologna, Sunday afternoon without motorized traffic, 1988.

the city center to motorized traffic on Sundays and as a result I experienced the city the way it had been from Roman times until the early twentieth century. My first photos of the Piazza Maggiore were made that day and it made me think that ideas such as Whyte promulgated were second nature to Italian urbanists who had been designing cities for hundreds and hundreds of years.

In the meantime I have returned to Bologna on more than twenty occasions, and I have always photographed Piazza Maggiore with a sociological eye, looking for "things people do," "elements that influence social action," and "sub-regions in the piazza and their social uses." There was always something different going on, and it was almost never without throngs of people; that is, except when on a national holiday in December I went at the first light of day and found it largely deserted. My photos from that morning have an eerie sense of having transported the viewer to the nineteenth century. On the Saturday evening preceding Easter, I found it lit with a massive TV showing the Pope addressing the faithful. Before Christmas there was a skinny, drunk Santa and a photographer offering to pose with children for a fee (I saw none take the offer). For two years the steps in front of the cathedral were blocked off from pedestrian use and police monitored everyone entering the piazza at a checkpoint set out in front of the doors. There had been terrorist threats to bomb the church because it contained a painting found objectionable to some Muslim visitors. This changed the nature of the piazza and led to public outcry; eventually some but not all of the barriers were removed; but the social life on the steps of the cathedral did not recapture its prior character. In the summer denizens of the piazza seek shade; in the winter they move with the sun to remain in its warmth. Children use the piazza as their playground, chasing pigeons, batting balloons, or kicking soccer balls back and forth to each other. In the winter of 2010 a rare snowfall left a foot of snow in the piazza for several days and it became a temporary winter playground; I photographed a snowball fight that lasted for nearly an hour. Returning in the summer of 2011 I found that the piazza had been taken over by a huge movie screen, hundreds of portable chairs fastened together and a projection room as large as a small cabin, all to show movies each evening. It felt to me, an outsider, like the ruination of a public space but the seats were full for the evening showing. In other words, the piazza is a living, breathing space, adapting itself over time, weather and even political contexts to one purpose after another. It is clearly successful, but vulnerable.

The themes of action (what people do); actors (different groups); sub-regions of the piazza; and factors influencing social uses are, of course, all intertwined. Even coding several hundred photos on these themes often led to conundrums in which every coding decision is partly correct and partly incorrect. Still, the result was an overall portrait of a complex social arena, constantly evolving.

I also thought about my own reactions to the piazza; how my feelings evolved from that of an outsider to a seasoned visitor. Because Bologna is off the common American tourist route it largely avoids the marching armies of outsiders that take over the piazzas of Rome, Florence, Siena and Venice. As an American I was a minority even among visitors and felt that my presence (or the impact of others like me, that is, American tourists) had little impact on the piazza.

Like Whyte I have been interested in cataloguing social behavior through photography. His research teams treated images as objectively as the teams could make them. The cameras were mounted on fixed vantage points and recorded images at predetermined intervals. The resulting photos still embodied human intentionality (the subjectivity of a point of view), but having said that Whyte's research teams used the photos to record what passed by, purely and simply.

My photography was different: I interpreted as I observed. For example, I often framed photos of children from their height or lower, and I photographed into the sun in late afternoons because people faced the sun when they interacted with each other. I tried to communicate the subjective nature of the piazza; what it feels like to be there, as well as information on who is there and how they interact. Though I have been making photographs for this study now for twenty-three years, it is not yet finished.

What follows is a small excerpt from the visual study of the piazza that focuses on uses of specific sub-regions. From the 3,000 images currently in this project I could have chosen several directions for this excerpt, such as activities, or factors influencing change in the piazza.

When I began photographing the piazza I often wished I could hover in a balloon over the square to photograph it. Aerial photos were hard to find! With the advent of Google Earth the aerial view became available and surprisingly detailed, though pixelation is visible in images downloaded from the system.

The Google Earth view allows us to see the physical relationship between the piazza and the city; the core from which streets radiate to the ancient wall, now a ring road. The remarkable detail of Google Earth allows us to gain an appreciation

Figure 4.11
Piazza Maggiore from
Google Earth.

for the various elements that make up the piazza, such as the intrusion of tables into the piazza from the restaurant on the northern border, or the presence of police vehicles on the northeast corner of the square. What is particularly useful is seeing an overview that reduces the piazza to a series of rectangles, some a bit out of square, joined where the piazza changes its character.

We enter from the northwest entrance to the piazza, passing through the adjoining Piazza del Nettuno, past a sub-region of the greater piazza containing a wall of memory dedicated to the more than 300 Bolognese partisans killed by the Nazis in the waning months of World War Two. On the anniversary of the end of the war in Europe (May 8), the wall was decorated by wreaths and potted plants and visited by elderly Bolognese, who studied the ceramic images that commemorate those killed more than fifty years before. Perhaps they were studying the wall to find the face of a friend or a loved one.

Usually the partisan region is frequented by teens. The presence of teens in this space is so common that it seems they have claimed it as their own; indeed at the height of the 2010 snowstorm they were the only people in the piazza. In Figure 4.13 they ignored me as I approached and photographed them, even from conversational distance.

One passes from Piazza del Nettuno into Piazza Maggiore by navigating to one side or the other of the dramatic Fontana del Nettuno, a place where tourists and natives rest on low steps or pause to admire the fountain. Because of its central location it is a meeting place both for those familiar with the piazza and newcomers. Often tourists sit on the surrounding ledge and read guidebooks, and others just enjoy the vantage point.

The long wall on the western side of the piazza is the elegant façade of the Comune di Bologna, the city's administration building. It is a region that is passed through more than occupied, though on several occasions jugglers, actors doing mime and other street performers located themselves in this region of the piazza.

On the far southwestern corner the piazza opens up to a secondary tiny and unnamed piazza. On the southern side of this sub-piazza is a shop for hats, the Cappelleria Dante Barbetti. The antiquated fonts that decorate the store front and the old-fashioned hats give the location the feeling of a set from an Italian movie from the fifties. The distinctive feature of this mini-piazza is benches set at regular intervals. The benches are located in the only place in any of the spaces in the Piazza Maggiore that is formally designed for sitting and they are nearly always occupied. The arrangement of the benches discourages face-to-face conversation, since the conversers are side by side rather than facing each other.

While it is perhaps an error in urban planning, it has not been fatal; the benches are used. Occasionally teens use these places to make out, which teenage Italians have made into an art form. As a liminal urban region it carries some of the rules and traditions of the regions it borders; there are often cars driving sneakily through the piazza, which is confirmed by Google Earth aerials and several photos in my collection.

Figure 4.12 (opposite top)
An elderly man studies photos of partisans, victims of Nazi violence, on the anniversary of the end of World War Two.

Figure 4.13 (opposite bottom)
Teens in the partisan memorial area.

Figure 4.14 (opposite top)
Neptune as a resting place.

Figure 4.15 (opposite bottom)
Mimes busking.

From the small piazza by the hat shop we pass to the east in front of a small bar (Bar Romano) that often extends into the public space, usually with tables intruding directly into the piazza. The tables introduce the issue of the fluctuating boundary between public and private uses of the piazza. The piazza, of course, is public space, and the bar is a commercial establishment. People use and expect tables in this situation; occupying them is almost a public pastime in Italy. Either bureaucratic rules or more likely unwritten norms guide how far Bar Romano or other establishments can extend themselves into the piazza. The largest restaurant in the piazza on the northern border has sometimes gone so far into the public space that it threatens the character of the shared areas. These would be the questions that a sociologist like Whyte would be preoccupied by: How do the interests of the public and the private intersect in a question as to the proper and optimal extension of tables into the piazza?

The cathedral across from the small bar (the Basilica di San Petronio) is the historical basis of the piazza, and the spiritual center of the city. A famous if not beautiful cathedral, it was once the largest in Italy and several centuries ago was considered the leading candidate for the center of Italian Catholicism. The front of the piazza has been the most active social region of the piazza.

The steps provide seating for a wide variety of people. Some lounge, (seeking shade in the summer and sun in the winter, using the slight elevation to observe

Figure 4.16
The hidden piazza.

Figure 4.17
The steps and entrance to
Basilica di San Petronio,
unimpeded.

the activity in the piazza). As is evident in the photo, the ledge around the front of
the cathedral becomes a bench.

Others use the elevated position to present their political views (Figure 4.18)
or to present special worship spectacles, especially during the Easter holidays, where
the Pope may appear via a huge television screen, or religious luminaries may appear
to address large crowds in the piazza.

Figure 4.18 (opposite top)
Steps as stage for protest.

In recent years, since the threatened bombing, the steps have become a
policed space with a path established by markers that all entrants to the piazza must
pass through, and a metal detector that examines all entrants to the cathedral. The
steps and the small flat area between the cathedral and the top of the steps have

**Figure 4.19 (opposite
bottom)**
Altered entrance.

lost their special place in the piazza and one can say that this change has profoundly affected the social life of the piazza. While some of these restrictions have eased, the entrance to the cathedral has not returned to its prior openness.

The long span on the eastern order of the piazza is typically devoid of humans. That is partly due to the portico (the covered sidewalk), invisible in the Google Earth photo. There is occasional bus or car traffic sneaking illegally along this path as well. The photo shows a particular characteristic of modern Italian piazzas and streets, where large, sparklingly clean shop windows reflect the surface to passers-by. As a result the window becomes both a view inward at displayed products, and a mirror showing the piazza.

On the eastern boundary an important side street leads to markets and food shops; the taxi stand invites the urban traffic into the edge of the piazza and on the northern border a large restaurant commands the view of the center of the piazza and the cathedral. The restaurant expands into the piazza, often by the depth of six to ten tables, and tourists and others sit at the tables to be entertained by the public square before them. I complete the visual inventory of the piazza with two panoramic photos that face each other across the expanse of the public space. After the details of the previous images these provide a sweeping context.

I end this brief sociological tour of the piazza with an image (Figure 4.23) that shows one of many ways in which the piazza has been transformed in recent years.

Figure 4.20
The portico area as liminal space.

Figure 4.21 (above top)
Facing southeast; in the
foreground the restaurant
intruding into square;
background center
San Petronio.

Figure 4.22 (above bottom)
Facing northwest; overlooking
the steps of the cathedral into
the center of the piazza.

Here the piazza becomes an outdoor movie theatre; several hundred chairs are linked
together and remain in place during the day through much of the summer; a semi-
permanent building houses the projection system at the western side of the piazza
and the huge screen occupies the eastern boundary. Hundreds of Bolognese attend
these movies (one evening in 2010 the film was *Fargo*, though classics of Italian
cinema are more typical) and thus they escape their sweltering apartments in the
evening hours. Showing movies in piazzas is an Italian tradition dating to the 1930s,
so this is not revolutionary in and of itself. Yet the effect on the piazza is profound.
The screen, chairs and projection facility has taken over the scene completely. Some
people who would have hung out in the piazza before it became an outdoor theatre

Figure 4.23
A tourist alone in a
transformed piazza.

still do but for the most part the piazza has lost its identity as a pulsating region in which many very different groups congregate, interact and otherwise experience Italy. Some auto traffic had begun to creep in as well, which I think is partly a result of the precedent set by the now common military and police vehicles that patrol the piazza.

This brief journey offers an introduction to an ongoing study. Given the number of years involved, the study makes me aware of change. Some are modest: changing hemlines and hairstyles, and fabrics for the suits men wear on Sundays. Others are profound, threatening an end to a central feature of Italian cultural life.

The project on the Piazza Maggiore makes a case for an empirical visual sociology. I photograph the piazza to remember my observations, and often to discover elements in my photos I had not seen. For the most part I am an unobserved observer, a fly on the wall. Occasionally people react to my presence, but not very often. Others are in the piazza, photographing each other or just hanging out being tourists (usually German or Eastern European, and they often have cameras) or, of course, Bolognese. So there is an identity I can blend into; the piazza is a public space that I can be part of, and making photos there does not violate the norms of public life in that situation.

However, the project seems limited if left in this form. The photographs could be the basis of a public forum or discussion that would question policies regarding

Figure 4.24
The outdoor movie screen, for several weeks each summer, dominates the eastern region of the piazza, transforming its use.

vehicular traffic, the expansion of restaurants into the public area, the use of the piazza for outdoor movies, the policing of the entrance to the cathedral (and the security system in place which ruins the steps as a public area) and other issues related to the role of the piazza in contemporary Italian life.

The study will expand in 2011 to include elicitation interviews with people who are all connected to the piazza in one way or another: kids, mothers, teenagers, old men, tourists, sanitary workers, city politicians, homeless people, refugees and others. We expect to show the piazza as a contested but largely harmonic urban region that solves many problems and provides many entertainments, and expresses the quintessential urban Italian experience, worthy of considerable preservation efforts from one or another force that threatens it.

Two projects have recently followed this path. One was completed by several sociologists who studied British city-center conditions[8] by having participants complete photo surveys of the city centers. Eighty-four participants produced what the researchers called a "sea of data," and at this stage a research report that describes the project is largely what has been produced. Its most important side may have been the way it galvanized researchers and activists to think about and engage in improving the city centers they photographed, interviewed people in and re-imagined. The challenge for visual studies of this scale is that it is often easier to generate a lot of visual information and text in the form of interviews and analysis than to distill it into findings. An excellent solution was created in the exhibition and website OPEN/CLOSED: Public Spaces in Modern Cities,[9] by Russian sociologists and photographers Lilia Voronkova and Oleg Pachenkov, which asks such questions as "What is public space? What makes a space public? What does it look like or what are the new aesthetics of urban public space? What role does public space play in the life of cities today? How is public space changing and why? Who organizes and who rules public space? Are we witnessing a decline of urban public space?" and so on. The exhibition (which was displayed at the Department of European Ethnology of the Humboldt University in Berlin) presents the work of seven researchers who studied Lviv, Manchester, St. Petersburg and Sofia. Their goal was to include images and they are on the website as answers to questions or musings on themes announced in the text. The website, meant to raise questions rather than to answer them, is beautifully designed and includes large-format, analytically captioned color images. The project offers a fine example of how to present material once collected, and how to preserve it, at least to the degree that the Web can be depended upon.

I have presented human spaces from above and at eye level. There is also the matter of being in space and both visual sociologists and documentary photographers have explored this territory. Because I'm going to explore this subjectivity and visual representation in greater depth later, I'll just mention books like documentary photographer Bob Adelman and Susan Hall's *On and Off the Street*[10] in which two ten-year-old boys, one black and the other white, move through their urban universe (New York); have an argument and make up. It tells the bigger story of the world as experienced by kids in the city in the form of a photo narrative; a wonderful strategy, seldom used. Sociologist Helen Stummer, a white middle-aged photographer, immersed herself in the toughest ghettos of Newark for more than a decade and told stories both in words and images of black, marginalized ghetto residents.[11] The images are unsentimental and full of hope. Camilo José Vergara's *Subway Memories*[12] begins as a recollection of hundreds of trips on New York's subway with his two children before becoming a meditation on the evolving machines, public art, levels of deterioration and the guarded companionship of other riders. He is well known for his large-format portraits of declining urban areas, which are discussed later, but this work shows how photos grabbed with a small camera (at least I assume it is—he doesn't say) record and interpret what it feels like to be in a particular urban space. When one reads an essay like sociologist Murray Melbin's "Night as Frontier"[13] one imagines the night as inhabited in the city, with different norms, different stresses, different patterns of social control and different kinds of friendships and relationships. Books such as Ken Schles' *Invisible City*[14] provide visual referents to these ideas, framed by commentary by Lewis Mumford and Jean Baudrillard. The list could go on and on; my point is that when social space is imagined it can be represented visually, though the means to do so will tax the tools used by most sociologists. There remains a treasure trove of documentary examples to point in new directions. It remains for visual sociologists to educate themselves and to apply some creative redefinition to old tasks of understanding the material world we inhabit.

Chapter 5

Comparing societies

We turn from material culture to the visual study of social change and the visually comparative method. Many fundamental ideas in sociology, for example Marx's theories of dialectical materialism, describe change with visual metaphors. For Marx the essential idea is a sequence of societies that come apart and take new forms. Whether sociologists think much about it, the imagination of change and comparison is always partly visual. Our mind conjures up elements of a time and place and imagines it giving way to another. Recently visiting the Lake District in England I was struck by a water wheel preserved in a local museum from 1830 that visually summed up the origins of the industrial revolution, before internal combustion engines took over. It was a modest technology, but seeing that one element made it possible to imagine the entire system. Later, on a path called Corpse Road, we came upon what looked to be a worn stone couch that a small plaque identified as a "coffin rest." It was a platform where pallbearers had paused to rest the coffins they were carrying several miles to a village with consecrated land, since their village had none. The ancient churchyard in that village was bordered by a stone fence that marked the consecrated land, and inside the fence the graves were so crowded they were nearly stacked upon each other. The power of the church in the pre-industrial period to publicly announce who would be welcome at the pearly gates was shown in these crowded burial spaces, now neglected and covered with moss. These were all visual traces of history at one stage, implicitly moving to another.

The past is much with us, but it leaves messy records and understanding them takes a great deal of effort, coincidence and luck. There are occasionally simple references: the coffin stone, worn smooth by hundreds of years of service, and the crowded graveyards are examples. We learn from other records that it was only in the 1830s, with the industrial revolution-based urbanism in the UK, that the church lost its monopoly over burial and thus much of its social power. The stone is a visual reminder that one can look at, describe and photograph the past, but it takes some sociological sniffing about to ferret out the meanings of these visual traces. The population increase in Manchester (as noted by Engels in his depiction of the working

Figure 5.1
Coffin rest, Lake District, UK.

Figure 5.2
Graveyard, northwestern UK.

class)[1] was rapid in the early eras of industrialization and with it came the decline of rural society dominated by religion. The state established burial laws and huge graveyards for the citizens of the new cities. A space would be consecrated inside these graveyards for the burial of the officially blessed, but all of a sudden one's membership of the elect was not as easily seen or as important as before.

It should also be said that little sociology can be drawn from these visual traces if they are left to themselves. They are so much more than their clues allow. We can visit the ruins of a third-century Roman bar in Ostia Antica, but we don't know who drank there and what conversations or business would have taken place. We can admire the ornate architecture of a Venetian guild house, but to know what went on inside we need more and other kinds of information.

Gillian Rose suggests that discourse analysis, attributed to Michel Foucault, may be a helpful direction for historical visual analysis. She summarizes discourse as "a particular knowledge about the world which shapes how the world is understood and how things are done in it."[2] The statements that create the basis of discourse can be visual as well as textual.

This perspective acknowledges that seeing embodies power; in Rose's words, "A specific visuality will make certain things visible in particular ways, and others unseeable . . ."[3] This is demonstrated, for example, in informal displays of power that normal gender interactions include. Rose quotes John Berger's 1972 essay: "a woman must continually watch herself. She is almost continually accompanied by her own image of herself."[4]

Rose references studies of late nineteenth-century East London, an area of persistent urban poverty that recorded what was happening there and how the discourses about the situation were framed. Because the situation contradicted expectations (the poor remained poor despite the increase in wealth in the UK) the poor were blamed for their poverty. Discourse analysis is not a matter of simply seeing various points of view, but understanding how these were constructed and used in power struggles between institutions or communities. For the historian, understanding discourses takes painstaking research. Rose suggests that the researcher study virtually all texts,

> . . . contemporary newspapers . . . contemporary accounts of visits to the East End by journalists, clerics, philanthropists and others, which often take the form of travel diaries and could be published in pamphlet or book form as well as in newspapers; novels and, less often, poems; documents produced by various branches of government such as the census, reports by local medical officers of health and other sorts of government reports. Many of these written sources are illustrated with images—often engravings—or with maps, cartoons or other images. Almost all of these historians also use photographs of the area, some taken by philanthropic institutions and some by journalists . . .[5]

Rose, via Foucault, suggests that the most effective way to understand the past is to study how people in the past saw, experienced and defined their worlds. It is necessary to abandon a perspective grounded in our time and place, and to create another. The interpretation of visual information is a crucial part of this process.

Studying social change

Photography's ability to record what is viewable encourages its use in the study of social change. The idea is simple: photograph what was photographed before, and do it very carefully, matching lenses, camera formats, precise framing, weather and seasonal variables and other elements that affect how the photos will look. All the elements that make a photo look a certain way can be controlled, so the only source of difference in appearance is the difference in time between photos made at different times.

But because photography was invented in the mid-nineteenth century, rephotography (as it is known) only reaches back about 150 years. Occasionally there were extensive photo surveys that lent themselves to rephotography. For example, landscape photographers in the 1970s rephotographed sites throughout the American West that had been photographed by the US Geological Survey 100 years before.[6] This became a mini industry which was redone and expanded some twenty years later, and republished as a third view in 2004.[7]

The original archive referred to above existed because the national government had been sufficiently interested in boundaries and new lands to make a record of the expanding nation. Photographers included Timothy O'Sullivan and Henry Jackson. The rephotography project completed in the 1970s produced a record of American settlement and sprawl, as well as ecological change in water levels and patterns of plant growth. Most towns had grown and spread out; some had declined and disappeared. A viewer comes away with a sense of impermanence and change in a particularly American version.

The ideas explored in the American West project are straightforward: first there is no settlement and little trace of human habitation; then there is settlement and its various effects. It was not until the work of sociologist Jon Rieger[8] that sociology had its first visual studies of social change. His ongoing study of an isolated region in northern Michigan has shown details of a rapid and profound social change, and his methods have largely defined a method for visually studying social change.

Rieger was a member of a research team from the University of Michigan when he was a graduate student in the late 1960s, studying why young people were leaving an isolated region in the Upper Peninsula of northern Michigan. The largest settlement in this region in 1970, Ontonagon, had at that time a population of just over 2,000 people, and the towns of the region were economically viable, with local businesses connected to mining, logging and farming. Rieger photographed about seventy sites in the research area using black and white film. At that time, he writes, he did not expect to return. In the meantime, however, his interests in social change and visual sociology led him to rephotograph the county several times. The result is a remarkable (and ongoing) project, showing the rapid decline of rural America.

Among Rieger's insights is the recognition that social change is not always visible, and the visual dimension of change does not always coincide with the actual change. An industrial plant may close and the visual outcomes might not register for five or more years. Some social change is not visual, and subtle visual indicators may indicate deep social changes. Finally, the steps in the process of change are as important as the beginning and end points. In many non-visual studies of change only the beginning and end are significant, but in visual studies of change it is understanding intermediate steps that often provides the most insight.

Figure 5.3
1970: Soo Line Railroad, Ewen, Michigan. At the time of this photograph, the Soo's trans-Upper Peninsula railroad still served as an important economic link between industry in this rural region and the outside world, especially for shipping wood out to mills and processing plants. The railroad passed through Ewen and all of the other communities in southern Ontonagon County—Merriweather, Bergland, Topaz, Matchwood, Bruce Crossing, Paynesville and Trout Creek. By 1970 some of these communities had declined to mere remnants of their former selves, but the railroad still maintained and staffed stations in Ewen and at least two other communities. Ewen was also the location for crew changes on trains that passed through, providing steady business to the hotel shown at left in the photo. (Photographs and captions for Figures 5.3–5.5 by Jon Rieger.)

Rieger argues for coordinated data collection, where images stimulate ideas, which lead to non-visual data collection, which in turn leads to additional photography. Though he does not name it as such, his method is visually grounded theory.

Although it is situated in one location, Rieger's research suggests a larger story of decline in rural America. His attention to methods makes his work especially useful. Rieger revisits exact locations, places similar cameras mounted on tripods in the same position, and waits for the light to approximate what he'd photographed years before. Field notes and data from local archives supplement observations and photographs.

Rieger suggests two additional approaches to photographing social change. The first is to photograph change retrospectively; that is, trying to see backwards in time. Rieger asks: What did an earlier version of the same process, or the first steps in a changing environment look like?

Figure 5.4
1990: Abandoned railroad, Ewen, Michigan. By 1985, the Soo had discontinued its rail service through the central part of the Upper Peninsula. In 1990, when this photograph was taken, the ties and track were being salvaged from the roadbed and the railroad had relinquished the right-of-way to the State of Michigan. A similar scene of abandonment existed in each of the communities that the railroad had passed through across the southern part of Ontonagon County. In examining the visual changes in the scene, I noticed that the station, including the windows, had been painted and that a planter with a tree in it had been placed beside the building: Could this be an indication that it had been converted to a new, perhaps important, use? No such luck: After the closure of the railroad, the former station had also ended up in the hands of the state and was vacant and deteriorating. The building exterior had been spruced up and the planter positioned by local volunteers to keep the place from being too big an eyesore during Ewen's 1989 Centennial Celebration.

Figure 5.5

2005: Location of former Soo Line railroad and station, Ewen, Michigan. While there had been some discussion in the community about turning the old railroad station into a senior citizens' center, nothing came of it and eventually the State of Michigan razed the building. The hotel by this time was out of business but a bar remained open on the ground floor in the part nearest the street. At the time of this photograph, the roadbed of the former railroad survives only as a hiking, biking, ATV and snowmobile trail. This is a fairly common pattern in this region where a number of railroads have ceased operations. Trail maintenance has been managed by volunteer groups. This saga is emblematic of the economic decline and population loss that has occurred across the breadth of Michigan's Upper Peninsula.

To recreate the past it may be possible to find an archive that documents the earlier stage of the process under study. For example, Rieger became interested in pulp harvesting, the current form of local lumbering. It was a less respected form of woods work, overshadowed by logging operations that had cut the huge trees of the virgin forests. As a result, pulping had been photographed very little. Eventually Rieger was able to collect a visual record of pulp harvesting in northern regions of Michigan, Wisconsin and Minnesota from several regional historical collections. These allowed him to create a visual baseline from which to evaluate change in the technology of pulp harvesting then revolutionizing the industry.

Rieger's other suggestion for visualizing an obsolete form of social life was to recreate it as if in a play. Rieger asked people to re-enact old routines with old technologies, even wearing the clothes and using the props of the earlier era, which he photographed. Rieger's approach was similar to the method used in docudramas such as the 1978 film *Northern Lights*,[9] which portrayed the founding of the

Nonpartisan League in North Dakota, using locals to act out parts that were written from the diaries of their elder relatives.

Camilo José Vergara, a Chilean sociologist living in the US, has produced a large body of work on social change in the American city, often by rephotographing sites just a few years apart.[10] Vergara primarily uses a view camera mounted on a tripod and he works in color so his images are extremely detailed. He photographs buildings "eye to eye," often climbing on the roof of his (rented) auto, and he uses perspective-correcting cameras that appear to move the viewer to a position suspended in mid-air.

Vergara, who has never, to my knowledge, used the term "visual sociology," has done more visual sociology, and more effectively, than perhaps anyone, as the penultimate explorer of forgotten urban landscapes. He focuses on the cities and regions of cities (particularly Newark and Camden in New Jersey, Detroit, New York and Chicago) that have changed quickly in the past forty years through abandonment, deterioration, boarding up, collapse and teardown. Many of the buildings Vergara photographed were spectacular examples of American architecture; the Corn Exchange Bank in Harlem, the Blackstone building in Gary, the Michigan Central Railroad Station, to name a few. Vergara's most well-known book, *American Ruins*, often presents three views of a building in advancing stages of deterioration, five to eight years apart, and then an empty lot after its teardown. He enters abandoned buildings and finds how they are used as squats, by artists who leave behind sculptures, murals and graffiti, and as marketplaces for drugs. Now and then he includes people in his photos, usually as small actors far off in the lost urban landscapes, seemingly more leftover debris in a larger landscape of abandonment. Occasionally he includes a story that interprets the change he records. He quotes the late Calvin Earle of 11th Street in Camden, who inhabited the last standing building in a neighborhood that had disappeared before his very eyes: "This used to be all houses around here. You had stores all around. Within five blocks you could buy everything you needed."[11]

There are oddly beautiful images of nature reclaiming the deteriorating buildings. In the former Camden Free Library trees are growing: in summer leafed out; in winter barren and dormant; in fall beautiful with changing leaves. The surrounding building with a caved-in roof seems like a protective container for a delicate organism.

Vergara explains that the abandoned cars he photographed in Los Angeles tell a more complicated story than they appear to. Poverty has its function: the old cars were used as extra rooms or rented to the homeless. He writes:

> For those who knew the neighborhood when backyards were grassy lawns, this signals deterioration, but the car owners regard the backyard vehicles with nostalgia. Not only are they reminders of happy times, but there is the ever-present hope of one day fixing them up and selling them for a lot of money.[12]

His view could be ironic, serious or bitter; it is hard to tell:

> Declining cities could learn from the Middle Ages. Michigan Central Station and a few dozen surrounding acres of old parking lots and railroad tracks should be turned into an abbey or monastery. Government or foundation money would help a group of monks to stabilize the ruin and establish living quarters in it. I envision local farmers willingly cooperating, assisting the monks in setting up their farm, chicken coops, and barnyards. I see strawberries growing between the rails along the train tracks; I see lambs and cattle grazing on the overgrown parking lots and goats on the roof and staring out the windows. I cannot wait to eat Michigan Central brand eggs, butter, chicken, tomatoes, and strawberries. I would even expect an enterprising order of monks to set up a micro-brewery and market their own brand of jam . . . Michigan Central would bring visitors from all over the world to Detroit. Motown would become the "city where the Middle Ages work."[13]

Vergara's visual sociology of American urban deterioration is summed up as seven unique features. He writes: "The form these take, the frequency with which they are found, and the manner in which they cluster together and reinforce each other, contribute to the distinctiveness of these urban spaces." These elements are:

- *Fortification*, buildings are turned into fortresses by sealing the ground floor and the roof, erecting fences and adding surveillance and guard dogs.
- *Ruins*, which he defines as buildings left open for decay, and that are subsequently filled with discarded materials.
- *Empty lots*, the empty spaces left over after demolition.
- *Social containers*, the reuse of old structures such as hospitals, schools, hotels as care-taking facilities for the homeless, as drug treatment facilities and as shelters for the addicted and the sick.
- *A visual language of art and advertisements*, memorials made by residents to dead gang members and those caught in the crossfire of gang wars, the work of artists working independently, and projects created by schools and civic organizations to improve the city.
- *Public service billboards*, which Vergara says, "teach the ghetto residents how to live. The admonitions in these billboards are a contemporary equivalent of Ben Franklin's Poor Richard's Almanac."
- *Suburbanization*, which Vergara sees as coming to the inner cities in new developments, malls, big box retailers, entertainment centers and "new gated or fenced communities that introduce suburban construction and values" to inner cities.[14]

Vergara's visual elements show an overall pattern of change that can be compared to other cities and circumstances. Vergara doesn't claim that all change is visual, or that he explains it completely. But he offers a visual vocabulary for understanding a complex social phenomenon, and it is one that can be developed further.

Rephotography projects have also examined the lives of those who had become inadvertently famous in earlier documentary projects. Bill Ganzel was the first to seek people and places whose images had become cultural icons as part of the FSA (Farm Security Administration) and to rephotograph them nearly forty years later.[15] The most famous image revisits Florence Thompson and her daughters, whom Dorothea Lange photographed in a migrant camp in 1936; then dirty, fearful, and with her children hiding their faces. It had become the image that represented, in many people's eyes, the Great Depression. Ganzel's photograph in 1979 shows Thompson and three of her daughters prosperous, chubby, well scrubbed and thoroughly middle class. Journalist Dale Maharidge and Michael Williamson completed a similar project, using Walker Evans and James Agee's *Let Us Now Praise Famous Men* as a model.[16] Their focus is on cotton farming, the plight of tenant farmers, and the poverty of the rural Alabama. They also rephotographed many of the same people Evans had photographed in the late 1930s, fifty years distant, and they recorded reactions and memories, not all favorable, about being the subject of such a famous project.

The most touching, personal and sociological rephotography project has been done by Milton Rogovin, who died in 2009 at age 101. His four-part rephotography of several families in Buffalo's low-income West Side was but one of his many projects that focused on the conditions of the poor and working classes in several parts of the world (an early project came on the invitation of Pablo Neruda and combined his photographs from southern Chile with Neruda's poems). The rephotography project began in 1972 and just a few years before Rogovin's death.[17] The more than thirty years that spanned these images seem to compress whole lifetimes: children become adults; couples almost merge into a single physical presence. Middle-aged couples begin to disappear in the last photos as new generations suddenly resemble the elders photographed earlier. What one takes from these images is the resilience of these families and the stability of their social locations. Not much has appeared to happen to them speaking of social mobility, yet there they are, decade after decade, looking directly into Rogovin's 6 x 6 Rolleiflex camera, obviously pleased to be at the center of the photographer's attention. Rogovin asked his subjects to place themselves where they wanted to be photographed, and we thus learn about the significance of things and places, and how those values evolve. In some later photographs his subjects have posed themselves alongside their prints from an earlier Rogovin session and, in fact, many of the later portraits are posed around family photos. They are quiet, respectful images, and the medium-format Rolleiflex, under Rogovin's control, produces images of remarkable beauty. The quality of these photographs may result from Rogovin's personal humility and his obvious empathy with the poor; branded as a dangerous communist by the House Un-American Activities Committee in 1952 (and his optometry practice essentially ruined as a result), he turned to photography to explore the condition of the poor and working classes. But these are more than touching portraits; they are a sustained visual ethnography of a single community on the lowest rung of the American social structure.

Finally, the film series *Seven Up* examined the lives of fourteen English children, aged seven, from various social ranks, each born around 1957. Director Michael Apted revisited most of the original participants in seven-year cycles and the series now has seven installments filmed at ages 7, 14, 21, 28, 35, 42 and 49,[18] becoming what could be called "living rephotography." Apted's series has been very popular in the UK and elsewhere, and has attracted sociological attention, including reviews by ethnographer Mitch Duneier and sociologist Jon Wagner. The series inspired similar programs in Russia, South Africa, Japan, the US, Australia, France, Denmark, Holland, Sweden, Germany and several other countries, and may be the most viewed example of unrecognized visual sociology to date. Interest in these programs may be due to the human preoccupation with knowing the end of our sociological and personal stories (Apted's original goal was to see how social class played out in the lives of the children he interviewed) but the success may also derive from an audience's feeling that they have come to know people who appear and reappear, telling their changing stories. The effect of being in the program is also intriguing: are these people trying to live to a higher standard as they anticipate the next round of filming? Are they able to, even if they try?

Visual sociology and archives

The archive is not an innocent repository of information; rather we know, since Allan Sekula's essays[19] that photographic archives embody institutional power because they organize knowledge. His perspective owes much to Michel Foucault, who earlier characterized the archive as a form of *discourse*: that is, part of the constellation of meaning that constitutes both an argument for meaning and the meaning itself. Sekula's primary message is that archive influences historical scholarship because it directs how a society comes to know and represent itself. In becoming part of an archive a photo is taken from its original context and placed into another, where it becomes equivalent to other images found there. The organization of the archive defines and orders all aspects of life that it documents. Finally, archived photos gain legitimacy as documentary evidence because they are located there.

Carol Payne's research on photographic archives[20] is an excellent example of Sekula's insights applied to the politics of an important archive. For several years Payne worked with the National Film Board of Canada (NFB) Still Photographic Division, which during the second half of the twentieth century produced thousands of photos and hundreds of documentary stories about Canada. About 10 percent of this cultural production was about Inuit people who, she notes, were categorized as Eskimo (a generic term that lumps many different groups together) by academics living in southern Canada. Her focus on the hidden stories in the archive sees a background narrative of nation building and a patronizing attitude toward indigenous people. The text for a story, for example, describes the "childlike, yet rugged, simplicity of the Eskimo."[21]

Payne calls her work visual repatriation, a process through which native researchers use photographs to reclaim native memory, to name community members and historic figures, to question the imperialistic intrusion of southern Canadian society into Arctic communities and to encourage communication between generations. The researchers are generally younger Inuit who use NFB images in interviews with Elders. Payne describes the photos as having strategic indexicality, which means that they *really* mean what they are supposed to; they identify people and as a result they give agency to people who recognize their nearly forgotten past. The interviews are a form of photo elicitation designed to produce oral histories. In any case, the research is a powerful example of deconstructing the power of the archive, turning it inside out to create new uses and meanings.

Eric Margolis' research on documentary archives also draws heavily on Sekula. In one study, Margolis analyzes four projects that documented Native American boarding schools from the late nineteenth century to the mid-twentieth century. Margolis begins:

> It is essential to remember that the children subjected to the peculiar educational institution of the Indian boarding school were a conquered people . . . Defeated by the U.S. Army, the Native Americans lost control not only over their land, but over the education of their children and in many respects the ability to reproduce their culture. [22]

The photo archives document the natives before and after their removal from natural landscapes and their transition into white culture schools, where practical trades are taught, patriotic symbols abound, and there is an air of military like discipline and order. Portraits made over time show native clothes, hairstyles and postures replaced by Anglo postures, clothes and settings. As policies of cultural extermination were replaced by more progressive policies, the photos highlighted educational principles including "child-centered and active education, inquiry-based learning and the use of manipulatables . . . students involved in laboratory experiments, life drawing lessons, sculpture, shop and home economics; . . . nature study trips, and visits to museums and workshops."[23]

Margolis is interested in what the photo archives communicate, as well as how the meaning of the archives has been defined. How, Margolis asks, "did Indian school photographs come to be seen as evidence of an oppressive system rather than progress in the civilization of savages?"[24] Cultural genocide has been replaced by multiculturalism, while the open racism of the past has become more muted. Both Payne and Margolis' publications include many images, and as a result we can evaluate their arguments by seeing what they are talking about as well as reading their arguments.

Barbara Norfleet's study of the post-World War Two American culture[25] relied on the archives of professional photographers who documented the daily lives of clients "rich enough to hire them." Norfleet imagines a dialogue between her collected photos and those of Robert Frank (cited earlier), a photographer of the same era whose images commented critically on American culture.

Norfleet presents an American middle class preoccupied with new suburbs, autos, cocktail parties, teen life, dances, swimming pools and public events. The photographers whose work she draws upon were not public historians; they were private photographers working for clients, and their large negative images portrayed subjects without grain, blurred movement or extreme contrast. By contrast, Robert Frank's 35 mm photos "display a gritty, unappetizing man-made landscape and a sad, alienated people," a view of America where "there is no energy, no hope."[26] What is remarkable in Norfleet's eyes is that the two messages, made from very different perspectives, different styles and even cameras, are so consistent, despite their different subject matter and editorial focus.

Norfleet interprets the images from her own perspective as a young woman coming of age during the era, and with statements by social scientists including Robert Nisbet, C. Wright Mills, Vance Packard, David Riesman and Erik Erikson, and novelists including Jack Kerouac, James Baldwin, William Styron and J.D. Salinger. The result is a collective self-portrait of a historical era that stresses its underlying tensions.

Norfleet's study can be favorably compared to the work of Michael Lesy, who has edited several books of photos chosen from both private and public archives. His most well-known project is his published dissertation[27] that presents 200 photographs of Wisconsin town photographer Charles Van Schaick (the original archive consisted of 30,000 glass plate negatives) made between 1890 and 1910. Lesy's focus was on derangement, insanity, suicide, pyromania and other psychological manifestations that he says were a result of economic unrest, isolation and other dysfunctions of the frontier life. The photos (including Lesy's peculiar homemade collages) show children in coffins, women with wild hair and mad eyes, horses, old-fashioned advertisements and other typical images of rural life. At the time of publication in the early 1970s Lesy's book caused great controversy and there continues to be disagreement as to whether the photos are an eccentric collection, often manipulated by the author, or whether the images can be read as an interpretation of frontier culture.

Robert Levine's study of nineteenth-century South American culture[28] is one of the very few historical studies to draw almost exclusively on photography. Levine began by examining a huge body of early photographic work in South America to see what social transformations, urban development and other processes looked like. It is a fascinating approach and it shows a great deal that was only implied previously. One of his main conclusions, however, is that you can only study what the photographers of the day photographed. As a result his is a history of what was photographed, and given the limited use of photography at that time and in those locations, what is left out is as telling as what was included.

In a recent study, Patrizia Faccioli and I used historical photos to make several arguments about the evolution of the meaning of food in Italian culture.[29] We visualized key ideas, including the *mezzadria* and the *latifondi* systems of land tenure, with photos we saw as visual ideal types. In seeking to understand the historical roots of the poverty and retarded economic development in southern Italy we spoke in detail about how the *mezzadria* system, the traditional feudal structure in northern Italy, balanced its exploitation of the Italian peasantry with security and, in periods of good harvests, a viable living. Our photograph from the grape harvest in Tuscany in 1930 (Figure 5.6) shows six harvesters who appear to be an extended family (there are two young children and a teen) as well as a middle-aged man in a white shirt and a fedora, who appears to be the agent of the landlord.

The workers and the agent are sharing a meal of beans or soup and bread, and they are drinking large glasses of wine, being poured by a smiling, clean and attractive woman. The workers are similarly tidy, even dapper in appearance. If the photo is telling the truth, it describes a system of contented, well-fed workers, sharing food and wine with their respected friend, the landlord's agent. The exploitation built into the system (the peasants are tenants and pay the landlord half their crops) is hidden.

The facing image (Figure 5.7) portrays the peasantry in southern Italy in roughly the same era, that is, before the post-World War Two agricultural modernization. The southern Italian peasants appear not to have washed in some time, and they wear worn and ragged clothes, their matted hair covered by scarves and crude hats. Some of their clothes look as though they were made from feed sacks and they are suspicious; their postures mildly aggressive. They are carrying sacks slung over their shoulders; one assumes they are walking on their way to work. The image only includes women and children, reminding us that in the *latifondi* system men often worked in locations far from their families. Unlike the *mezzadria* peasants the *latifondi* peasants did not live in landlord housing, did not have land to grow their own crops on and hired themselves out at barely subsistence wages to do daily labor typically several kilometers from the crude, crowded, dirty rooms, seldom with running water or other rudiments of civilization, where they live jammed together with their families.

We have suggested that an agricultural system can be summed up in a single image; that a Weberian ideal type can be represented in an image. Weber used the ideal type concept to understand a concept abstractly rather than to create a definition that fits all cases. To be successful, the photograph of the ideal type must shift attention from the details in an image, or the relationship between elements, to a conceptual generalization.

We were also able to document important aspects of food production, including the processes of hand-driven pasta manufacture in Naples and early factory production of pasta in Milan. The image from Naples confirms stereotypes of southern pasta manufacturing; the pasta hangs over long poles, drying in the sunlight.

Figure 5.6
Peasants in the grape harvest,
mezzadria system, mid-central
Italy.

Workers will move it into different rooms with less light and more humidity in certain stages of the days-long process. The questionable hygiene of drying the pasta outdoors is evident.

An image depicting the factory production of pasta,[30] however, questions several common assumptions. First, it places factory manufacture of pasta much earlier than is normally assumed (the industrialization of pasta manufacture is usually dated to the late 1930s). It also describes a manufacturing process that appears to be rational and efficient in contrast to the image of the hand production in Naples. The ten pasta machines in the second photo are lined up in a spacious, clean, orderly and brightly lit room. Women in white uniforms and hats operate machines that appear to be rolling *sfoglia* into large sheets, which are then turned into the *tortellini* that are drying on the small bins lined up in front of the machines. While it is a production system that is machine-based, humans appear to control the pace of the work and undoubtedly apply their skill and working knowledge to the process.

Finally, an image from 1950 (Figure 5.8) communicates the craft of Parmigiano manufacture. Here the visual details tell the story of a centuries-long production system that *looks* efficient, pleasant and rational. The workers wear clean work outfits; the master grader who is evaluating the cheese wears a pressed white shirt and dress pants. The cheeses are stacked to beyond the top of the photograph (more than 12 feet high) on wooden shelves, and the workroom has an orderly and

Figure 5.7
Peasants in the *latifondi* system, southern Italy.

pleasing atmosphere. From the caption we learn that the cheese graders spend twelve years apprenticing; these are careers rather than casual jobs, and we infer that the positions are sought after and provide a middle-class income. There are seventy-two Parmigiano wheels visible in the photo, spaced carefully across the shelves. Each would be worth several hundred euros in today's world, and would be proportionally expensive in 1950. We don't know how large the room is, or how high the stack of cheeses extends beyond the framing, but the effect of the framing of the photograph is to communicate wealth and order.

These and other historical photographs analyze such concepts as peasant development, craftwork and political struggle around the edges of food systems. Often they add information that escapes written description. The looks on the faces of the peasants in the two systems, or their postures and clothes, fill out the understanding of more complex arguments. Having the images side by side encourages sociological comparison. They become a visual constant for various readings of the history: a common locating point for a definition of a sociological and historical reality.

It is difficult, however, to use photos made by various photographers, gathered into an archive, to make visual arguments. We are drawing conclusions from bits of data that could be described as informational flotsam. The archive the photos are drawn from, Corbis-Bettmann, consists of millions of images gathered

Figure 5.8
Parmigiano grader, Emilia
Romagna, Italy, center of
Parmigiano production since
the thirteenth century.

into a single (virtual) location and made available for sale. We don't know the conditions under which the photos were made; we do not know if they are representative of the event or situation they portray. Perhaps the happy wine harvesting peasants described above are an exception; perhaps the desperate peasants of the south are similarly untypical. Our best defense for our approach is that as we looked through hundreds of examples we studied images that challenged our assumptions as well as confirmed them. When we finally chose images we were confident that they represented the main themes the archive communicated.

The final example is perhaps the most ambitious use of visual imagery to understand social change. The study is John Grady's analysis of the depictions of black Americans in *Life* magazine from 1936 to 2000, the final year of the magazine's publication.[31] He created a database by analyzing every advertisement in *Life* that pictured an African-American, a total of 590 ads. These were coded using grounded theory, which involved working with the images chronologically and identifying each for variables that were assigned values. When new variables emerged, Grady returned to the first images and recoded the entire collection. While this sounds extremely tedious, Grady notes that most variables were discovered during the beginning of the coding and that few variables were subsequently added.

The variables reflected attitudes toward racial segregation and integration. What is remarkable about the study is that Grady discovered that the ads mirrored trends identified in national censuses and other attitude surveys, but they told a more complete story than the surveys do. Grady points out that surveys indicate what people say they do, which often differs substantially from what people actually do. A survey often presents an imagined future and asks the respondent to indicate their imagined actions. Because there can be no check on these claims, Grady points out the disconnect between assertions and reported behavior. Grady's analysis includes the topic of the advertisements, the specific actions taken by white and black figures within the ads and their social desirability or attractiveness. Decoding the advertisements suggests that racial integration has moved ahead at a slower pace than the surveys indicate, yet Grady believes they suggest a stronger commitment to racial integration. The study also suggests that there are areas of social interaction where racial integration is less advanced than others.

There are several admirable aspects to this study. The visual data both elaborate trends identified in questionnaire-based surveys, and also suggest different conclusions. The study uses a large but manageable data set, sufficient to answer the questions posed. The ads are visually complicated and rich with potential meaning, making their analysis a challenging but doable research activity. Seeing examples of the ads published in the article allows the viewer to analyze visual information in addition to evaluating written arguments.

Grady's work leads us to reflect on the issue of coding. Coding assumes that a researcher is able to uncover latent meanings through systematic, rational study. One of the best examples aside from Grady's is Catherine Lutz and Jane Collins' analysis of 600 photos published in the *National Geographic* magazine over three decades.[32] Lutz and Collins claim to have discovered a pattern of meaning implicit in the *National Geographic* photographic tradition, working from the assumption that content analysis and coding are scientific methods that uncover pre-existing and more authentic meaning than casual looking does. This viewpoint is often uncritically accepted, yet it is important to remember that coding produces only another example of situated knowledge that reflects an historical moment and an institutional way of seeing. Even though academics often claim that our way of seeing interprets a more profound or correct vision, it is indeed just another argument for a point of view.

While sociology draws heavily on history, there are only a handful of sociological studies of the past that draw primarily on imagery. We have spoken about this briefly in reference to Foucault's method of discourse analysis. Focusing on the visual leads us to archives of forgotten or otherwise unremarkable photographers—professionals who did their jobs well but never expected to be

Figure 5.9
Hong Kong: high-rise slum.

known outside their communities, who may have produced some of the most telling histories of the times. I remember the lone professional photographer from my Minnesota hometown who was the photographer of all town events with his Hasselblad and his big flash attachment. He was a technical master and used the best equipment money could buy to photograph Homecoming queens, 4th of July parades, school events and town rituals. His photos illustrated the weekly town newspaper and high school yearbooks, and his services were purchased by hundreds of people for weddings and other family events. He belonged to the era just after Norfleet's project, when a small town still had a photographer who was highly skilled and photographed everything of interest. I learned with dismay that his negatives were thrown in a dumpster when he died. Now that even the newspapers are disappearing, this public record and its potential for sociological analysis will disappear as well.

As these projects show, reading the past through archives is not as simple as decoding a simple visual record. Images mean something in their original context, and those meanings evolve as the images appear and reappear in new contexts. A sociological view is attentive to the way images contribute to various discourses on power. Payne's work with the archives from the Canadian National Film Board can be one inspiration to use images from archives to interrogate their origins and redirect their power.

Figure 5.10
Hong Kong: high-rise
capitalism.

Comparative method

The comparative method in sociology has usually referred to studying complex social processes such as revolutions in different societies or historical eras. It is hard at first to imagine photography contributing in a meaningful way to these studies. Comparative methods, however, have a place for imagery, if we think of Weber's concept of the *ideal type* and Durkheim's rules for sociological methods. Weber's ideal type is a construct that is, in the end, a picture, and Durkheim stressed the potential for the comparison of social phenomena, each maybe photographable, in different settings. While few visual sociologists have photographed the same phenomena in different settings, societies or even nation states, many of us have drawn upon documentary and other sources to construct comparative arguments for our teaching or research.

The mind-numbing number of images now available via free Web sources would make it possible to experiment with comparative analysis in a newly creative way. Photos have the disarming capacity to ask what sociological concepts look like in the concrete. The challenge is to locate images by sociological topic, which they are seldom catalogued for. This requires developing the ability to see images analytically, past their obvious topics. While searching through thousands of photos in archives such as the SONJ (Standard Oil (New Jersey)) or the Corbis-Bettmann

archives I became more and more accustomed to this kind of seeing; an image of peasants harvesting grapes, for example, becomes an image that represents a kind of feudal social organization.

One can dream of richer possibilities. One model would be a visual version of the Human Relations Area Files, founded in 1949 at Yale University. The HRAF is a classification scheme of cultural information that gathers vast written data on all cultures and cultural phenomena that have been studied. For many decades this was accomplished by hand, and it is now digitized. If your university belongs to the consortium it is possible to browse through all information on a single culture, or to investigate a theme (there are 700 searchable topics) across cultures from the

Figure 5.11 (above top)
Hong Kong life.

Figure 5.12 (above bottom)
Mong Kok market.

Figure 5.13
Downtown Hong Kong, two banking interns from the UK, whose work they described as, "shifting your Yankee dollars to the Chinese."

convenience of one's personal computer. What HRAF suggests as a possibility is a vast searchable catalogue of images organized by sociological idea, location, date and perhaps photographer. Were this to become a reality (and I am not the first to think of such a possibility) comparative visual analysis would expand mightily.

A small number of visual sociologists have done comparative field studies. A convincing example is Charles Suchar's study of gentrification in Amsterdam and Chicago. Suchar had lived in Amsterdam for a year early in his career, and had also photographed the evolution of the neighborhood of Lincoln Park in Chicago for several years. He returned to Amsterdam two decades after his first experiences there and photographed many of the same locations, so his study became a comparison of how specific areas of two cities changed over time. Suchar asks:

> In neighborhoods that have gone through extensive gentrification, what occurs in the end-play of the process, particularly in post-industrial corridors and areas that are often contiguous to housing development? How is gentrification in these neighborhoods related to changes and redevelopment taking pace in each of the cities involved?[33]

His images showed how policies guided by different values produced contrasting versions of similar processes.

Caroline Knowles and I used a comparative visual approach to understand the experiences of immigrants in Hong Kong.[34] Hong Kong changes from one urban reality to another more rapidly than any other city I've visited. Hong Kong immigrants flow between these visual universes depending on what they do and where they live, but because the city is so compact and the public transportation is so efficient, there is a social fluidness that was key to understanding how people live in the city.

To visualize this idea I used lenses that recorded information in a distinctive way: in this case a very wide angle lens, aimed in the same direction, to show the slums of Mong Kok (Figure 5.9), almost adjacent to the gleaming high-rises of international capitalism (Figure 5.10).

After being unsatisfied with conventional photos of street life (the hustle and bustle of life was either too close when using conventional lenses or too abstracted by the optics of wide angle lenses, where the center of the frame is moved away from the viewer and vertical lines are distorted) I began to use a rotating lens panoramic camera, which records the width of human vision (about 150 degrees) and with objects in the left, center and right in the same perspective an eye would see. The panoramic camera technology is very old and the cameras are awkward to use. It is also possible to knit adjacent images together (Photoshop has an easy way to do so) to create panoramas that have the optical quality of an image made by the rotating lens camera, except that the rotating lens camera makes its image at one time, so the social action taking place inside the image is captured as it happened. In any case our technique allowed us to compare neighborhoods on a visual basis in a way that approximated to the way we saw these places through our eyes (Figures 5.11, 5.12, 5.13).

In these examples the comparative idea is explored by using the same camera and lenses to record an idea in the same way in different places. I suppose one can go too far with this point, but I'm struck by the fact that Robert Frank's photos of American culture were all made with the same camera, same lens and same film, which meant that his point of view did not change (his 50 mm lens was neither a wide angle nor a telephoto; it is about what one eye sees); his Leica was small and quiet thus his ability to photograph without disrupting people was the same in all instances, and the interpretative influence of grainy Tri-X film was consistent from image to image. In this way one could say that his photos were a technologically comparative study of various ideas such as the public demonstration of our politics; our racial tensions; the character of life in places like diners and cafes, and so forth.

What has been implied in this chapter is that photographic images tell the truth; they show what is in front of the camera (commonly referred to as indexicality). Is implication intended? Well, partly yes and partly no. To the extent that I suggest it is true we can use photos to learn about the world; to compare times, views, places and to look for sociological inferences from what we see. That is one side of the coin, but the other is that it is important to remember that even the most indexical photos have a simultaneously subjective character created by point of view, lens and other camera features. Like all truth claims they are situated and partial.

Chapter 6

Ethnomethodology, semiotics and the subjective

So far I've spoken about how a visual approach works in fairly conventional social science, and I have concentrated on photography rather than imagery. In this chapter I expand the perspective. I first discuss ethnomethodology, which for many sociologists is still fairly exotic, and where photography, film and video are useful because they represent an interesting form of empiricism. I also suggest that there is a potential overlap between documentary street photography, or photography of the casual glance, and ethnomethodology.

After this discussion I turn to the relationship between semiotics and visual sociology, which is intended to make concrete many of the ideas discussed in this volume.

Finally, sociology has approached subjectivity by studying emotions as a part of group life, and more recently as an aspect of autoethnography (autobiography + ethnography). I suggest that art photography that draws on feelings, emotional reactions and conditions is a parallel to the study of emotions that emerges from some visual sociology.

Ethnomethodology

Ethnomethodology (EM) is the study of sense-making in the social world, and as such turns to the raw material of the world for data. EM in the form of conversation analysis explores how people make sense of social settings in normal conversations, either on phones or overheard in social situations, so in these instances the data are the words, pauses, tonalities and so forth. However, ethnomethodologists also study the details of action; the accomplishment of social action, which is largely mediated through sight.[1]

An example of how sight and ethnomethodology are connected is found in David Sudnow's research, as he begins his study of the practical activity of jazz:

... the sight of my piano-playing hands is familiar. I know their looks, not only in those intimate ways in which we all know our hands' looks, but as my jazz-making hands. It is the ways of the hand that I watch now. For a long time in learning to play jazz piano, I was busy watching my hands and the terrain of the keyboard to see that they did not get into trouble; or I was looking at the keyboard in order to find places to take my fingers, so that instructional work was occurring as a form of guidance in which my looking was very much implicated. Then my look became preoccupied in more subtle ways, party to an imaginary conceiving of various aspects of the territory in which I was moving. Even when looking away from the keyboard, I would conceive visual "gestalts" of pathways for use as I was playing.[2]

Sudnow draws on two visual collections in his book: drawings or charts of a piano keyboard where the actions of his hands are centered, and photos of his hands "accomplishing" jazz. The visual material provides a way to study what ethnomethodologists often refer to as the "local, temporal and sequential;" it provides what Deirdre Boden called a "microscope . . . [to glimpse] the fine structure of the social universe."[3]

While I was not performing ethnomethodology per se when I studied Willie's world, or when I later studied how Italian women cook, I was interested in the practical activity of work and food preparation, and I used photos that "broke the frame" of the subject's normal view of their lives with photos that zoomed in and reframed. In other words I moved from Sudnow's self-reflection to interview situations in which the point was to encourage people to shatter their taken-for-granted views and become analysts of their normal activity. Photos are especially useful in these circumstances precisely because they freeze a moment that can then be seen in a new way; a person can objectify their own experience. But it is not an automatic process; not any close-up can produce the kind of insight that comes from objectifying one's experience, as illustrated in Figure 6.1.

But Sidé, a working-class Bolognese woman, reflected on the personal politics of her relationship with her live-in mother-in-law when she saw the photos of her preparation of *sfoglia* (the pasta dough) and *tortellini* (Figure 6.2). The photos reminded her of decades of competition and eventual guarded peace between the two women of the household rather than the details of the work involved. Because she made *sfoglia* and *tortellini* several times a month, and had done so for years and years, perhaps it was so ingrained in her consciousness that it was not easily made into spoken narrative. Here the important issue was what the work represented in the micro politics of her family life.

The natural connection between EM and visual sociology has been more and more obvious to both fields. In 2003 a special issue of *Visual Studies* was devoted to ethnomethodology, which included Carlin's[4] ethnomethodological approach to the workplace, focusing on the organization of documents and forms, and the objects

Ethnomethodology, semiotics, subjective

Figure 6.1
Willie's hands on the file, close up, which inspired Willie to comment: "You've got to shift that pressure from one hand to another. As you go across the saw the pressure shifts on your file. If you hold it hard you can't feel the pressure. You're not gripping the file, you're more or less letting it float or glide right through."

workers use to organize them. Hester and Francis' contribution explores what they call "the visually available mundane order" on a walk to the supermarket, including the understanding that their observation and presence in the setting is part of what they are observing. They note examples of Goffman's "civil inattention," where "people pass each other with only the barest of glances necessary to avoid collision and usually without even eye contact and talk rarely occurs between persons who are not together."[5] These were the most accessible studies to sociologists of culture; at a recent visual studies conference in Berlin,[6] the majority of presenters were British ethnomethodologists who had little awareness of the sub-discipline of visual sociology and their presentations were driven by the opaque language and sometimes extreme focus of EM. For example, one paper was a twenty-minute reflection on a thirty-second video depicting the exchange of a scalpel between a nurse and a doctor. The need for a metalanguage in ethnomethodology, in which description is itself described, puts demands on expression that not all sociologists are willing to undergo.[7]

Charles Goodwin usefully summarizes the range of visual thinking in ethnomethodological research:

> Within . . . ethnomethodology visual phenomena have been analyzed
> by investigating how they are made meaningful by being embedded

Figure 6.2 (opposite)
This and other photos of Sidé's hands on the roller did not lead Sidé to describe the work or the skill it involved, though it inspired a lengthy comment about the role of *sfoglia*-making in her challenging relationship with her live-in mother-in-law.

within the practices that participants in a variety of settings use to construct the events and actions that make up their lifeworld. This has led to the detailed study of a range of quite different kinds of phenomena, from the interplay between gaze, restarts and grammar in the building of utterances within conversation, to the construction and use of visual representations in scientific practice, to how the ability of lawyers to shape what can be seen in the videotape of policemen beating a suspect can contribute to disruption of the body politic that leaves a city in flames, to the part played by visual practices in both traditional and electronic workplaces.[8]

Goodwin's papers show us that it is not a simple matter of turning on a video camera and then analyzing what has been recorded, but creating a visual record in a wide variety of ways that serve specific questions and studies.

Certain photographic traditions are in effect an ethnomethodological take on cultural studies because they are as much about looking as they are about the subject being observed. They are about seeing casual occurrences and interactions in public or they juxtapose elements ironically or cynically. The point, in one way or another, is to comment upon culture (cultural studies) by looking at the performance of routine actions (ethnomethodology). Robert Frank's previously discussed photo essay *The Americans* is an example. Cultural themes included race, class and gender, including a black nanny and a white child; a black motorcyclist and a white girlfriend; and people of different racial identities, ages and social classes occupying different seats on a bus, looking out of different windows with expressions that seem to mirror their social positions. Robert Frank's politicians are framed with exaggerated symbols and their gestures are flamboyant. Workers, diners, entertainers and others are shown in the back stages of their social lives. Frank made the snapshot a window into culture, and I use the term snapshot to take note of his one-camera-one-lens technique (50 mm lens on a Leica camera); and his casual, quick shooting technique that did not intrude into the scenes he recorded. Robert Frank's work led to a tradition of street photography that includes, among many others, Lee Friedlander and Garry Winogrand.[9] What I find interesting is how they both seemed to look with an ethnomethodological eye; a radical reframing that sees new patterns, associations and meanings. For example, a Winogrand photo of Elliot Richardson (a nationally important American politician from the 1970s) shows him at a press conference, sitting at a bare, cheap table that holds several microphones linked to tape recorders arranged on the floor. Richardson, an elegant Cary Grant-looking man, leans forward earnestly, but his stern authority is mostly lost because of how the photo is framed. Normally he would be photographed with a telephoto lens, and his earnestness would be clear in the tightly cropped portrait. Winogrand's photo shows him in the context of the mundane production of daily news, and as such makes him seem insignificant. Seeing politics in this way makes it seem like a spectacle.

Winogrand normally worked on the street, photographing strangers as they passed each other. Mason Resnick, who was to become an editor of *Modern Photography*, wrote a description of a workshop he took with Winogrand in which he describes how he walked and photographed through a crowded New York street:

> Incredibly, people didn't react when he photographed them. It surprised me because Winogrand made no effort to hide the fact that he was standing in their way, taking their pictures. Very few really noticed; no one seemed annoyed. Winogrand was caught up with the energy of his subjects, and was constantly smiling or nodding at people as he shot. It was as if his camera was secondary and his main purpose was to communicate and make quick but personal contact with people as they walked by.[10]

Winogrand seemed to see without editorializing; he is quoted as saying he photographed "to see what the world looks like photographed." In fact he developed a way of seeing that sociologists try to develop; noting the incidental, momentary fragments of interaction, always in a new context.

As a young photographer I was inspired by Henri Cartier-Bresson, in many ways the first important figure whose work led the "visualization of the momentary" later developed by Winogrand and others. Cartier-Bresson, who worked in the 1950s and 1960s, coined the term "the decisive moment"[11] to describe his style of photography and his way of being part of the public he photographed. Cartier-Bresson worked with an unobtrusive camera and one senses that he blended into the scenes he photographed, raising the camera to his eye as a visually compelling arrangement of elements came into view. Cartier-Bresson did not complete photo essays except in the sense of a series being located in one place or another; rather his photos were like spare, black and white paintings that recorded how people inhabited a place and a moment in history.

Cartier-Bresson was not a cultural theorist, rather an observer with a camera who found a way to make photos that we remember. Figure 6.3, an image I made in 2003 in Shenzen, China, comments on the then new China: the pace of people on the sidewalk; clothing styles of global bureaucracies and international fashion; and even gender roles of the new Chinese society. The material backdrop of the photo suggests that the new cities of China seemed to be all surface and repeated forms. It calls upon what Cartier-Bresson offered as a photographic practice, though I feel immodest to say so.

Victor Burgin is a rare street photographer of the Winogrand/Friedlander genre who also writes as a cultural theorist. His books[12] combine what a critic called a

> meditation on cities that is at the same time an autobiography, a work of cultural criticism, an essay on the history of industrialized culture, and a dramatic enactment of the functions of irony, humor and political

Figure 6.3
Street scene, Shenzen, China.

analysis in a world irrevocably altered by the mobility of people, things and ideas in our time.[13]

In fact *Some Cities* meanders from British to American cities and back to European and Communist bloc urban centers before visiting the Far East, a volcanic island off Sicily and other spots. Casual observations draw casual meaning from the photos: Brits love sunlight because there is not much of it so Burgin photographs people on the street with their faces turned in bliss toward the sky; in Berlin there are many forms of surveillance (this was when the wall remained in place) and this leads Burgin to photograph a peep show where the observers of the nude dancers are unseen, leading to commentary on Foucault's ideas of internalized imprisonment where inmates are watched but are never aware of their guards. He uses images to construct a free-floating cultural commentary. In fact the book is dedicated to "the woman in the hallway" who appears several times in the book, which seemed to this viewer to be a cool reference to the unknowable. But Burgin's considerable reputation in cultural studies suggests that for many his approach is convincing.

In this discussion I've ranged from photography's usefulness as a way to gather data in ethnomethodological research to photography's use in cultural observations. The link between these has to do with how sociologists define, see and record the social world, and how photography can be part of that process. As both EM and visual sociology develop, their connections will likely increase to their mutual benefit. It may be that the informal take on ethnomethodology I've suggested offers a path that is less intimidating to those for whom the culture and language of EM remains abstract.

Semiotics

Semiotics refers to a theory of signs, an element of ancient philosophy that became, in the nineteenth century, an approach to linguistics. From the semiotic view, language works because a community or a group agrees that a word represents something specific, which is called its denotative meaning. A word communicates within the grammatical structures and codes of a language, which are referred to as syntax and semantics. Our words both denote something specific and connote further meanings. All human communication has this double feature: denotation and connotation. When connotation becomes especially complex in a combination of symbols and meanings we have what Roland Barthes called myths.[14]

Language may be easier to analyze than other communicative systems because its syntax and semantics follow rules, at least at some level. It is more complicated to understand how photographs or other visual texts communicate, in part, because there is not an agreed-upon visual syntax, and also because we use words to describe the communication of images and in doing so mix two symbolic systems.

The denotative meaning of words is based on an understanding of what they are agreed to mean (most simple form: "stop!" means "cease movement now"), and the denotative meaning of an image refers to how it registers in the mind of the person who sees it. But images never denote like the word "stopsign" and thus semioticians refer to connotation when speaking about how visual symbols operate.

Connotation refers in part to the cultural lens we use to interpret an image. The context of the image contributes to its connotation and the context includes its relation to other images; its text or caption, its location in a particular magazine, journal or book, or art gallery or other factors. Connotation can not only affect the degree to which an image makes a statement; it can also reverse its meaning.

Semiotics invites us to study hidden meanings, which implies that images have both a primary and a secondary meaning. This further implies that image meaning is knowable and exists on at least two levels. This allows semiotics to become a critique of power and implies, for example, that the party making an image understands both what the audiences will take from it and what they intend by sending it out. An obvious example would be advertising, which, if successful, guides one to consume a product or an experience not for what it may mean intrinsically but for what the advertising images say it will. You buy the beautiful and powerful car because in doing so you will become the person portrayed in the car advertisement: powerful, sexually attractive and of a certain lifestyle. It's not the car; it is the second level meaning that takes you to the purchase, and, from this perspective, because it is a phony promise the consumption will be empty and meaningless.[15]

At its most deterministic, semiotics tends to support a view that academics can read truer meaning into activities like watching daytime soap operas, adopting certain fashions, or watching certain cinema styles than the audience members can. It is also possible that while some of the deconstruction of semiotic signs makes a great deal of intuitive sense, academics are often seduced by their own commitment to a symbolic way of seeing. Marx intended the term *false consciousness* to refer to the inability of the working class to be conscious of the structural (economic) realities that construct their lifeworlds. In Marx's case these economic realities, consisting of a class system that was often obscured, did in fact exist, whereas the second level meanings that modern semioticians refer to may or may not.

Said more directly, when specific groups, such as the working class, consume popular culture they may do so for the reasons academics often say they do (and by doing so they are reinforcing their false consciousness and their subservient position in the society), or they may be consuming popular culture for a host of other reasons; maybe they find daytime TV narratives compelling! It is a larger issue than can be resolved in a few paragraphs but it is important to evaluate and use semiotic analysis of cultural consumption with a view of its potential determinism.

I will discuss the semiotics of visual signs in three ways. The first analyzes how humans create symbolic meaning in their dress, gestures and other ways of presenting themselves to others. Semiotic analysis points out hidden messages behind the obvious ones; the most famous example is Erving Goffman's study of gender politics in advertisements.

I will next discuss how semiotics suggests the messages of visual environments, whether architectural, otherwise humanly constructed, or occurring naturally. I will discuss a current study of fascist symbolism in contemporary Rome as an example.

Finally I look at the semiotics of images. This includes the semiotics of photos, films, paintings or other visual media. Common themes would be the analysis of power relationships in family albums, analyses of hidden meanings in advertisements, or analyses of meanings in propaganda films.

Semiotics one: The presentation of self

Erving Goffman wrote what was the seminal and still influential study of gender politics in print advertisements in the 1970s.[16] His study is based on a number of assumptions, the most important being that people continually and unconsciously perform social roles that are defined in part by gender. Secondly, Goffman assumes that there is a correspondence between the human actions he sees in magazine advertisements and those that occur in normal social life.

What did Goffman discover in his analysis of hundreds of ads? Women touch in a restrained, ritualistic way and men touch in a more utilitarian way. Women appear to guide daughters into adulthood; boys have to fight their way there. Rooms in ads are organized in a symbolic way, with lower levels assigned to ritually polluting tasks (storing dirty laundry, being walked on) and beds taking the role of a space where women more than men make themselves sexually available. Women's postures more often include elements such as knee bends that suggest subordination, psychological removal and dependence on men.

In these and many other examples Goffman studied the physical grammar of subordination. While the themes may not have been totally new they had never been studied empirically, using an imperfect database that certainly had its strengths. There remains the question of whether people in advertisements and people acting in public can be taken as equivalent, but the patterns Goffman saw were certainly there. There were many follow-up studies using Goffman's method, in several cultures and using several sources of data. Though seldom identified as such, Goffman's study of gender display in ads is one of the most influential contributions of visual sociology to the sociological mainstream.

Patrizia Faccioli and I created a research project that we hoped would be something of a real world test of some of Goffman's ideas.[17] For this research I photographed about twenty public display ads in Bologna, Italy, that included interaction or reaction between men and women. We subsequently showed these photos to Italian and American women to elicit reactions to the gender politics implied in the images. The themes were variations of common themes of seduction, flirtation, male domination, sexuality and beauty but generally the interpretations and reactions of Americans and Italians to these images were quite different.

For example, in reaction to Figure 6.4 an American woman commented:

The ad does not work for me. I would not buy the product advertised.
The relationship between the man and woman is purely sexual, based
on physical appearance. The man has greater power. He is taller and
looks stronger than the woman and he is looking at her in a very sexual
way . . . I hope I am never viewed like this.

Another American woman commented in reference to this ad: "The ad makes me a little angry: The woman is in her underwear: the man is dressed. Her only power is sex. He can't think clearly, only because the woman is undressed."

The Italian women viewed the ad much differently. One said: "The ad does not challenge my identity at all. It makes me glad to be a woman, knowing or feeling that we have the potential to be alluring."

Another Italian woman commented:

The message is: if you would like to be appreciated, wear this stuff.
All people love to be admired, the men too. They are playing and

Figure 6.4
Man with many bananas.

enjoying. Maybe the bananas give a touch of originality and define the relationship as a game. The message suggests she is the winner and he is seduced: I think it's an equal relationship. The bananas remind me of the natives of any lost island, so it confirms the message: He seems to be a slave to passion. He's a primitive, who doesn't resist his impulses. She looks like a self-confident woman, not afraid to show herself; she's brilliant. The slogan puts the passive and the active together: To be admired is passive, but to love to be admired is active.

Figure 6.5 (opposite top)
American women were all offended by the ad; considering it a mockery of violence against women and a glorification of male domination. One viewer noted the figure from the 1940s in the foreground and recalled the gender roles the ad seemed to be idealizing. Italian women tended to see the aggression as connected to passion, and also the ad itself as symbolizing the violence and uncertainty of the modern moment. The Italian women found the visual construction of the ad to be ironic and even powerful; American women only saw the threat it implied.

Figure 6.6 (opposite bottom)
The photo shows two ads; on the right is a swimsuit and on the left is a personal ad by an individual who presents himself as a transvestite, offering sexual services, which is not illegal in Italy. American women did not see a connection between the two ads and were astounded that sexual services, deviant or otherwise, could be publicly advertised. The Italian viewers saw the ads in relation to each other; the transvestite as "brave and honest" and the swimsuit as a callous manipulation of women who attempt to achieve an impossible physical ideal.

The reactions to all of our twenty-some photos followed these general patterns; Americans saw the gendered interactions as threatening and demeaning and the Italians saw them as mutually seductive and often funny. There were some photos of male–female interaction in public display ads in which men seemed to be asserting themselves in a threatening way against women; Americans were upset by the implied message whereby the Italian women tended to see physical power as integral to sex. Finally, one photo showed a billboard in which a transvestite sex worker posed in lingerie and listed her phone number, and this large poster was framed alongside the bikini ad next to it. The Italian women saw the sex worker as heroic; the American women could hardly believe such sexual forwardedness existed, and were put off by it.

It was a modest study because of the small sample of women interviewed in both the US and Italy, not to mention the need to match age, social class position and other attributes to make meaningful comparisons between Italian and American subjects. It is also important that the ads emerged from Italian public life and Italian women are used to such imagery, while American women are less so (or were, in the late 1990s, when the study was completed). Still, the study provides an example of moving from assumed meanings of images to studying how meaning is created in the situated act of viewing. It goes beyond the assertion of meaning to research on what different people actually see in the same visual universe.

Semiotics two: Symbolic environments

"Little boxes on the hillside, little boxes made of ticky tacky, little boxes on the hillside, little boxes all the same." The 1962 hit song *Little Boxes* by Malvina Reynolds that began with these lyrics connected suburban sprawl to middle-class conformity. The song implied that living in suburbia meant consuming suburbia's symbolic meaning (conformity and cultural thinness), which was at odds with what suburbia was supposed to symbolize, an escape from urban crowding, access to fresh air and bucolic calm. Until Bill Owens photographed his own suburbia,[18] the association of suburbia with a type of material reality, and the implication of what it meant, had to be inferred. Owens and others who have subsequently photographed several forms of community life have all challenged easy assumptions with often contradictory and certainly complex symbol systems.

Looking in another symbolic direction, postmodern architecture combines elements from different eras and traditions in forms that are strange, discordant, ironic or humorous. Postmodernism as a symbol of creative irrationality was intended to replace the hierarchy, bureaucracy and conformity that were communicated by the rationalist architecture of the skyscraper. For some, postmodern architecture is a delightful and liberating experience. Michael Graves' Humana Tower in Louisville, which combines references to ancient Egypt with skyscrapers of the early and late twentieth century seems like a terrific joke and I'm thrilled every time I see it. John Burgee's PPG Place in my home town of Pittsburgh executes Gothic design in iron and glass, and seeing its pinnacles pierce the cloudy skies always gives the old downtown a great splash of visual excitement. In other words, consuming the postmodern symbol in some instances achieves its intended result. But for most, I suspect, the strange buildings are simply seen as peculiar if they are noticed at all. As such they are failed symbols, having little consequence.

Urban environments have often been manipulated to communicate a specific message. When Mussolini's urban designers cleared slums from around monuments like the Colosseum they were intending to encourage awe in the population and to connect their regime to the glories of the past.[19] Buildings with streamlined shapes, curved glass and san serif fonts connected fascism to Futurism with the obvious message that fascism was modern and progressive. Buildings or whole neighborhoods (EUR, the University of Rome or the sports complex at Foro Italico)

Figure 6.7
PPG Place, Pittsburgh.

Ethnomethodology, semiotics, subjective

Figure 6.8
Palazzo della Civiltá Italiana (Square Colosseum), EUR, Rome. The Palazzo was intended as a fascist interpretation of the Roman Colosseum, a combination of arches, or loggias, in a rationalist package. Around the base of the building are nearly thirty statues, each representing an element in the fascist conception of the corporate society. The building has been recently restored and is the centerpiece of the prosperous suburban neighborhood of EUR, a community planned and largely constructed during the fascist era.

were only the first step; fascist designers added bas-relief sculptures, mosaics, or murals that defined the ideal family, the proper organization of rural life, the glories of athletics and military battle, the confluence of fascism and Catholicism, Mussolini as the savior of Italy and the corporate organization of society itself.

Making several thousand photographs of fascist symbols, buildings, neighborhoods and urban redesign in modern Italy led me to wonder: how are these symbols seen and understood by modern Italians; or, how are they consumed? This is, after all, an empirical question, which, working with Roman sociologists, I am studying.[20] Preliminary analysis of more than 600 interviews shows that fewer than 10 percent even identify the buildings, symbols and other architectural features as fascist. Further work on this ongoing project will analyze the attitudes toward the fascist symbols by social class, age and political self-definition. The photos are organized in levels of abstraction; the most abstract being the design of neighborhoods, which it is likely only a student of architecture would identify as fascist, followed by the fascist buildings, symbols and, most specifically, words and names. Mussolini's name and likeness remain predominantly displayed in many parts of Rome, which one would imagine to be recognizable to all.

Because the research will explore the potency of symbolism in a lived environment it may influence policies that will decide what modern Italians will do with these remaining symbols from a discredited past. The larger question concerns

Figure 6.9

Free-standing bas-relief depicting an idealized vision of rural life in a fascist society, EUR, Rome. The wall was to be the entrance to an institute of agriculture, which was never completed due to the collapse of the fascist regime. The wall is a floating signifier in a seldom-visited corner of a large park, but the themes detail the fascist view of rural life. One panel after another details cooperative peasant life, self-sufficiency, diversification of crops and animals, the nobility of hand labor, and the bounty and satisfaction of farming. Interestingly enough, the mechanization of agriculture under Mussolini's "Battle for Grain" and other policies was bringing to an end precisely these characteristics of rural existence in Italy.

Figure 6.10

Mosaic, Foro Italico, Rome. Mussolini used sports to recruit the young into proto-fascist groups. Fascism idealized athletics, and Mussolini's large sports complex, Foro Mussolini, was a pride of the fascist regime. It has now been renamed Foro Italico, the site of a new stadium in which professional football is played. The entrance to the stadium passes over mosaics, such as this one, that celebrate fascism. The "M" pictured stands for Mussolini, here integrated with the symbol of fascism. Other mosaics extol the mostly male athletic form, the invasion and subjugation of Ethiopia, the creation of an Italian empire and other claims of heroism, honor and greatness. One mosaic reads: "much honor, many enemies."

what collective memory will be preserved, and in what form, and what forms of collective memory will be redefined or even eliminated. For example, Mussolini is currently buried with his family in his home village, which has become a destination for hundreds of thousands of neo-fascists from the entirety of Europe; several politicians on the right (including his granddaughter, who carries the name Mussolini) have lobbied to have his tomb moved to Rome. The question of what to do with the past becomes largely a question of preserving or eliminating visual traces of collective memory.

The relationships between buildings and their political messages can become a semiotically driven historical study. One of the most accomplished examples is by Alick McLean,[21] who showed how the rise and fall of the Italian city-state in the commune of Prato was negotiated through buildings. Various groups vying for power (the Holy Roman Empire, local aristocratic families, the church and the rising bourgeoisie) all claimed their legitimacy partly through physical structures they created and displayed in the urban fabric of medieval Italy. McLean's study details how secular/economic, religious and political architectural forms were played off against each other, often in a desperate struggle to maintain the upper hand. For example, at one point in the eleventh century the bishop in charge sold off church lands, relics and other resources to finance a building campaign that left the church in dire economic straits. The secular buildings in the democratic city-state

Figure 6.11
In the 1930s Mussolini, who had been dictator of Italy since the early 1920s, created a culture of sports for the youth of Italy. As a result thousands of young Italians journeyed from the far reaches of Italy to participate in games and competitions in Rome, many situated at the complex that carried his name. Mussolini's name still adorns the 130 foot obelisk that welcomes sports enthusiasts to the modern soccer stadium.

Figure 6.12 (opposite)
Mussolini's likeness is found in many sculptures, mosaics and murals in contemporary Italy. This bas-relief sculpture, which places Mussolini atop a horse, piles the entirety of Italian history on his shoulders. The sculpture, about 50 feet high (the door on the left is about 8 feet high), adorns an office building in the neighborhood of EUR, built in the fascist era, but operating effectively today.

that evolved during its 200-year-old existence edged up against symbols of religious power and borrowed from their legitimacy. Porticoes had architectural references to religion, but became protected spaces where commerce took place and which the rising bourgeoisie claimed.

Sociologists have sought other ways to decode the symbols of built environments. Adam Yuet Chau's study of what he calls "an awful mark"[22] analyzes the secondary meaning of the character (in the meaning of a Chinese symbol) that is painted on buildings about to be torn down by the Chinese government. Chau's

focus is on ". . . the relationship between forms of public writing and power, physical violence and symbolic violence in the context of urban spatial transformation in China."[23] He sees the huge, sloppily written characters as examples of official writing in a society where words on buildings are traditionally blessings, Daoist talismans, or political slogans. The demolition character is seen as an expression of arrogance; a demonstration of the unchecked power of the state. The symbol communicates that a certain building is slated for destruction, but it also sends out a secondary, or connotative, meaning. Chau calls this communication a "text act;" it does not just communicate, but it acts on people. Chau notes that public reaction is often to confront the character with a battle of words (graffiti) or symbols such as hollowed out portions of walls, which represent a large bald head with exaggerated features, a mockery of state power.

Finally, Luc Pauwels studies the connotative meaning of corporate offices,[24] noting how objects and their layouts communicate the values and norms of the organization. International corporations display world maps and flags to show the global reach of the company and the connection of the company to a nation. The placement and decorations of offices communicate the status of the person who works in the company, and the hierarchical organization of the company. Corporate boardrooms gain an almost sacred quality via their furniture and decoration. According to Pauwels, these are readable codes that reveal a consciously created symbolic environment.

These examples demonstrate that the connotative meanings of built environments are moving targets, changing with history and circumstances. McLean's study shows that historians can read these meanings through a lens nearly 1,000 years old; our current study of fascism in Rome show that symbolic meanings have shifted radically in fifty brief years. The corporations or universities we work in do their best to send messages through their architecture or decoration; we may give an ironic nod when our university adds some wrought iron filigree to an old building to give it a more historical look, but when it is completed we are perhaps surprised to experience the space in a new way; buying into a symbolic dimension it lacked before. Interestingly enough (though it has not been studied) one of the most notable semiotics of the modern university is its bland emptiness, which is very different than the Oxfords and Harvards of the world. My current university office is in a building that was a parking garage in its previous existence: its reincarnation as a center of learning was partly convincing and partly not!

Semiotics three: Reading visual texts

Perhaps the most common use of visual semiotics is to decode photos or other visual texts. It has been typical to see advertising images from this perspective and the secondary or second level meanings are not complicated in these situations: if you purchase product X you get the object, but you also become like the person in the ad. One consumes the object but more, the argument goes, one purchases the meanings of the object as represented through advertising. These assumptions vary in depth. Linda Kalof and Amy Fitzgerald's semiotic analysis of the messages behind the photos and drawings of dead animals in hunting magazines[25] leads them to conclude: "Instead of love and respect for nature and wildlife we found extreme objectification and marginalization of animal bodies."[26] It is not clear what "extreme objectification" or "marginalization" means in this analysis, aside from the fact that Kalof and Fitzgerald clearly think that one cannot kill wild animals and at the same time "love" them or their natural setting.

Often semiotic researchers also stretch our imagination or sometimes restate what is commonly taken for granted. For example, historian Simon Schama asserts that objects in seventeenth-century Dutch paintings—such as globes on the wall, small pets or silver chalices—were codes for the anxiety experienced by a Calvinist society adapting to the wealth of early capitalism.[27] This may be true (and his work is deeply informed), but it is difficult to know if the objects were, in fact, interpreted (and by whom) in the way he asserts. It's a provocative idea, and armed in the present with new ideas and insights we are certainly tempted to explore its logic. Vibha Arora's semiotic analysis of postcards from Sikkim, the northeastern province of India,[28] asserts that through the cards Sikkim is presented as a Himalayan Shangri-la, a hidden paradise, a land of peace and tranquility and the ultimate eco-tourist destination. The postcards are really an advertisement. They communicate place but with the connotation of an idealized and unattainable reality.

A particularly convincing study is Anu-Hanna Anttila's analysis of Finnish vacation propaganda films from the late 1940s, which she interpreted as directives to the working class to use a paid holiday leave to revitalize themselves with sun, fresh air, bodily culture and hard work on the relative's farm; in other words to become happier and more productive citizens. A second example is Anna Szorenyi's analysis of several coffee table books on refugees,[29] specifically three well-produced photo studies of forced migration in contemporary times. These include *Images of Exile*, a product of the United Nations High Commissioner for Refugees; *Migrations*, which world famous documentary photographer Sebastião Salgado spent several years photographing, and *Exodus*, which was produced by Signum Fotografie, a photo agency devoted entirely to the refugees.

Szorenyi refers to critiques of the tradition of photo documentary of suffering written by Martha Rosler, Abigail Solomon-Godeau and Susan Sontag, and adds Walter Benjamin's comment that "photography . . . has succeeded in turning abject poverty itself . . . into an object of enjoyment."[30] She suggests that while the books purport to emphasize empathy and sympathy, she finds that they communicate a feeling of distance between refugees and readers, who are mostly in affluent countries. The books simplify the refugee experience, implying that there is a kind of person who is a refugee who thinks and feels in a particular way; that the central feature of their lives is victimhood; that the problem is one of human rights; and that the "state of being" of the refugee is "persecution, flight, exile," and, finally, "rescue and resettlement."

Szorenyi suggests that refugees as people are obliterated in the process as they become a symbol for first world guilt. They do not speak in the books; they are often presented as distant and faceless objects, and simple markers indicate their exotic, third world status. They are victims acted upon by tragic forces and circumstances.

A closer look at these publications, Szorenyi asserts, is more complicated; there are photographs in each collection that question the standard refugee trope. For example, Szorenyi describes a photograph of human skulls and moldering rags in the killing fields of Cambodia and comments:

> . . . if I had seen beauty at first, that sight is now rendered tasteless by the revelation of the subject matter. In this way this photograph can be read as narrating its own critique of the practice of turning atrocity into aesthetics.[31]

Szorenyi points out that the introduction to the book *Exodus* anticipates the now common critique and she finds photos in the book that negate that critique; where refugees are making decisions, acting in purposeful ways and in many ways confronting their victimhood. The photos show the surveillance system in a Europe that helps to dispel refugees, and we can read narratives in the photos that describe how refugees overcome unimaginably hard circumstances. What then is the problem with the book? Szorenyi asserts that despite the progressive messages in the images, the refugees are not empowering themselves through their own actions, but being empowered by photographers who present them a certain way.

Szorenyi was clear about her own ambivalence regarding the refugee projects; while her view of "misery photography" is critical she also recognizes that invisibility gains nothing for those caught in the crossfires of history, and she hopes for "more productive representational structures" for refugees and presumably for others.

Cultural studies

There remains the question of visual sociology's relationship to cultural studies. On the most basic level it is fair to say that cultural studies interpret texts, whether they are written or visual. Written texts are typically literary (many cultural studies departments are part of or an adjunct to departments of English or languages) and other forms of texts are photos, films, paintings, body adornment and buildings, so there seems to be a natural connection between visual sociology and cultural studies. Cultural studies have been criticized for lacking a method (Pierre Bourdieu notes his distance from cultural studies for that reason) and visual sociology is an integration of method and theory, as is hopefully clear by this point in the book. Cultural theory is heavily theory laden and if there is a single theme that connects much of the sub-discipline, it concerns how people in lower social classes internalize their subservience by consuming messages that legitimate the system and their place in it. The first generation of cultural studies researchers in the UK in the 1970s drew inspiration from Antonio Gramsci, jailed (where he eventually died) during the Italian fascist era for political dissent, who questioned in his writings why Italian peasants and workers supported fascism. Cultural studies researchers were perplexed by the UK's turn to the right in the 1980s, and especially by the working-class support for right wing PM Margaret Thatcher. But cultural theorists tend to assemble ideas and contemplate their connections rather than to do field work. The influential texts[32] make almost no mention of sociology, not to mention visual sociology, but when they do, their view is incomplete. For example, in what is considered the most important collection on cultural studies, a paper by Simon Watney entitled "the sociology of photography" presents a determinist caricature of sociology that would be rejected by anyone working in the cultural end of the discipline. Fortunately an insightful visual sociologist, Elizabeth Chaplin, examines early visual sociology in the context of cultural studies, and her masterful study begs for an update as it has been more than twenty years since its initial publication.[33]

Maybe the best way to explain the distance between visual sociology and cultural studies is to note their singular focus on the relationship between images or texts and power. Cultural studies writing can be arcane to the point that a parody submitted by the physicist Alan Sokal was regarded as legitimate and published by the cultural studies journal, *Social Text*, in 1996, which showed at the very least that the vocabulary is easy to satirize. Nevertheless much of what visual sociologists study is consistent with cultural studies and hopefully the barriers between the two sub-disciplines will erode in the near future.

Interpreting the subjective

Several years ago I suggested a typology of visual sociology,[34] adapted from Bill Nichols' similar overview of documentary film,[35] that consisted of four approaches: empirical, narrative, reflexive and phenomenological, or subjective.

There has been, in the meantime, an increasing interest in the subjective within sociology itself. At first there was the study of emotional labor, best represented by Arlie Russell Hochschild's research on occupations such as airline stewardesses. This was followed by a movement which called itself autoethnography—a combination of autobiography and ethnography. More recent sociological studies of emotions include poetry, first-person journaling and other forms of self-expression, embraced with a near religiosity by a small number of sociologists. The expression of the subjective in visual sociology has been a parallel development, though it is unclear from citations and other evidence that the movement toward subjectivity in non-visual sociology has yet to draw upon visual sociology.

The idea is that visual expression, whether through painting, drawing or modes of expression like photography, is a way to express oneself, and that much expression has sociological content. Alfred Stieglitz' claim that the clouds he photographed in the 1930s were equivalents to his moods or emotions does not have a great deal of sociological cachet, but his student Minor White's stark photos, intended as a mirror of his emotions, could plausibly be seen as a manifestation of the alienation he felt as a closeted bisexual man.

How have sociologists used images to explore the subjective side of social existence? There are at least three ways: by using images as visual metaphors; by recounting the details of experience; and by using photos as a bridge between researcher and subject.

In the case of visual metaphor, Richard Quinney's recent books[36] describe his transformation from a critical criminologist to a philosophical wanderer, finally finding his way back to his home spaces of Wisconsin. His photographs depict landscapes and objects, often from or around his parents' farm, where he grew up and which he left to become an intellectual. They depict mood and feelings grounded in the depiction of seasonal change, aging buildings and the land. His writings borrow from philosophy and literature, and reflect both his inner and outer journeys, and they offer a parallel to the images.

The first of these books, published in 1991, was a radical departure for Quinney and for sociology. He is credited with introducing a Marxist approach to criminology and had authored several still influential texts in that area. I was then editor of a book series on visual studies of society and culture published at Temple University Press, and Quinney's was one of the first manuscripts we published. It seemed like a revolutionary moment for both sociology and visual sociology; a respected criminologist suddenly writing a memoir in the first person, illustrated with photos he'd taken throughout his life. Quinney's visually based autobiography led to six more (at this writing). His themes have been an examination of life's purpose, and the importance of place in his identity. At one point Quinney accepted an academic position in northern Iowa, close to his family landscape, without even a job interview, to rediscover and re-experience his roots. The job went sour (the department may have thought they were hiring the criminologist, not the visual sociologist) and the landscape initially lacked the roots he sought. Quinney's work from that period tells of loneliness in an empty small town on the border of Wisconsin, and an academic job he no longer wanted. As retirement has led him back to the landscapes he spent his life yearning for, the images and texts regain energy, as though winter has become once more spring.

Quinney's autobiographical reflections in images and words are currently the most formal work by a visual sociologist using visual metaphor to explore identity. If one were locating his work in sociology per se, it would find a home in the growing area of autobiographic ethnography. Quinney's photographic work, however, makes his contributions very different than the confessional work that usually characterizes what is now called autoethnography. Quinney's images are thoughtful constructions that communicate his instincts and feelings, akin to the work of Minor White and others who pioneered this tradition in the fine arts.

Sociologists and others have also used images (usually photos, but also drawings, paintings, X-rays and other images) to show the insider's experience, especially during transitions that are difficult, traumatic or terrifying. One thinks immediately of the project of writer Dorothea Lynch and photographer Eugene Richards[37] who together described the experience of cancer that eventually took Lynch's life. The autobiography and photos documented her discovery of cancer; her hopeful experience of recovery, and the terror of remission, as well as her experience in hospitals, clinics and other settings of the medical system.

The transition from health to death is also told in the images and text of Jo Spence.[38] Many writers have described the transitions that come with serious disease, but these projects use photos (in Lynch's case, by her partner Eugene Richards) to show the view from the hospital bed looking outward, of the bodily assault that cancer represents and of the re-aligned sense of self that diseased-based change brings. The images show how the self is rooted in the body and how the experience of illness is mediated by institutions. They show the emotional labor of illness in the faces of participants, the performance of professional work, and the experience of those who are left behind.

Perhaps the strongest example of imagery used to detail identity and illness was done by Jon Prosser,[39] well known for his visual studies of schools. Prosser suffered a nearly fatal bacterial infection of the heart, and a subsequent stroke that changed how he experienced and viewed the world, now as an impaired person in a several year recovery process. He analyzed the experience of illness and recovery with narrative and imagery, which he refers to as mediating his experience of illness. Prosser's memories of the first days after the stroke are mental movies that played as repeating film loops in his mind, showing mountain climbing experiences in which he was fearful and anxious. When his family finally reached him in the hospital, his daughter drew a picture in which Prosser was reduced from her memory as, "big and strong" to small, vulnerable and "tied up to machines." During the long recovery Prosser saw the world differently; normal images of brain scans became evil faces; groups of people were transformed into images of the brain. His visual apprehension came to reflect his inner torment. As he recovered he began to study the fine arts: in his life-drawing classes he drew women with "soft lines and relaxed bodies," but men were "contorted, deformed or exploding."

In the publication of the article, images are not captioned, because, as Prosser explains, "I saw the words as secondary and the visuals were there to explain the words even though the 'reader' would have to worker harder . . . the figures are for me far more important than the words ever were."[40] For this publication, given that I am limited to a short excerpt, I asked Prosser to add captions to two images.

It took Prosser years to recapture his ability to lecture or write. He found a path back to higher cognitive functioning in part through mental mapping where he was able to visualize ideas and their relationships. To write the article discussed here, Prosser produced a mind-map (Figure 6.14) that connects the paragraphs, images and narrative texts that became his unified expression.

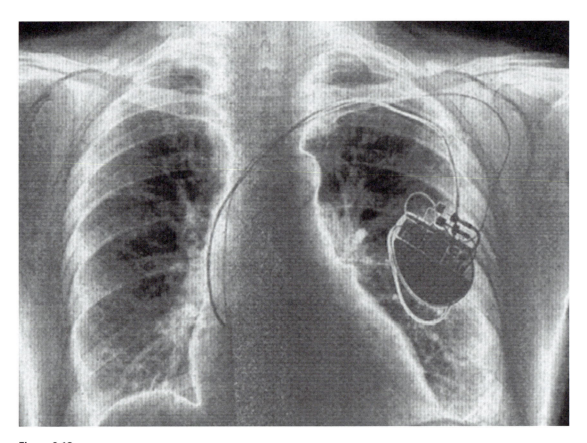

Figure 6.13
X-ray with pacemaker. Using the objectivity of a medical image and its subjective interpretation in the process of self healing.

When I was in hospital I became disillusioned with doctors' narrow interpretation of visual evidence. So figure 6.13, originally used for clinical purposes and selected for its objectivity/reality, is really fulfilling its role as a healing device through my processing of it. I saw it initially as objective/medical data (the pacemaker as an alien device inside my body), then, face to face with my worst nightmare, I came to perceive it as something small and comical, eventually feeling "is that all?" Hence using the objectivity of a medical image and its subjective interpretation in the process of self healing. (Image and caption by Jon Prosser.)

Prosser experienced illness and recovery in part visually and also found a way to communicate it that way. As a result the reader and viewer understand the experience of illness in a far more complex way than words alone would provide.

Ricabeth Steiger used images to explore the routine experience of the one hour and six minute train ride from her home town of Basel, Switzerland, to Zurich, where she works, which she has taken several times a week for several years.[41] Steiger writes that

> photographs may reveal what we are normally unable to perceive, because our perception is too slow or because we are unable to focus on two things simultaneously. On the other hand, the photographs freeze moments that are meant to communicate the personal

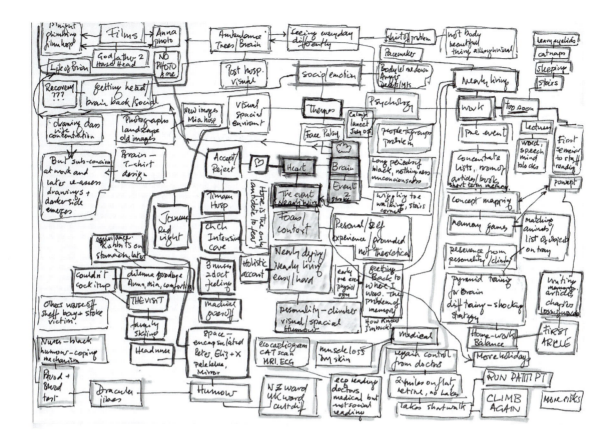

Figure 6.14
Using what remains
functioning after brain injury
to aid healing: adopting mind-
mapping to encourage the
development of ideas, and
provide a rationale and
structure for an academic text
(Jon Prosser). Original coded
in four colors.

experience and a sense of the social space on the train. In this way the
project is both an empirical record and an interpretation of social life on
rails.[42]

Steiger made several hundred images over several months and then categorized
them, discovering several categories of activities including "navigating through the
crowd at the station," "looking out of the train," and "looking into the train." The
large windows of the train car provide a moving picture of Switzerland and allow
passengers to disconnect from others and perhaps daydream. Looking into the train
invites interaction with others. The analysis of images led to understanding norms
surrounding how space is claimed and used. Categories of people photographed
included "people only seen once," "people seen regularly but not interacted with,"
and "commuters she sits with and communicates with." Most of those
photographed were commuters she came to know, who became implicit co-
conspirators in the project, acting out their routines for the camera.

By using the same 20 mm lens (an extreme wide angle) Steiger was able to
capture people in their environments. Using the same lens, black and white film and
image development made the images equivalent in framing and perspective, giving
the impression of the human eye drifting across the intimate landscape of the train.

Figure 6.15
Train ride from Basel to
Zurich (1). (Figures 6.15–6.17
by Ricabeth Steiger.)

The project was presented in two ways: seventy-six black and white photos printed as thumbnails on three pages, and, in a first for visual sociology publication, as a CD, included with the journal that autoloaded into the then-current MAC or PC computer and played as a slideshow/movie.[43] The experience of seeing seventy-six images blend into each other at twenty-second intervals lulled one into the subjectivity of the train experience. The silvery black and white reproductions made the experience into something approaching a dream. In fact this discussion could also be placed in the following chapter on multimedia, since it was a unique and successful application of multimedia to explore the subjectivity of routine behavior. The photos were presented without captions or conscious organization in the slideshow/movie and the excerpt offered here simply provides a sense of the larger project.

Images have also been used to explore the subjective by bridging the worlds of the researcher and the subject. The best demonstration of this new direction is in Sarah Pink's recent work, where she has used video and photography to record the mundane aspects of experiencing the world. She refers to the future of visual anthropology as vested in "engaging the senses,"[44] attuned to human "place-making" in which people tell of their environments. An example of her method is

Figure 6.16
Train ride from Basel to
Zurich (2).

found in her study of "walking with video" through a garden with two elderly people.[45] They describe the experience as they walk, and later they reflect on the video Pink had produced of the experience. The article describing the research includes a few excerpts from the video: a person in a small garden; an empty landscape; feet hitting the soil.

The images are not meaningful in and of themselves; rather they provide a way for person A to explain to person B what was experienced. Pink attempts to refigure anthropological ethnography to include the study of experience, and ethnography in this instance is based on sharing the lives of those studied. Sharing, in her view, means tasting, feeling, touching, walking; that is, being in the world of those one hopes to understand.

A future direction for research on visual and subjective aspects of social life includes studies of virtual experience, for example, in the interactive game *Second Life*. So far this work is more speculative than empirical, yet the work of sociologists Giovanni Boccia Artieri and Laura Gemini[46] establishes the groundwork and suggests future strategies.

Including ethnomethodology, semiotics and the study of the subjective in a single discussion makes sense partly because they are equally distant from

Figure 6.17
Train ride from Basel to
Zurich (3).

other practices of visual sociology but they also share the goal of grasping the taken-for-granted aspects of life; investigating the normal process of seeing and being in the world.

Chapter 7

Multimedia and visual sociology

Recently an NPR story caught my ear: a twenty-eight-year-old woman from Yemen, Amira Al-Sharif, had secured funds from Kickstarter[1] to finance a year in America photographing women her age. It was an engaging story of crossing cultures in a way that Americans are not used to hearing about; it's us, after all, who usually do the crossing.

Her photos were well described in the report and one could click on to the NPR website to see them. There were eight photos on the site that showed veiled women in Yemen juxtaposed with informal, hip, sexy twenty-somethings in New York, as well as a touching photo of her American friend, Anna, sprawled on a large bed with her grandparents during a Thanksgiving visit to her home. By the time a reader of this book comes to this reference the NPR story will be long gone, but it will be possible, of course, to Google-search Al-Sharif, and see if she has been successful in her dream to become a professional photographer.

This is the character of images in the twenty-first century; they are everywhere, they are extraordinarily impermanent, and their social impact cannot be anticipated. The old way images were made, on a physical surface (now referred to as an "analogue" technology), produced a semi-permanent trace. My father's film negatives still produce the images they were intended to, because the technology to make images from negatives was so pervasive and so simple, it will probably always exist in some form. The CD that was part of a special edition of the journal *Visual Sociology* just ten years ago is now unreadable.

Despite these troubling trends, analogue technologies have now largely been replaced by digital technologies, manifest in everything from several thousand dollar cameras that mimic old film cameras to picture-making cellphones carried by most people. Not only are the images everywhere but the means for making them are as well.

Images made by digital technologies are less rooted in realist assumptions because they are very easy to change, and they also flow up continually in a vast cloud, around and through the global community via the Internet. The images produce a kind of ubiquitous seeing that inspires revolutions (the 2011 revolution in Egypt is a recent example) and they provide a way for people to express themselves in ways that often have dramatic outcomes. As I write this, Congressman Anthony Weiner's self-destruction via his posts of lewd self-portraits has just occurred. He will be forgotten by the time this text is read; his images will be a micro visual footnote of 2011. This is partly due to the sheer number of digital images circulating in cyberspace; it is estimated that more than seventeen billion analogue images were made in the US in a typical year in the early 1990s and that in 2011 "about 5 million pictures are uploaded to Flickr every day . . . 2.5 billion photos to Facebook each month . . . and YouTube . . . serves 2 billion videos a day to millions of viewers around the world."[2]

Sociologists are only now beginning to study what all of this means. Some trends are obvious, though their implications are not. Teens build their identities via the latest social network sites. Traditional journalism and photojournalism are giving way to net-based journalism and in digital form stories are shorter and more ephemeral; little is preserved and there are fewer guarantees that traditional journalistic ethics will oversee what is posted. Advertising is everywhere in the digital world, yet it is hard to make a living as a photographer, even when a Web posting may generate millions of viewings. Careers and the moral policing they imply have given over to a free-for-all with few standards or assumptions about truthfulness.

But multimedia in visual sociology is more than a discussion of the impact of digital technologies on mass culture. Since the 1990s, visual sociologists and anthropologists have begun to use multimedia to study the world and to present their work. Multimedia first appeared as adjunct materials for texts, adding data, visuals or other information; adding *more* rather than something *new* to a standard book. That has slowly given way to new forms of imagining and imaging the world.

Many of the successful experiments in multimedia have been created with software programs such as Macromedia's Director, which began more than twenty years ago as HyperCard, a program bundled with early Apple computers. The key to HyperCard was that it allowed information to be organized in a nonlinear manner; the now familiar links in websites and other multimedia suddenly allowed one to go sideways into new material as well as ahead or backwards, as books and movies require.

Relevant forms of multimedia for visual sociology and anthropology include written texts, still photos, video excerpts, maps, graphs and tables, and interviews, all interconnected with live links that allow a viewer a nearly limitless number of paths through large bundles of information. Multimedia ethnography exists as DVDs or CDs or, increasingly, as websites, where links connect ideas not only to other information inside the document, but also to documents outside. The e-book, that can include video as well as other forms of images and texts, is beginning to appear. These new forms of scholarship and expression have great potential for visual sociology, which I will show below, but they have not replaced books, articles, films and video.

Howie Feeds Me

I first examine Dianne Hagaman's CD-Rom *Howie Feeds Me*:[3] it is part love poem to her husband, Howard Becker, part reflection on their experiences together and part expression of her sentiments about being a couple. Hagaman combined photos into what she calls sonnets, which viewers scroll through at their own pace. Each sonnet contains fourteen photos, and there are fourteen sonnets in the CD. Hagaman has structured the document to limit the viewer's choices, so the experience of viewing the CD resembles watching a movie while negotiating one's way through some of its major pathways.

The images communicate mood, allusion, sentiment and memory. They began as black and white Tri-X film images, and their glowing silvery texture translates beautifully to the computer screen. Anyone viewing the project feels as though they are looking into the private lives of old friends, whether they know the couple or not. The project reflects design choices that take advantage of multimedia's ability to achieve specific ends; there are few words and images, but they are constructed like an elegant three-dimensional puzzle. The material could not have been presented in any other format, which is its point. Hagaman's project also shows how a multimedia expression can be artistic and sociological, getting at the essence of a relationship like a fine short story.

Paris: Invisible City

Bruno Latour, an influential French social scientist, has produced what one could refer to as a visual ethnomethodology of urban spaces in *Paris: Invisible City*.[4] The book has been published conventionally, but is also available as a free multimedia document, which is easily found on his website. It is the electronic version to which I turn.

The webbook has a conventional cover that shows what appears to be a bureaucrat manipulating several small objects on a table. We see only his hands, his light blue shirt and the unidentified objects. As we study the book we realize he's one of the many bureaucrats, social scientists, engineers, politicians and accountants on which the existence of the modern city depends. It is the reality of his (and her) worlds that Latour investigates. Latour explains:

> One could just as well recruit one's students at random off the Boulevard St. Michel, or forecast the weather by raising one's head to a corner of the sky. The gradual change from this cheerful chaos to the impeccable roads [of] maintenance service is not a move from disorder to order, nor from rich sociability to cold efficiency; it is the transformation of a sixteenth century town of four hundred thousand inhabitants to a city of four million. Whereas the four hundred

thousand could use one another as landmarks, memories, archives and caterers, the four million can no longer do so.

The webbook's strength is in the multimedia organization. On the cover are four numbered parts, *traversing*, *proportioning*, *distributing* and *allowing*, verbs that show the ethnomethodological orientation to the study of the accomplishment of routine life. The points of view from which this reality emerges include the tourist, the resident, the worker and the outsider.

Each of the chapters contains a curving path (perhaps representing the Seine) with nineteen clickable blocks. These are links to small essays and photo sequences. Clicking on the first essay begins a sentence: "You can find anything at the Samaritaine;" which entices the viewer to click to the end of the introduction: " 'You can find anything at the Samaritaine' is this department store's slogan. Yes, anything and even a panoramic view of all of Paris . . ." Latour then interrogates the idea of panorama to say that, well, yes, the famous panorama of Paris is there but it only shows the surface of the city. Latour's focus will be on the arteries of wires and tubes, electronic simulations, paved streets and records, and more records that organize vast levels and densities of information.

The photos that border the essays show scientists in lab coats fiddling with machines; social workers looking up records; stuffed birds in ornithological museums looking out in frozen poses; engineers controlling the flow of water via computer programs; and surveillance systems making photos of pedestrians as they walk through the city. We see the taken-for-granted aspects of modern urban life, both what is organized bureaucratically and what takes place informally. A large number of the images show computer screens, because that is where a lot of the modern work of running a city takes place.

A conventional book was published from this material but it seems less compelling. Why does the Web format work so much better? On the Web version of the project the viewer treats the material like a puzzle; figuring out how to navigate through levels of information. One is invited to open parts as though they were windows of an Advent calendar. The photos are sometimes redundant, but so is the reality they describe, so that may be their point. There are small surprises; Latour's friends Howard Becker and Dianne Hagaman are shown "acting out a cliché," by photographing young lovers "just like a Doisneau." I found myself easily thinking about the four themes around which the book is organized, and evaluating the various parts as levels of abstraction. There seems to be just enough information, but not too much, and the construction of the site carefully controls the paths one can travel. The fact that the virtual book is available on the Web is enticing and it begs the question of who, in the end, pays for the enterprise? Is visiting a website the same as engaging serious scholarship? Have there been any of the normal academic reviews that are supposed to guarantee that at least at one level one's work has been vetted?

The Ax Fight

In 1997 Peter Biella, Napoleon Chagnon and Gary Seaman produced the first fully integrated multimedia visual ethnography, based on Chagnon and Tim Asch's classic ethnographic film, *The Ax Fight*. The original was a ten-minute film showing a hostile interaction between two groups of Yanomamo tribespeople in Venezuela. *The Ax Fight* was an unusual example of ethnographic filmmaking, an unshaped piece of visual data at odds with narrative models of anthropological filmmaking originating with Robert Flaherty's *Nanook of the North*. *The Ax Fight* had typically been taught by having students view the footage several times, at normal speed and in slow motion. The film's potential as a teaching tool increased in multimedia because students, working from their own copies on their own computers, were able to create their own analyses. The *Yanomamo Interactive* CD-ROM includes three versions of the film, 380 paragraphs that describe the events as they unfold (these are viewed alongside the scrolling film), more than 100 captioned photographs of the participants in the ax fight, genealogical charts that plot the participants' relationships, and maps of the village that detail what happened in the fight. Students can flip from filmed events to biographical sketches, maps of important places and ethnographic explanations, which invite them to create and test theories. It allows students to imagine how they would film a similar event in different settings. For example, when I last studied the CD, I selected a participant in the fight and traced his genealogy in the village through his participation in village groups. I felt that the medium had invited me to become a researcher with primary data, though it had been, of course, set up previously. Still, the example shows how well multimedia can combine elements to create a teaching and learning environment.

Oak Park

Jay Ruby's ethnographic study of Oak Park, Illinois, uses several forms of multimedia to disseminate the results of a field study initiated in 1999 and completed in 2006 (Ruby http://astro.ocis.temple.edu/~ruby/opp/). Ruby set out to study the Chicago neighborhood where he had spent the first eighteen years of his life. It was, he felt, a community with high degrees of social integration across class, ethnic, racial and gender barriers. Ruby writes that:

> The more I learn about Oak Park, the more I learn about myself . . . the study will also enable me to pursue a number of anthropological interests. Among them are: the limits of reflexive methods, the value of ethnography in studying a contemporary U.S. community, how an ethnographer can visualize culture and make a film about it.

The project draws upon interviews, photographs, observations historical commentary and video segments. The methods Ruby used were standard ethnographic techniques: interviewing, photographing, filming and studying archives.

In the early years of the project the website included a community listserv, ongoing segments of interviews, observations and field notes. The website had been organized around modules which were broad categories with scroll-down subcategories. As the project came to completion, the website evolved. It is now smaller, and organized around a table of contents that resembles a written ethnography, moving from the study of the historical background of Oak Park to discussions of race, gender complexity, schools, odd and interesting facts about the town and a report from a minority perspective. The chapters are brief and text heavy, but include links to additional imagery off site. Other chapters link to current Web newspapers and the local government website that serves the community, which has the effect of continually updating its own ethnography.

The website includes papers Ruby presented from the project when it was in progress, and quarterly and monthly reports with images of people he was interviewing. The heart of the project became five "Oak Park Stories" available on DVD from a commercial publisher. The DVDs tell the story of a middle-class African-American family, a gay family, a middle-class white family and several institutions in the community. They evolved from the earlier modules to become freestanding digital documents designed to be seen on the computer.

Ruby's design choices encouraged several communities to participate in the ethnography. These include his graduate students in visual anthropology, the readership of his listserv and, significantly, the community under study. The website had a rough draft feeling, which invited exploration and comment. The final product CDs are professionally produced and do not depend on a website for future use.

Biella's and Ruby's projects show that visual ethnography comprising many forms of visual and textual information can work well as multimedia. There is not much point in presenting a long film in multimedia but it would be reasonable to add background material in the same way that modern commercial films are packaged. That multimedia works well for some projects, however, does not invalidate book or film based visual ethnography. There is a limit to how much unshaped data most audiences can work with and just because it would be possible to install all of one's field notes, photographs made during field work and background information on a multimedia site does not mean one should. Architects of multimedia need to make the right choices so an audience can face the data with a good chance of making sense of it. More traditionally oriented visual ethnographers have spoken of the need for a "coherent itinerary" for these products, and the best multimedia visual ethnography (*Yanomamo Interactive* is a great example) is packaged with instructions that guide a viewer through the mazes the data present.

"Landscapes of Capital"

I turn to a recent essay by sociologists Stephen Papson and Robert Goldman, and multimedia designer Noah Kersey,[5] in which the authors, well known for studies of the semiotics of advertising, reflect on their experiences in designing, implementing and consequently modifying a Web-based research project entitled "Landscapes of Capital: Representing Time, Space, and Globalization in Corporate Advertising" (http//it.stlawu.edu/~global/).

There has been a great deal written about the supposed liberation from master narratives brought about by hypertext.[6] What this means simply is that in hyperdocuments readers enter and exit where they choose, and they skip to other regions of a document, or venture outside to other websites when they see fit. This is usually cast as an escape from the tyranny of authorship, but Papson, Goldman and Kersey suggest that it brings with it a style of reading they call surfing, or zipping from a section of text or an image to another as links direct a reader to other articles, ideas or expressions. They note, however, that "association does not necessarily enhance critical thought, deep readings and reflexivity,"[7] and that ". . . traversing a world of white noise composed of fragments and factoids is not necessarily empowerment."[8]

The hyperlinked character of these projects has also not eliminated their narrative structure. Biella and his colleagues created webs of information around a ten-minute visual narrative, the original film of the ax fight. Ruby posted film clips, filmed interviews and other visual material during the years of research, but in the end decided to package the research as CDs which are narrative in character.

The "Landscapes of Capital" website has 200 pages of text, nearly 1,000 TV commercials, a database and a glossary and excerpts of relevant social theory. The authors note their efforts to create a writing style that is appropriate for a hypertext website, and they have created an aesthetic where the page represents "a set of visual relationships."[9] They question, however, whether their short texts and large number of visuals leads to a fragmented and unwieldy document. They ponder whether viewers read entire text blocks, or skip the theory to focus on what they call visual spectacles, such as the camel imagery in their module on the semiotics of advertising. When the authors published an analysis of their site in 2007 they had decided to "go backwards" to write a book from the website, in addition to redesigning the website as a database. Their decisions were partly practical; the website had not been reviewed in academic journals despite what they felt was its intellectual legitimacy. One senses that they felt cheated by the discipline after the huge effort their project had required. They write that "books make work legitimate in a way that the Web cannot yet—and may never—do."[10]

They also came to question how well the site performed, and they were led to wonder whether a conventional book might not have been more effective. They write:

The site is so large that no one can sit in front of a computer screen and read through it. The printed page, the book on one's lap, is much more amenable to a complete reading and more pleasurable for longer engagement spans . . . We are continually told readers don't bother to scroll down a page. Simply, the book, in all its physicality, is superior for engaging a reader in an extended theoretical narrative, and it was frustrating to try and shoehorn that element of the project into a webpage-based structure. As authors, we want to allow the unfolding of an argument across many chapters . . .[11]

Having videos of the ads available communicates their pacing and full content. But because videos are memory hungry they have to be small, about the size of a 35 mm film negative. This was also the case with the filmed interviews Jay Ruby included in his website, as well as in the Biella project. Their small size encourages a "nanosecond glance" rather than detailed study.

"Landscapes of Capital" could be an effective instructional tool. My own reaction, however, was that the quantity of information decreases its usefulness. Why, for example, are 1,000 examples of TV ads needed? Would not a small number, presented in larger size and analyzed in detail, be more useful? I also found it difficult to read social theory on a computer screen; the dense material begs for a solid surface. Perhaps one message from "Landscapes of Capital" is that a website is hard to put borders around; it is more difficult to exclude information. Its strengths—providing a platform for vast quantities of different kinds of information—can be its undoing.

Issues in multimedia visual sociology

The impermanence of websites, and their need for constant maintenance, poses other problems. Links that connect them to other websites often go dead, because the websites they are linked to have changed or disappeared. For example, in Sarah Pink's discussion of hypermedia ethnography that appeared in 2001,[12] of the three websites referenced (one that documented Michael Fischer's field note summary in Pakistan, a second that presented "peasant worlds in transition," and a third that integrated photos and written text by Richard Chalfen) none were running by 2011. This means that the text written by Pink is now obsolete as well. Papson and his colleagues write: "Think of the tons of website detritus reflected by nonfunctioning links. Perhaps at some point, despite our best intentions, our site will join the electronic rubbish heap . . ."[13] As I complete this manuscript I have learned that, alas! the Biella CD no longer works on the operating systems of current computers, and the project is in search of an update. Without the update, it will indeed become an unreadable addition to, as Papson put it, the electronic rubbish heap.

There is no doubt that multimedia offers interesting possibilities for visual ethnography and other forms of visual sociology and anthropology. To a great extent the projects discussed above have produced visual sociology that could not be done in any other way. Papson and his colleagues have included the media—the TV ad—so, in their words, they can "show, not tell." Biella and his colleagues offer a variety of visual data to complement their written analyses. Ruby made his presentations about the research available during the process of conducting it which encouraged community dialogue through his website.

There is more material, and different kinds of material, available on these websites than is found in a book. Multimedia can be packaged as a CD and combined with books[14] and other forms of media collaboration are possible. The now emerging e-book, designed to be read on an electronic tablet like the iPad, seems a natural form of multimedia visual studies. But while future visual sociology will explore topics that require advanced forms of visual presentation (particularly video or film excerpts, or large numbers of photos) it is unlikely that multimedia will replace the book, article or freestanding film. Papson and Goldman write that "the printed text demands that we focus and refine our argument";[15] to give the text the shape, form and content that have survived as books for several hundred years. Their book, *Landscapes of Capital*, is going to print as I complete this project. I note that one of the most compelling visual sociological/historical projects in the history of the discipline, Susan Meiselas' 400-page "family album" of a hundred years of Kurdish history, began as a website and was, after many years of Web development, transformed into an artfully designed large-format book that integrates historical accounts and images, official tracts and contemporary images.[16]

Images, graphic display or photographs

Visual sociology began with a strong orientation to photography, but that has evolved to an orientation to all forms of visual representation, which can be thought of as non-digital multimedia. For example, the visual presentation of data takes place in charts, graphs and tables; these are a form of knowledge largely taken for granted in the social sciences. An important exception is found in the work of Edward Tufte, who analyzes existing forms of the presentation of visual evidence and offers ways to do it better.[17]

While sociologists are used to presenting quantitative information visually they are less accustomed to explaining ideas in innovative visual formats. Frustrated by the challenges posed by teaching concepts in sociological theory courses, I constructed visual texts to explain ideas like dialectical materialism.

The following visualization, an example of what I've taken to calling idea portraits, presents the movement of history from feudal to capitalist to socialist societies. One self-imposed rule is that I must fit each visualization on to an 8 by

11 inch piece of paper and thus in this instance I left off an earlier stage of the dialectic to make the rest fit. The Marxian idea of superstructure and substructure are presented as vertical relationships. Elements that led to transitions between eras are presented in slanted texts. With InDesign or Illustrator these are easy to make, and students report that seeing the relationships of ideas visually helps them create an overview that can be later be elaborated upon.

Other visualizations developed for the social theory course include Weberian theories of charismatic and bureaucratic authority, Engels' ideas about the evolution of families in different economic systems, Durkheimian theories of the division of labor, and timelines that include significant books, events, eras and personalities from prehistory to the present. The visualizations simplify many aspects of complex ideas (and students have often spoken positively about how they made complex ideas more understandable) but at best they provide a kind of intellectual skeleton on to which students may hang the details.

Figure 7.1
Dialectical materialism.

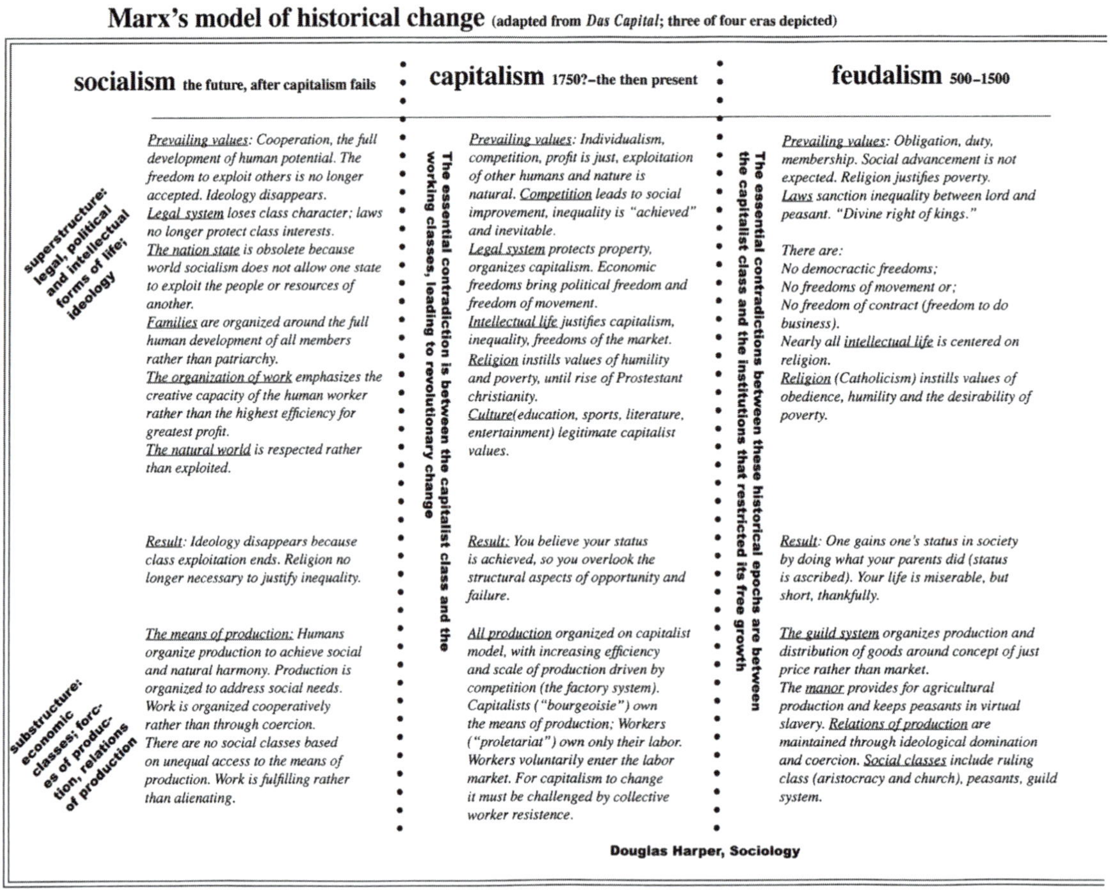

Marx's model of historical change (adapted from *Das Capital*; three of four eras depicted)

socialism the future, after capitalism fails

Prevailing values: Cooperation, the full development of human potential. The freedom to exploit others is no longer accepted. Ideology disappears.
Legal system loses class character; laws no longer protect class interests.
The nation state is obsolete because world socialism does not allow one state to exploit the people or resources of another.
Families are organized around the full human development of all members rather than patriarchy.
The organization of work emphasizes the creative capacity of the human worker rather than the highest efficiency for greatest profit.
The natural world is respected rather than exploited.

Result: Ideology disappears because class exploitation ends. Religion no longer necessary to justify inequality.

The means of production: Humans organize production to achieve social and natural harmony. Production is organized to address social needs. Work is organized cooperatively rather than through coercion. There are no social classes based on unequal access to the means of production. Work is fulfilling rather than alienating.

superstructure: legal, political and intellectual forms of life; ideology

substructure: economic classes; forces of production, relations of production

capitalism 1750?–the then present

Prevailing values: Individualism, competition, profit is just, exploitation of other humans and nature is natural. *Competition* leads to social improvement, inequality is "achieved" and inevitable.
Legal system protects property, organizes capitalism. Economic freedoms bring political freedom and freedom of movement.
Intellectual life justifies capitalism, inequality, freedoms of the market.
Religion instills values of humility and poverty, until rise of Protestant christianity.
Culture(education, sports, literature, entertainment) legitimate capitalist values.

Result: You believe your status is achieved, so you overlook the structural aspects of opportunity and failure.

All production organized on capitalist model, with increasing efficiency and scale of production driven by competition (the factory system). Capitalists ("bourgeoisie") own the means of production; Workers ("proletariat") own only their labor. Workers voluntarily enter the labor market. For capitalism to change it must be challenged by collective worker resistence.

The essential contradiction is between the capitalist class and the working classes, leading to revolutionary change

The essential contradictions between these historical epochs are between the capitalist class and the institutions that restricted its free growth

feudalism 500–1500

Prevailing values: Obligation, duty, membership. Social advancement is not expected. Religion justifies poverty.
Laws sanction inequality between lord and peasant. "Divine right of kings."

There are:
No democratic freedoms;
No freedoms of movement or;
No freedom of contract (freedom to do business).
Nearly all *intellectual life* is centered on religion.
Religion (Catholicism) instills values of obedience, humility and the desirability of poverty.

Result: One gains one's status in society by doing what your parents did (status is ascribed). Your life is miserable, but short, thankfully.

The guild system organizes production and distribution of goods around concept of just price rather than market.
The manor provides for agricultural production and keeps peasants in virtual slavery. *Relations of production* are maintained through ideological domination and coercion. *Social classes* include ruling class (aristocracy and church), peasants, guild system.

Douglas Harper, Sociology

Drawings

Drawings have been useful in ethnographic studies because they can leave out much of the visual information that a photograph contains, and because they reflect the imagination of the artist and produce yet another form of interpretation. One of the best examples is Richard M. Swiderski's ethnography of the "African poetics of technology,"[18] in which the author's spare renderings show urban Africans fashioning technologies around improvised machines in a wide range of circumstances. Some are standard repairs, a welder fabricating a mount beam for a disk harrow (page 107); others show how the tasks of daily life are carried out (roasting maize on a grill) and how people adapt to machines always in trouble (page 115: men pushing a disabled bus). I had the impression that the pictures also captured perspectives that Swiderski may have imagined rather than actually saw, and that this freedom allowed him to tell the best story of a moment or an event. In other words, the drawings seemed not to be just simplified photos; they seem to be visual interpretations that captured a new point of view through perspective shift or scale.

Swiderski's drawings can be compared to those of folklorist Michael Owen Jones, who used drawings to describe and study the work and life of a southern chairmaker.[19] His book was typeset in hand lettering, repeating the notion of a handmade object. Just as Swiderski's drawings communicate an aspect of improvisation that his text explores, Jones's tell of chairs and the people who make them. The images fulfill our expectations of what crafts people look like in the rural south, and we imagine them playing a mean harmonica in off hours. That Jones presents his book as a handmade object (hand lettered and illustrated) is certainly ironic given its mass production in the same print shops that produce any other book.

When I was studying a small mechanic's shop,[20] I struggled with how much to tell about the machines Willie built, modified and fixed. It was easy to get lost in descriptions of the work because words easily create layers of meaning that only a technical expert could understand. Indeed, the technical design of a car transmission or a manure spreader was not my point. Yet I realized that to understand Willie's work one needed to understand something about what he was working on. The photos served that purpose, especially when I used close-up lenses, and when I organized the photos in sequences. I came to realize, however, that they were not the only or best way to visually represent the world I was trying to describe.

I turned to drawings because of several advantages they have over photographs. It is possible in a drawing to leave out information included in a photograph and to peel back a surface to allow the viewer to see inside an object. The drawings often explained entire photo sequences: one drawing showed the whole machine (a corn chopper), so Willie's repair (and what he said about it) made much more sense. Seeing inside a repair allowed a viewer to better understand the engineering involved in routine repairs. It also made the skill demands of routine work more obvious: when drilling out a broken stud in a brake repair one must not destroy the threads, or a larger repair will be needed. The artist, Suzan Harper, had to interview Willie to learn what to include in the drawings, and had to talk to farmers about the farm machines she drew to understand how they worked. The drawings, artful and clean, also relieved the visual tedium of the black and white photos of often dark and cold workspaces, and invited the reader/viewer to a higher level of understanding, as shown in these two examples (Figures 7.2, 7.3).

Sociologists have also asked people to draw as a way to understand their taken-for-granted perceptions and experiences. This began several decades ago with research in which people were asked to create maps of specific environments,[21] and is similar to ethnomethodological studies of the routines of trip preparation.[22] Sociologists have asked children to draw maps that trace their routes through the city; to show where they feel more or less safe, to define the boundaries of ethnic identification,[23] to record their definitions of their own spaces and to see how they negotiate the modern city.

These examples are variations of what has recently been called visualization. Lev Manovich[24] shows how visualization, an old idea, has been transformed by advanced programming and increased computer processing power. This has been Edward Tufte's point for several years. Manovich's reference to the often-cited Charles Joseph Minard graphic showing Napoleon's march on Moscow (1869) demonstrates that powerful computers are not required for visualization. Yet computers and advanced programming have changed the nature of visualization, leading to new ways to see much greater amounts of data. Manovich references

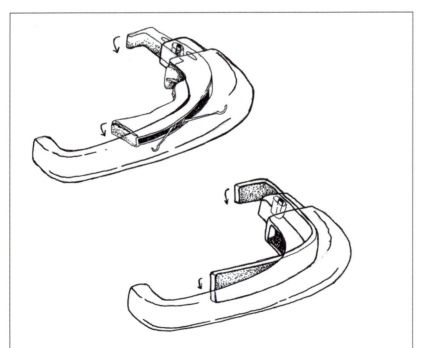

Figure 7.2
Re-engineered Saab door handle. The standard door handle mechanism on some Saab automobiles was poorly designed and often broke. Willie engineered a replacement part (lower) out of different material. The drawing makes it possible to see inside the parts to understand the engineering involved. (Figures 7.2 and 7.3 by Suzan Harper.)

Figure 7.3

The book includes several images and a discussion of the repair of a silo blower, but there is no overall image that shows what the machine is or what the repair was meant to accomplish. Figure 7.3 creates this visual overview.

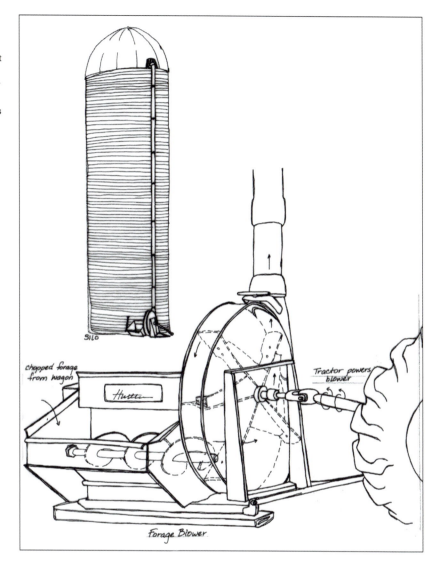

an example entitled "Flight Patterns," made in 2005 by Aaron Koblin, that created an animated map of all commercial flights in the US over 24 hours, using flight schedules and trajectories. Here we see the visual structure of a huge data set and how it changes.

One of Manovich's projects involved the creation of a single image made by shrinking and joining 4,553 covers of *Time* magazine: every issue published between 1923 and 2009. The resulting image is beautiful, and a piece of it adorns the cover of the journal where his work is published. Yet what do we learn from this graphic? The predominant message is that the color saturation of covers increases and decreases over time so the example shows that the processes can produce trivial information as well as significant insights. Perhaps a better example appeared on art pieces the size of small billboards, mounted at eye level, which were on display in the spring of 2010 in Rome. There were several of these huge canvases on display near the tomb of Augustus, but the one that remains in my memory pictured life-size photos of all the cell phones thrown away in a single day in the US. The photo of hundreds of thousands of objects made a point about waste I had a hard time imagining in any other form. Another example of a stunning and intellectually satisfying visualization is the graphic that represents the Web, which illustrates Wikipedia entries on the Internet. The image, which looks like a cross between galactic formations and the nervous structure of an animal, was produced for the Opte Project by Barrett Lyon. The Wiki site notes that Lyon believes that what he calls network mapping

> can be used to visualize sites of disasters in the world, citing the significant destruction of Internet capabilities after a disaster. Additionally it can be used as an important gauge for the growth of the Internet and the areas of growth.[25]

The image is also visually stunning, attested to by its display at the Boston Museum of Science and the Museum of Modern Art in New York.

The old concept of visualization has made a conceptual leap with new technologies and creative rethinking. It is especially relevant to sociology, which is a numbers-driven discipline. In fact high-level visualization may be a way to overcome the visual–non-visual divide. Encouraging students or researchers to create visual forms of empirical information has and will lead to new ways of knowing. It may also demonstrate the trivial nature of much of the numbers-driven sociology in the contemporary discipline.

Summary

This chapter may have more to do with the future of visual sociology than the present. The rate of change in the image world is awe-inspiring or unnerving, depending on one's perspective, and future forms of images and their effects are completely unknown. There may be more to learn about this future from William Gibson's 1984 novel *Neuromancer*—where brain–computer interfaces are normal, and where one descends into cyberspace as an actual physical reality—than from now standard texts on visual methods. In any case it is very exciting to contemplate the future of these lines of inquiry and to include them in the normal canon of what we call visual sociology.

Chapter 8

Photo elicitation

In the next two chapters I describe research that uses images as a means to an end, rather than as an end in and of itself. The basic idea is collaboration: people using images in one of several ways to learn something together. In some instances researchers make conventional field-work type photos and talk about them with people they have photographed (*photo elicitation*; most of the examples in this chapter); at other times researchers give cameras to people and encourage them to photograph their own worlds (*photovoice*; the next chapter). Judging from what has been published to date, photo elicitation has been more about generating knowledge, and photovoice has had a subtext of empowerment; that is, a research process that is designed to empower those who traditionally were the focus of academic attention. There is no reason these secondary meanings will be maintained in the future, especially as photovoice emerges from research communities in public health, community development and other related fields to also become a part of sociology and anthropology per se, which is already happening.

Collaborative methods are slightly confused by the fact that researchers often use one method but call it another, or design projects that use elements of both. For convenience' sake I will discuss examples of photo elicitation that authors have named that way in this chapter, and do the same for photovoice in the next. What they share in all cases is collaboration, with images or image making at the center.

I would also add that these collaborative methods are among the most important innovations in visual sociology and anthropology. They often broach subject matter that could be studied in no other way, and when empowerment is the result of research (and I don't think it automatically emerges in photovoice research, but it certainly does in some instances) it signals a very big step for social sciences in general. I also add a word to the wary: I've tried to find ways to describe all of the photovoice and photo elicitation I've discovered, but my best efforts have sometimes failed to make summaries, critiques and analyses of more than 160 published reports seem lively.

Photo elicitation

In the early 1980s I had finished my book about railroad tramps and was casting about for a new project. I was living in a neighborhood of farmers in northern New York with my young family, quite separate from the university community where I worked. As I got to know the rural neighborhood I began to question the prevailing wisdoms of rural sociology, which I was called upon to teach. The rural sociological canon celebrated agricultural modernization and economic development; human capital was measured in the formal education of farmers, and, ultimately Big Agriculture was the unquestioned holy grail. Not that there was necessarily anything wrong with modernization and change, but I also felt that the old intelligence tucked into the nooks and crannies of the North Country, the old social norms and patterns of social exchange, seemed worth studying in their own right. Though this was clear to me early on, it took me a long time to find a way to figure out a way to proceed, especially with photography.

About 5 miles past our farmhouse lived Willie, who I later referred to as a "Zen master of junk." His shop was an irresistible place for a photographer, full of old machines rusting away or sinking into the landscape and a cast of regulars who were as tattered as the scene they inhabited. The first time I'd met Willie I'd pulled into his shop after closing time, gasoline pouring out of the carburetor of my old Saab, threatening to turn my car into a torch. After a brief conversation he invited me to use his tools to take the offending pieces off the engine and then he performed a quick and simple fix on the improperly designed part, before handing me back the tools and telling me to "button it up." In lieu of payment he invited me back for the evening to play guitars together, as he had seen mine in the back of the Saab. That night was the first of many.

I began spending a lot of time in the shop and became interested in studying it in depth. We had become friends, and Willie had seen me through the several rewrites of my first book. But I soon realized that while I found the shop very interesting, I didn't know what to photograph. On the tramp project there were obvious subjects: boxcars, hobo jungles, missions and Skid Rows; ways to ride trains, get drunk and find food; and cultural categories such as kinds of tramps and train workers. The visual ethnography had been straightforward, not to say that it had been easy. In Willie's shop, making the culture visual was a more elusive goal.

I was at that time teaching my first courses in visual sociology, and had read John Collier's 1967 text *Visual Anthropology*, and, in particular, his description of what he called photo interviewing.

The process involves inserting a photograph (or other image, though most are photos) into the research interview. A typical interview is a conversation where each party responds to what they think the other person means by what he or she says. But while this may accurately describe conversations between people who know each other well, many sociological interviews, especially when the participants come from different cultural worlds, are very different. Most social scientists have done interviews where pre-packaged questions have little or no meaning to the person being interviewed. This is satirized in Wayne Wang's 1982 film *Chan is Missing,* when the two Chinese characters are interviewed by a social worker speaking in social science jargon that leaves them both dumbfounded. It is very funny, but in a painful way for sociologists. The incomprehension can also work in the other direction: researchers often find themselves speaking to people whose vocabulary, syntax or inflexion makes their talk seem like a foreign language.

The PE (photo elicitation) interview radically redefines the sociological interview because it centers on objects in a photo that both parties are looking at and trying to make sense of. Often neither party understands the limits of the other's comprehension or, more often, incomprehension. Usually the researcher asks the subject to identify, explain, or reflect on elements in a photograph that the researcher has made during the research process or found in an archive.

After several unsuccessful efforts, I found it most effective to ask straightforward questions. In the case of the study of Willie's shop, these included:

- *"Who is this?"* (Does he come here often? Does he have a job? Does he pay you for work you do for him? Is he good at mechanical work? Do you like having him around?)
- *"What is this?"* (Where did you get it? Did you buy it; find it; did someone give it to you? Why did you use it in the repair? What are you going to do with it?)
- *"What are you doing in this photo?"* (Where did you learn to do this? Is it difficult? What are the particular challenges of this job? Can you describe what you see, feel or sense about the materials you are working with? How much are you charging for this work?)
- *"How do you work for neighbors and others?"* (What labor do you charge for and what do you give for free? How do you figure what to charge? How and what do you trade? What goes well and not so well in these dealings?)

If the PE interview goes well the person being interviewed sees himself or herself as the expert, as the researcher becomes the student. The photo becomes a bridge between people who may not even understand the extent to which they see the world differently. That was exactly what happened with Willie and me; one of the first things we learned was how little I understood about what he took totally for granted.

The approach was first used in the 1950s when John Collier, who was then a photographer attached to a Cornell University research team, was asked to contribute to a study of mental health in changing communities in the Maritime Provinces in Canada. At first he was asked to help researchers agree on a rating system for the housing in their study area; researchers found that they defined "dilapidated" or "above average" housing in different ways. To solve this problem

Collier photographed 200 houses and the teams then studied the photos to agree on which elements in the photos would mean one rating or another (this was as simple as defining a porch that was crooked as middle class or lower). This is a remarkable idea seldom used in social science interviewing: creating a concrete referent to a statement or a rating on a questionnaire. Collier's method worked so well that they decided to integrate photos into the research interviews themselves. To test their method they did both elicitation and conventional interviews with the same families, which Collier described:

> The material obtained with photographs was precise and at times even encyclopedic; the control interviews were less structured, rambling, and freer in association. Statements in the photo-interviews were in direct response to the graphic probes . . . [whereas] the control interviews seemed to be governed by the mood of the informants.
>
> Collier further noted that "the pictures elicited longer and more comprehensive interviews but at the same time helped subjects overcome the fatigue and repetition of conventional interviews . . ." and that the photos had the capacity to "prod latent memory, to stimulate and release emotional statements about the informant's life . . ."[1]

The elicitation interviews reveal many things about images as well as interviews. They demonstrate that the meanings of images are not fixed, but emerge in conversations and dialogues. The meanings vary from one viewer to another. A photographer points a camera and exposes a frame, but the choices that led to the creation of that image may have had little or nothing to do with cultural meanings inside the image, and as a result the photos may not mean much to people in the culture. That was evident as Willie and I began discussing photos I had made of his shop. They contained interesting shapes and patterns of light and shadow, and they likely had some relationship to my social science thinking: here was craftwork; here was a negotiated relationship. But Willie knew the history of every piece of metal and every machine, building, or person who appeared in the frame, and how these histories were intertwined in long patterns of buying and selling, trading or giving things away. One could say there were layers of meaning in an image, from the literal object they described, to the social processes behind events they appeared in, to the values that were represented in the actions that surrounded the object.

Willie may have been the perfect research partner: intelligent and interested, and inhabiting a world that was rich for study. He took the interviewing seriously; his family would dutifully leave during the evenings when we discussed the photos, and he even turned off his CB radio,[2] his single link to the world, so we would not be interrupted and I could hear the tapes we made. We eventually taped more than thirty hours of interviews. Over the years I worked on the book we had many other conversations while working in the shop, bowling on Wednesday nights, or just hanging out, and these became a backdrop to the elicitation interviews.

I came to believe that the photo elicitation interviews did more than stimulate deeper and sharper memory, as John Collier noted above. Rather, our conversations created what Max Weber called *verstehen*, loosely translated as understanding, and usually interpreted as capturing the point of view of the other. As I listened to our taped discussions, I learned to put aside my assumptions, and to see Willie's reflections as a window into his world.

It is very easy to get enthusiastic about photo elicitation, and I was an early convert. However, I quickly realized that PE interviews opened Pandora's Box because there are so many ways to do every project. How many photos should one use in a typical interview? What should guide the photography used in interviews? Who should take the photos? Should people be interviewed alone, or in discussion groups? How do you put a study together from the mass of information that the interviews produced? How much of the interview material should be presented intact, and how much could or should be summarized? How do you keep the PE interview from becoming a routine conversation about common issues?

There are no simple answers for these questions and researchers continue to find new ways to do image elicitation studies. I have concentrated my career on writing books rather than journal articles because they provide a lot of space for photos and long interview segments, but others have done effective elicitation studies in articles and chapters.[3] I have come to think that photo elicitation produces something resembling documentary film, where there is a conversation running under a series of images, and in both of these examples the design of the information is key to its success. Others have approached the task in very different ways.

I will show how a PE interview works with an excerpt of a discussion of a tractor repair, which is adapted from the ethnography I wrote about Willie's shop. The passage begins with an introductory essay that places the repair in a larger context. It reads:

The tractor had been part of the landscape around Willie's shop for seven years. He had taken it from a neighboring farmer as partial payment for a welding job. When Willie got the tractor it lacked a starter, a three-point hitch, a number of control parts, and rear wheels. When the deal was made small tractors were not much in demand, and the farmer probably regarded it as a convenient way to get rid of a machine that had been allowed to deteriorate beyond usefulness. For Willie the tractor would be handy in the woods as well as around the shop.

It has been towed to Willie's on borrowed wheels and then sat beached on some elm logs, looking more and more like a permanent part of the landscape as the years went by. Parts and materials began to pile up around and on top of the machine, nearly hiding it. "Tractor still in there?" Raymond would needle Willie as he walked past. "Yup, and it's going into the shop just as soon as I get the _____ [any number of jobs that went in and out over the years] out of there." ...

In the meantime Willie came across a set of used truck wheels that he converted for the tractor, solving a major problem in the restoration project. Then one day a berth was cleared in the shop and the tractor was towed inside, its rear wheels skidding along because the engine and clutch had seized up in the years since it had been moved. The seized engine and clutch would mean an additional and perhaps expensive addition to what Willie had expected to be a straightforward restoration. I said it was too bad, but Willie answered: "What do you expect—you leave metal alone—metal rusts!"

... [the engine was rebuilt with the help of a man often at the shop] and ... A few repairs remained. The grille protecting the radiator had rusted away so the radiator was exposed to brush and low branches in the woods. The thirty-five-year-old radiator was extremely delicate and would be hard to replace if it was ruined.

A month later, on a Saturday morning, Willie's son Skip was telling Willie over coffee that they ought to do something about the front of the tractor. Willie had other ideas about his day, but Skip was unusually persistent and Willie finally agreed that the repair ought to be done. I worked alongside on a project of my own, pausing to photograph their work. Our discussion ... occurred a few months later.

> Willie: (looking at the stack of photos): "*That* looks like a Ford tractor."
>
> Doug: "I remember that Ford tractor being here eight years ago. It sat inside for ..."
>
> Willie: "It sat outside for five years. Inside two. I took that on a bill from Roger McLaughlin because I wanted a tractor. Hundred ninety-seven dollars."
>
> Doug: "Why did Roger give up on it?"
>
> Willie: "Well, he took the starter over to BOCES [an agricultural/vocational high school]—one of the boys that worked for him part time went to BOCES. He took the starter over to rebuild it. Never got it back. Got kinda disgusted with it. That's how I got it. It sat in his barn for three months, right in the free stalls. It got eat up with the acids from the cow manure—oh, that's bad on a machine. It was just like it had gone through a fire. That's why it rusted out."
>
> Doug: "You saw it as worth a lot of money fixed up?"
>
> Willie: "At that time you could get them pretty reasonable. But you can't now. I figured that if I put wheels on it, got a starter for it, and got it running I could use it for woods work—which is what I'm doing.

"The wheels are off a big truck—twenty-two inch. I had to cut the Ford wheels down to mount them on, to weld them in. And the front wheels are cut down to thirteen inches. I turned the cast iron hubs down to fit a thirteen-inch rim. The drawbar was missing; we built that out of parts. The throttle control was all rusted off, and the generator was missing. The radiator bottom was broke right off, so we took it off and rebuilt it. Soldered it back on. Gas tank was full of rust. Took that all off, cleaned it, blew it out. Cleaned all the manure out from in between the radiator and the hood—it was really full of manure. Changed the distributor over to where I had an exterior rather than an interior coil. Usually when it gets to be rainy weather they don't want to start with the other type of coil, and they burn out too easy. And I changed it over so that I'm using an eight-volt battery instead of a six. Starts in the wintertime now just like it does in the summer. The other day Ray Dean didn't think it would start—it was zero—but it started right up. Usually they say a Ford tractor won't start up after the first frost in the fall.

"We had to put a bumper on the tractor because Skip was using it too rough in the woods [laughs]. We were using it to get wood out, and he was driving it over little trees and everything with no bumper and no grille—he was going to spoil the radiator!"

Figure 8.1
Lighting up the Rosebud.

"We're getting ready to cut the parts for the grille. Skip got the metal and stuff ready and hunted up some of the pieces to use. I'm lighting the torch . . . They had the old mailbox out there—that old overgrown mailbox—and they were cleaning that down to paint it. Julie and Sheila [Willie's daughters, but only Sheila is in the photograph]. Sheila looks a little sour, but it's more or less that she's watching what I'm doing. She got full interest in what's going on . . . and Christopher's [Willie's grandson] looking at that flame. In fact, all those eyes are coming down to that flame. Mine too. I'm setting it, adjusting it. You're supposed to use a Rosebud torch for heating, but if you use a Rosebud on light metal it's just a waste of heat. And there's the ring [a seventeen-inch piece of metal behind Willie, outside the shop; right side of photo, middle] that we used for the bumper—the arch . . .

"You could have fixed the old piece but you would have spent more time on it than it was worth. There's about three inches gone off the bottom—it was eat right into the crank hole, so bad it wouldn't hold a true form to work from. You would have had to do a lot of building back, adjusting, measuring—because there are little pins that come out of each top corner that sets up into the top of the hood to hold it in place—they'd have to line up just right for it to work."

Doug: "I always wonder what you see through the helmet when you're welding. Can you see the details pretty well?"

Willie: "Perfect. I wear the lens that lets you see all your melting metal and everything. If you can't see what's melting, what's blending together—that is where a lot of people run into problems. They don't blend their metals together—they don't flow 'em. And that's why a weld doesn't hold. You've got to be able to see that flow of metal. You've *got* to be able to see it. There are different lenses for the helmets—they go by number, a code that tells how dark it will be. I use one of the darkest ones they've got. If you get too light a lens you can't see the full flow of your metal—it's just like not wearing any at all when you're brazing. You can't see what you're doing—you can't study it. The glow is too bright—it's like looking at the sun, almost . . . but you know, you can photograph more than you can see. In fact, sometimes I think the photograph shows more than *I* see."

Doug: "When I look at these photographs I see you close down, studying."

Willie: "You've got to be. If you don't see your metals and know how they're flowing you haven't got a weld. You get what I told you before—bubblegum weld—if you don't flow it. It just bubbles on and it doesn't

Figure 8.2 (opposite top)
Welding the new bumper to the tractor.

Figure 8.3 (opposite bottom)
Willie cuts an arch from the metal ring.

Photo elicitation

penetrate to hold your metals together . . . you've seen bubbles in metal on some welds—well, that's what they call a bubblegum weld."

Willie: "[If we'd used our first design] we'd have cut down a lot of wind—air to keep the radiator cool. If you cover the radiator too much with metal when the tractor's working hard it'll overheat. So we came up with the idea of putting the arch over it—that's when we came up with the idea of the ring.

"The ring was off an old stack flue—you can see it laying in the background in the first photograph."

Doug: "Stack flu?"

Willie: "Smokestack from Brasher Iron Works. A fella picked it up at Clotman's, a junk dealer up in Massena. He was going to make a furnace out of it, but he got discouraged in the middle of the job and bought one instead. He gave it to me and I made a furnace out of it, but I had to cut some pieces off of it. That was one of the pieces I cut off . . . [And] That's the furnace in the back of the shop—at least part of it. I had to cut more off when I put the hot water unit on the top. It's heavy, a quarter-inch, regular old smokestack . . ."

Willie: "I'm trimming it off the same thickness all around, more or less for looks. It was all rough—the way they cut it at the junkyard. I wanted to straighten it out; make it better than it was . . .

"Now I've got a tractor to use in the woods. I've used it a lot since it's been on there—an awful lot, for moving cars in and out . . . It's better than the original—you couldn't push a car with the original because it had a hitch on the front. I'll put the hitch back on, but I'll make it so I can snap it on and off. And the fact that it's solid all the way up there makes it work beautifully for pushing wagons or anything . . ."

This passage, shortened from the original and including fewer images,[4] can be expanded into a larger story of Willie's shop if we see the tractor in action, a crucial part of Willie's life. For photo elicitation to produce a convincing narrative the presentation needs to balance text and words, and this is challenging because there is more talk about some images than others. The design must accommodate the images and text within the conventions of book design. With the software program InDesign, the photographer/writer has the opportunity to offer a publisher a mockup of a manuscript, with photo sequences, sizes, captioning and other design decisions in place. Building these mockups has been similar to my limited experience as a documentary film editor: choices of text and images have to do with the flow of information as well as their content. There are artistic issues involved in the design

Figure 8.5
The tractor, three years later, about to power a saw on a frigid day.

as well as matters of content; in the end the filmmaker wants to make a film people will watch, and visual sociologists want to produce a book people will read.

In the passage from *Working Knowledge*, the conversation and photos delve into how and what Willie sees. Few of us have looked at molten metal through welder lenses, and Willie gives us a sense of what he sees and how it directs his work. We understand how de-industrialization leads to the recycling of junk that skillful people reuse. An example of exchanging things and money is described. Other narratives are in the background: a farmer who is not mechanically skilled lets a small tractor deteriorate in cow manure and pays his debt off by giving it to Willie; another person fails at building a woodstove from the smokestack and contributes his failed effort to what he owes. Willie uses his engineering skills, his talent as a welder, and his knowledge of tractor mechanics to rebuild a tractor while adapting it to his needs. Repair in this instance and many others means improving a thirty-year-old machine. Finally, the exchange shows how interviewer and subject don't come to the interview with the same knowledge or information. He says "stack flue" and I interrupt, "Stack flue?" which leads him to tell me, yes, it is a smokestack from an old factory, which existed when the town was an important industrial center.

The book that came from this project received favorable reviews in magazines such as *Scientific American* and the *Smithsonian*, as well as journals in sociology, the history of technology and related fields. The positive regard for the work was undoubtedly due to the sense that photo elicitation had created a bridge across cultures; a window from one culture into another. This was a very positive experience, yet when I tried to apply PE to my emerging study of dairy farming, it fell flat. I photographed farm work in fields, with animals and with machines, but the interviews that emerged from showing these images to the farmers were mostly uncomfortable restatements of the obvious. The research experience improved when I found a way to use images to look backwards, and to encourage an evaluation of the historical change they were all experiencing.

My neighbors referred to the system they had grown up with as "changing works," and in this system they traded labor, ate in each other's homes when they worked together, and farmed more as cooperative neighbors than individualistic competitors. The farms had been about the same size, and the farmers used and shared essentially the same machines. The old system had been in place in one form or another since the late nineteenth century, and had entered a period of rapid change around World War Two. By the late 1950s it was pretty much entirely gone, and by the time I studied the neighborhood it had one foot firmly in the future and the other groping around in the old system of the past. I wanted to know how farmers felt about the changes they had experienced; and whether they felt the new system was creating a viable future for the dairy farmer and for rural communities.

PE and historical memory

There have been several historical studies based on photos, as noted previously. They are usually analyses of archives, both formal and informal, and the research is mostly a matter of interpreting the images based on other information, including the nature of the archive itself. The people in the images are usually long gone, so their interpretations are no longer available. But what about the more immediate past? Might it not be possible to use photos to elicit the memories of the elderly now living in very different worlds?

There was indeed an archive that included images that described the worlds my farm neighbors had experienced. It was the Standard Oil of New Jersey (SONJ) photo archive, which had documented American culture between 1941 and 1953.

The photos had been made at the behest of Standard Oil as a public relations project to improve the image of the company, which had made deals with German companies prior to the war that had almost appeared treasonous once the war had begun. The company wanted to show how oil was part of the fabric of American life, and that Standard Oil was a patriotic company doing its part to preserve the American way of life. With that broad mandate about ten photographers (at any given time) were hired to photograph anything they observed that was related to the use of petroleum; which, of course, was virtually any aspect of American society. At the time the photos were used to illustrate Standard Oil's corporate magazine, and some found their way into high school texts, but they had very little use or influence beyond that. In fact several years after the several-million-dollar project was completed, the negatives were nearly thrown away. They were saved at the last minute by the

Figure 8.6
Gathering corn for ensilage,
Brooklea Farm, Kanona, New
York, September 1945.
(Photograph by Charlotte
Brooks.)

University of Louisville, where they are archived and made available to researchers. I was able to spend a week searching through the 67,000 photos to find about 200 that depicted the daily life on family dairy farms in neighborhoods geographically close to those I studied in the 1980s.

The director of the project, Roy Stryker, had also directed the Farm Security Administration project in the 1930s, and had been a close colleague and friend of Robert and Helen Lynd, sociologists who had written important community studies in the 1920s and 1930s. Stryker had developed the idea of visual ethnography from his association with the Lynds, and the SONJ photographers were encouraged to record daily work, home life, community activities and other sides of life that, as Stryker noted, were not of particular interest then, but would be of interest later. For example, I asked many dairy farmers if they had photographed the dinners they had shared during the harvests, but they were surprised by the question. Why would one have photographed what was so unremarkable? They showed me grainy black and white photos from their family albums: *Here is my new tractor in 1953; here is a cow that produced 14,000 gallons of milk; here are my kids taking their livestock to 4-H.* Of course there was sociology in their depictions, but the photos were too close to

Photo elicitation

Figure 8.7
Farm hands at dinner after threshing wheat on the Shaughnessy farm, Warsaw, New York, August 1945. (Photograph by Sol Libsohn.)

their experiences to generate in-depth discussion. They were photos of the typical things people then photographed; something noteworthy, rather than the routine.[5]

The SONJ photos were very different, and they produced different interviews. The photographers used 6 x 6 cm Rolleiflexes or 4 x 5 inch view cameras, and the detail in the images was vastly better than the snapshots farmers (or anyone, for that matter) were used to seeing. I had 8 x 10 inch prints of the images to use in my research and their scale and detail encouraged the farmers to study them seriously. So the detail was excellent but the photos were also different because they recorded aspects of farm lives that were so taken for granted they had not been deemed worthy of a photograph.

Willie became an informal research assistant, as he had been a farm laborer as a young man and knew a lot about agriculture from his work as a mechanic. He sat in on many of the interviews, often with old friends who were retired farmers, often directing an interview in subtle ways. For example:

Willie, studying the photo [Figure 8.6]: "You didn't have any time to bullshit! Especially on those corn deals."

Photo elicitation

Mason [Willie's friend, a retired farmer]: "When I was about sixteen or seventeen I went over to Delbert Johnson's to pitch corn. The cornfield started right there and went back, you know? And he had corn at least as high as this ceiling. And bundles that big [*spreads arms*].

"I think I was about seventeen and Jesus it was hot that day. One of them days in the fall when the old sun was beatin' right down. There was two of us pitchin' and three wagons. Two pitchin' and three wagons."

Willie: "That's a killer."

Mason: "Guy Moore and me was pitchin'. Well, we filled that goddamned silo full and about four o'clock we was all done. We had 'er full. Yes sir! And me and Guy come up and, of course, your clothes was just soppin' wet, the sweat run right off ya'. And, of course, I had a pack of cigarettes and book matches. I pulled out them book matches and they were just solid; the sulfur had just dripped off. Delbert smoked a pipe and he had them farmer's matches. So, [he] come around there—oh, Jesus, this made me mad—I said to him:

" 'You got a match, Delbert?' He says, 'What do you want a match for?' 'I want to smoke.' He says, 'You're too young to be smoking.' 'Well,' I said,

'I ain't too young to pitch your goddamned corn though, am I?'

"Never again. Never helped him again! I went home and I says to the old man, 'If that fella ever wants to "change works" again—don't send me; you go.'

" 'Why?' he said, 'What happened?' he asked. Of course, I didn't dare tell 'im about the smokin', you know. 'Cause he didn't know I smoked. But I told him about pitchin' corn. Mister, I never put in such a day in my life, I'll tell you. Along about three o'clock you pick up a bundle of corn off the fork and the tassles'd drag right on the ground. Honest to Christ, mister, heavy!

"Guy Moore says to me, 'Mister, you ever see me back here again, you bring the shotgun and shoot me right between the eyes!' "

The photo (Figure 8.6) pictures what was then a modern tractor, driven by a boy of eight or nine years old (the tractor is moving very slowly; he's mostly steering and occasionally, with a big stretch, pushing in the clutch to stop the machine). The four grown men are pitching bundles of corn on to the wagon; shadows suggest it is late afternoon after a long day. By itself the photo tells a story of neighborhood cooperation and it may idealize it; with Mason's story the scene becomes a bit more complicated. People take advantage of each other; not everyone appreciates the same aspects of the socially integrated neighborhood. The boy in the photo is smiling, likely proud to be in the photo, but it also likely true that the day on the tractor was trying for a pre-teen.

Similar deconstruction, both critical and otherwise, took place in many of the interviews. For example, Figure 8.7 shows a changing works dinner, what many farmers cited as the emblem of the idealized past when equally sized farmsteads, similar technology farm-to-farm and a spirit of cooperation led them to weeks of working together and eating feasts in one farmhouse after another.

Jim and Emily Fisher, a neighboring farm couple who had just retired, commented:

> "This is a great scene isn't it? The threshing crew sitting at their table eating."

> Doug: "Are these all farmers, or are some of these hired men? Can you tell by looking at it?"

> Jim: "Well, yes—there is a great variation in age. I would say all of the older men are probably the farmers; these young people are probably hired men or farmers' sons."

> Doug: "What have they just finished eating?"

> Emily: "Pie and coffee."

> Jim: "They probably had roast beef . . ."

> Emily: "Looks like cottage cheese . . . they made their own."

> Doug: "Looks like they are having cigarettes too."

> Jim: "Oh yes."

> Doug: "They are quite serious. What were they talking about, do you suppose?"

> Emily: "Well, it wouldn't be about the work they were doing—it must have been about politics. He doesn't care that he is taking the picture. Probably thinks what are things coming to anyway—making a sociological study of us!"

Women spoke about the friendships they developed with neighbors and relatives as they worked together preparing the food, and how that made their lives richer. Some women also saw the changing works dinners as a lot of hard work that was largely taken for granted:

> [Carmen and Marian were neighboring farmers]

> Doug: "Were you involved in making these dinners, Marian?"

Marian: "Well, yes, I always had to help."

Carmen: "They had a lot of fun with it."

Marian: "Oh, it was a drag!"

Doug: "Perhaps I am idealizing it?"

Carmen: "The crew was usually there for dinner and supper."

Marian: "Oh, yes . . ."

Carmen: "The women got a kick out of it!"

Marian: "Oh, baloney! I really created a stir in the community when I said I wasn't cooking for the men any longer after silo filling. I really got a lot of flack for that! Everybody brings their own lunch now, and nobody seems upset about it . . ."

In another interview I showed the same photo to Mary and Virgil, elderly farmers, and asked: "Was everybody a good cook?"

Mary answered: "I never heard it if we weren't! I didn't see anybody turn anything away! They were mostly good cooks up here at that time."

Virgil: "There were some places, though, you had to have an excuse to go home for dinner! I'd have to go home to feed the horses or something."

Mary: "He'd have to go home and feed his hens or do something! It was just unbearable!"

And Mason, in another discussion of the same photo, commented:

"There was an understanding that those with money put out less food. The better off didn't put their money on the table. The poorer farmers saved their best roast and brought out their best potatoes."

Arthur: "Harry Pierce owned the biggest farm and he was the cheapest S.O.B. in the neighborhood. I've seen him kill a chicken at eleven o'clock and have it on the table by noon!"

Clearly photos of iconic events spurred discussion, disagreement and various interpretations. Through these conversations the labor exchange escapes its idealization and becomes a human tapestry, full of contradictions.

For historical PE to work there has to be an archive that covers the topic of interest and a study population of the correct age: that is, old enough to have experienced what is in the photos but young enough to remember it clearly. Colter Harper's research on race and jazz in Pittsburgh[6] uses about 200 photos from the several hundred thousand image archive of African-American photographer Teenie Harris in elicitation interviews; in this instance his subjects were elderly at the point of the interviews and many struggled to clearly remember the subjects depicted in the images. Without the photos the interviews would have been impossible.

Colter Harper's research also shows the benefit of finding the right archive for a research project. The photos used in his project are the work of one of the most accomplished African-American photographers of the twentieth century, whose photos describe traditionally African-American neighborhoods, including jazz clubs. The jazz photos show the performers; the clubs as places in which races mixed and people dressed to be on display; and the interaction among members of the bands, and between the bands and the audience. Because Harris used a large negative camera and a strobe his photos have remarkable detail and clarity, which catches the attention of people studying them carefully.

The other example I'm aware of that uses archive-based photo elicitation is Carol Payne's study of Canadian National Film Board photos in interviews among Inuit peoples of northern Canada.[7] Her point was to repatriate visual memory among people who existed as objects of a paternalistic Canadian imperialism. As in the example of Colter Harper's research, the project begins with identification, but in this instance the individuals depicted are not well-known musicians but Inuit citizens who were unnamed when the photos were made in the 1940s, 1950s and 1960s. Naming them connected generations of families and showed the structures of communities.

The interviewers, university students, also used the images to create oral histories. These oral histories tell stories that sometimes surprised Payne, a Caucasian researcher. Payne implies that she expected a story about an Inuit school for English language instruction to be read by the Inuit as forced assimilation, but instead the Inuit defined the school in positive ways; as a place of discovery.

Payne cites Elizabeth Edwards' critique of photo elicitation[8] as "largely a one-way flow from informant to ethnographer," and she suggests that the interviews done in the Inuit studies were different because they were initiated by the Inuit and were done in close collaboration, often across two or three generations of the same family. One young researcher described the process:

> It was so exciting showing these Elders the pictures—it was almost like taking them back to the days when they were young. When I clicked on each picture, I watched their eyes. As they recognized an individual, they would have a big smile on their faces. They acted as if these pictures were taken just yesterday . . . Before now, I had not talked much with Elders. This experience was new to me, and I really enjoyed it. Each time they named a person in the picture, it made me want to go back to the time that they remembered.[9]

While Edwards' critique is important, I don't feel it justifies a rejection of the method. It is not only that PE interviews are efficient; the memories created by old images seem different. Payne describes a joy of discovery in PE interviews that many of us have experienced. Interviewees have a chance to explain, 'Yes, *this* is how it was . . ." and in the process interviews become a connection between people rather than a floundering intrusion.

Who should take the photos?

In most of the work discussed thus far professional photographers or sociologists made the photos used in research. Is their skill as photographers a necessary part of the PE process? Is this the best, or the only way to set up elicitation interviews? In some situations this seems reasonable. For example, Sol Libsohn's photograph of the changing works dinner (Figure 8.7) is visually remarkable and ethnographically rich because he framed the image from above, probably standing on a chair, which allowed the 80 mm lens on his Rolleiflex to record the whole table and much of the room. He used a flash held to the side to create light that was brighter than would have been in the room, but it appears almost natural (until you look carefully) because it comes from the side rather than the front. The bright flash allowed him to shoot at a small aperture (likely f-22) that created sufficient depth of field to put the entire room in focus. He had to know where to set the point of focus to take advantage of the depth of field afforded by the small aperture. He knew that the 6 x 6 cm negative would produce exceptional detail and working without a light meter in the camera he was able to expose the image correctly. When we look at the photo it appears to have been made by an invisible force; this was the result of Libsohn's success at getting the farmers to ignore him and his cumbersome equipment. This is not the only photo that might have been made of this scene of course, but it is a remarkable image because of what it tells us, and also because of how it connected to the memories of farmers. The photograph captures a culturally important moment because the photographer knew what he was doing technically, and he was also trained as a visual ethnographer because he'd worked with the Stryker/Lynd shooting scripts. He clearly also knew how to walk into the kitchens of farmers who were strangers until a few hours before, and win them over. None of these factors are inconsequential, and none can be assumed. Doing all of them well produces a photograph that tells a historical story of remarkable power.

This is also the case in the Teenie Harris archive used in Colter Harper's research: he saw the local community as an insider, and he was treated as an insider by those he photographed. He photographed the unremarkable, like common street scenes, as well as remarkable events like a national star appearing on a local stage. His large negative camera produced exponentially more information than snapshot cameras used then or now. His equipment was especially effective at night, and his strobe increased the detail and drama of his photos. His photos seem like a window into the past because the people pictured are doing what they would normally be doing; dancing, playing music, giving haircuts or just lounging against their cars in the then current fashions.[10] It is hard to imagine finding images in people's private collections that could equal Harris's images, though the exceptions do occur.

Figure 8.8
Balancing light from strobe
with natural light.

The view that skilled photographers should make the photos used in research
is not exactly a popular point of view in much collaborative research. The photovoice
movement is committed to shifting the photo-making process to those who are the
point of the study. Their perspective has a great deal to recommend it, but I do not
think there is an approach that works for all situations. At times I've made photos
that a casual observer/photographer would not have made: for example, using a
short telephoto lens with a strobe to photograph Willie's hands while at work (Figure
8.9), or even photos of Willie while welding or otherwise operating in tricky light
(Figure 8.8) (and, of course Willie could not have photographed himself while at work).
I hired small planes and learned the rudiments of aerial photography to add that
perspective to questions I've studied.

In some cases a middle ground may be the answer. In the late 1980s, for
example, I worked with a research team at the University of Amsterdam made up
of my students,[11] who used native-produced photos to study research questions
that were then common in Dutch urban sociology. I felt then, and still feel, that it
was a remarkable model that should be adapted and reused.

The researchers wanted to understand how residents of a neighborhood
named Schilderswijk, in the city of Den Haag, thought of their neighborhood and
each other. Schilderswijk was then the most economically depressed and poorly
maintained neighborhood in Holland, and was populated by a majority of non-native
Dutch from Turkey, Morocco, Surinam and other former Dutch colonies, as well as

Figure 8.9
Hands on the wrench.

a sizeable percentage of original Dutch (e.g. white) inhabitants. Some residents had spoken of the neighborhood as filthy, violent and hopeless, "as bad as an American slum." Other perceptions of the neighborhood were that it had an energetic street life where residents of various backgrounds mingled freely; where local pubs were meeting points for families and friends of many backgrounds; and where people watched out for each other. What was the best definition of the neighborhood? As the student/authors wrote:

> We knew that somewhere in these sets of images lies the reality, or, better, the realities of Schilderswijk. We hoped, with a method tuned

to gain an in-depth view of the subjects, to contribute a fresh view of the neighborhood.[12]

The team had studied the work of Sol Worth and John Adair,[13] completed during the 1960s, in which researchers taught Native Americans with little experience with photography how to operate 16 mm silent film cameras and editing equipment. Subsequently seven Navajo members made films depicting cultural activities and events. It is argued that the films show the Navajo interpretation of a given cultural activity, which may be communicated in what is photographed and even for how long. For example, when we watch the Navajo weaver make a rug we mostly watch the weaver caring for the sheep that will produce the wool, looking for natural ingredients for dyes, and other activities that set the stage for the actual weaving. It is certainly the case that when watching the films one "gets behind the eyes" of the subjects and immerses oneself in the activity itself.

Inspired by Worth and Adair, the Dutch research team sought to put image making closer to the hands and eyes of those they wished to study, but they did not give it over completely. To this end they asked their informants to

show us places and subjects in the quarter which they found to be important to them . . . to look through the lens of the camera to help . . . determine the angle which best created their desired photograph. Occasionally they took a photo themselves. Throughout we stressed to our informants (and to ourselves) that our photographs were not taken for their aesthetic value but to provide information.[14]

The five researchers identified five subjects who had lived in the neighborhood for at least three years, and who represented differences in age and ethnicity that characterized the quarter. In initial interviews they discovered that their subjects had a clear idea of what they wanted to photograph, and knew how framing would influence what the photos looked like. They also discovered that each individual saw the neighborhood in a different way. The initial interviews were followed by tours through the neighborhood as the teams made the photos that reflected the various points of view of the residents. The students then developed the film and printed and organized the photos for subsequent interviews, in which the subjects ranked the photos as to their importance, and told them why they had photographed the scenes they had chosen. They also discussed what themes and ideas could not be photographed.

Each subject examined the images made by the other four community members and gave their reactions. In reacting to the different views of the neighborhood, each resident began to understand how a common social space was defined by people they may never have spoken to, or even, in the case of the elderly ethnic Dutchwoman, a person (a Moroccan youth) she was afraid of. Creating five visual interpretations of the same reality reinforced the understanding that one sees from a cultural point of view; that neighbors from different cultural backgrounds see their shared urban spaces in different ways.

Figure 8.10
Suchar: "I've noticed that the house is filled with mementos, you know, things that you've collected . . ."Ray: "I don't call it collecting, it's like a disease. Like sores. They're there. You don't collect them but you can't live without them . . . We don't collect them for their money value. What they are, they're part of your life. All of it's part of my life. I think the house reflects what we do rather than what we think we should look like . . ."

The interviews were coded to topics such as "social uses of the material environment," "pollution of the street appearance," "ethnic integration" and "social interaction." The coding led to the layout of the eventual article that was sixty-four pages in length and could easily have become a research monograph. Including many of the photos in the research report invited the reader to experience the research process.

The researchers developed positive relationships with their subjects, and discovered they had stronger opinions about their neighborhood than they imagined.

It is to be remembered that the researchers were graduate students, and were experiencing in-depth research for the first time. The researchers and subjects gathered at a party at the end of the research project, where people from different backgrounds in the neighborhood met each other, often for the first time.

This in-between method was also used to great advantage by Charles Suchar, who studied the gentrification of Lincoln Park in Chicago (Figure 8.10). Suchar asked residents to pose in a place in their houses where they wanted to be photographed, and to add whatever objects they found meaningful.[15] In other words, he asked that their presentation of self be self-conscious, even staged. When Suchar returned with the images for interviews he asked them to elaborate on the choices they had made.

These are examples of collaborations between subjects of research and sociologist-photographers. In the case of the Dutch project, the students had thought a great deal about how to use cameras to capture a point of view or to express an idea. They mostly used tripods in the Schilderswijk project, which allowed them to study the exact framing with their subject-collaborator, sometimes changing lenses or angles of view as the team worked together. The result was that the images were the result of a great deal of planning; all parties took it seriously. In Suchar's project, the use of a tripod, medium-format camera and added light produced images of extreme clarity that engaged viewers in subsequent interviews. They represent a middle road in the collaborative model, in which the expertise and sensitivity of the researchers is preserved as some, or much, of the responsibility for picture making moves toward the subjects.

Photo elicitation, then, now and in the future

In the early 2000s I wrote an overview of elicitation studies that summarized what had been done and suggested what might lie ahead.[16] I had at that point discovered three dissertations, eight books, and twenty-eight articles in which PE was the principal research method.

In the meantime (summer of 2011), a renewed search produced eighty-four published articles in fifty-four journals. Of these articles, sixteen predate my earlier review (I missed them!) and four had been overlooked because they were published in foreign journals such as the *Scandinavian Journal of Educational Research*,[17] or in specialized professional journals. While I searched carefully in the updated literature review I undoubtedly missed some this time around as well.

While there has been a substantial increase in the number of photo elicitation articles and chapters, I am aware of very few books that have joined the handful cited ten years ago. Patrizia Faccioli and I did some photo elicitation in our study of Italian food ways,[18] but that is the extent of new books. Colter Harper's Ph.D. dissertation in ethnomusicology and Steven Farough's study of race and masculinity are among the few using the method. A small number of MA theses have been categorized as articles and join the list below.

About one-third of the articles analyzed below have subject-produced imagery, so they could also be considered to belong to the growing canon of photovoice studies. That really doesn't matter, except that, as we will see, photovoice studies often have a distinctive method (and ideology) that contrasts with the varied approaches that make up photo elicitation.

Any way you count it, however, the growth in photo elicitation studies—in journal publication rather than book-length studies—has been phenomenal. One wonders what a follow-up ten years from now will bring.

PE: The intellectual lay of the land

As far as I can determine, the first post-Collier mention of photo elicitation appeared in an article in which I described the methods being used in *Working Knowledge*,[19] although Jon Wagner had discussed photographs used as interview stimuli in 1979.[20] In the late 1980s and early 1990s, PE research was published very little in article form. Notable examples were studies by Charles Suchar on gentrification, Steve Gold on ethnic entrepreneurship and Megan Stiebling on the role of gender in kids' sports. These and a handful of other examples were published in *Visual Sociology*[21] and at the end of that era a few examples were being published in communication journals. Mainstream sociology, not to mention qualitative sociology, remained nuts left to crack.

Since that time PE has become more common inside sociology, published in journals including *American Behavioral Scientist*, *Qualitative Sociology*, *The American Sociologist*, *International Journal of Social Research Methodology*, *Feminist Theory*, *Human Ecology* and *Sociology*. More than twenty articles using or describing photo elicitation were published in *Visual Studies*. The remaining journals are in the fields of health, disability, educational research, leisure sciences, urban planning, travel research, communication, consumer behavior and in non-applied areas including field methods, ethnography, African-American studies, photography and culture and archaeology.

The authors of the newest studies were often working on research questions in which PE offered a new and better approach and they seldom affiliated with sociology or social science departments. About twenty of these studies evaluated photo elicitation as a method. Given that most of these research projects have several authors, the eighty-four articles show that several hundred researchers in a wide range of disciplines have successfully adopted what was just a few years ago a little known approach. Much of the research has been funded, which has also indicated the degree to which these methods have come to be seen as legitimate. Finally, the 2011 IVSA (International Visual Sociology Association) annual meeting has as its theme collaborative research, and the range and depth of PE studies at that well-attended conference was nothing less than phenomenal. It is clear that photo elicitation and its variations have passed from a status of quirky and esoteric to nearly the mainstream of several research traditions.

Overview by topics

I categorized each article or chapter as either applied or non-applied, and grouped them by topic in Table 8.1. I have categorized studies as non-applied if they were designed to produce knowledge for its own sake, as compared to applied studies that are devoted to solving a problem, evaluating a program, or understanding behavior in order to increase the efficiency of a social agency, business or enterprise. A quick glance shows that photo elicitation research has become common in health and education research, and in some applied studies of culture, particularly in the area of consumer behavior, tourism and sports. The non-applied uses of PE were used to study connection to place, family identity and the cultural studies of work. Clearly many articles could appear in several cells of the table and the split between applied and non-applied is seldom firm. It was difficult to finally categorize the studies in only one way, and clearly others facing the same task would do it differently.

Cell one: Applied studies of health

Health-related studies using photo elicitation often seek to break down the barriers between caretakers and patients, and to understand how people understand and experience disease, treatment, injury, threats to their safety and conditions such as obesity that threaten healthfulness. In just under half of the studies cited the subjects took the photos that they then narrated, discussed, or wrote about. In Dyches' (et al.) study of the world-view of kids with developmental disabilities, there were no words added to the photos made by the subjects. The point of these studies was to grasp an understanding across the divide between health and illness; between the institution of the hospital and an individual's places that were not associated with illness or recovery; or between the experience of living in a healthy way or not.

Most studies share a remarkable assumption that people can take photos of new experiences, many of which are upsetting, frightening or even terrifying, and use these photos to communicate what the experiences feel like or what they mean. These include the challenge posed by understanding how children face cancer (Epstein) and Frith's studies of how women experience chemotherapy.

Some of these studies, in particular Frohmann's study of women's safety, Fleury's study of Hispanic women, obesity and exercise, Johnson and her colleagues' study of the effect of female non-mother relatives on healthy eating choices, and Barnidge and her colleagues' study of the effects of poverty on health in a rural American county, are interventions as well as studies. They advocate for women, the poor or disadvantaged, and others, as well as seeking to understand an aspect of health. As we will see momentarily, these studies are similar in form and content to those listed as photovoice. Because they called themselves elicitation studies we included them here.

Twelve of the sixteen articles include photos; often an example or two to show how the method worked. Some striking exceptions were Oliffe's study of

Table 8.1 Recent research publications using photo elicitation (numbers in parentheses refer to the number of articles on this topic. First author only listed on the table. All articles cited in endnotes)

Applied	Non-applied
Cell one: Health	**Cell four: Defining culture**
– hospital patients, health (Radley)[22]	– family photographs and interracial intimacies (Twine)[36]
– children with cancer (Epstein)[23]	– how Italian and American women define Italian ads (Harper)[37]
– men with prostate cancer (Oliffe)[24]	– dynamics of families in Switzerland (Steiger)[38]
– overviews of visual health studies (3, Riley, Hurworth, Harrison)[25]	– how children understand and perform gender in sports (Stiebling)[39]
– definitions of alcohol use, Italy (Faccioli)[26]	– re-appropriating cultural memory among the Inuit (Payne)[40]
– women's safety (Frohmann)[27]	– defining youth style (Hethorn)[41]
– women's experiences with chemo, UK (Frith)[28]	– how white men see race and gender (Farough)[42]
– Hispanic women and exercise (Fleury)[29]	– how multicultural Norwegians interpret holy symbols (Vassenden)[43]
– kids with disabilities photograph (Dyches)[30]	– bullying from kids' perspective (Thompson)[44]
– people with spinal cord injury and drawing (Cross)[31]	– how refugees in the UK use and interpret urban greenspaces (Rishbeth)[45]
– needle exchange (Barrett)[32]	– how the Maasai define and use natural resources (Bignante)[46]
– heroin users contemplate Larry Clark's photos of addiction (Smith)[33]	– gender identity in physical education (Azzarito)[47]
– effect of female relatives on healthy food choices (Johnson)[34]	
– community members address health issues (Barnidge)[35]	
Cell Two: Teaching	**Cell five: Connection to place/things (culture)**
– reflection by teachers of adult education (Taylor)[48]	– ethnic identification (Clark-Ibanez)[54]
– creating inclusive global education in Africa and elsewhere (2, Kaplan, Miles)[49]	– identification with neighborhoods and the city (4, van der Does, Suchar, Moore, Kyle)[55]
– understanding freshman year experience (Harrington)[50]	– identity with community (2, Schwartz, Stewart)[56]
– students participate in school governance (Thompson)[51]	– landscape perception in archaeology, Sicily (Fitzjohn)[57]
– understanding kids' view of school (Cappello)[52]	– meaning of objects (Whitmore)[58]
– impact of grad school on beliefs about teaching (Taylor)[53]	– how three people define their home in Denmark (Wust)[59]
	– food deserts (Cannuscio)[60]
	– Fijian's sense of place in the face of tourism (Kerstetter)[61]
	– children's places (Rasmussen)[62]
	– 'viewscape' fetishism in Norway and Wisconsin (Van Auken)[63]
Cell three: Cultural behavior	**Cell six: Cultures of Work**
– consumer decision making among unusual consumers and in unusual situations (Rosenbaum)[64]	– attributing success in sports to race (Gonzalez)[67]
– evaluating leisure; evaluating experience of tourism, Canada and Scandinavia (3, Stewart, MacKay, Cederholm)[65]	– defining children's work in the underground economy, UK (Mizen)[68]
– consumer goods and identity among the youth in the UK (Croghan)[66]	– farmers define ecological farming practices in Australia (Belin)[69]
	– woods workers define logging (Rieger)[70]
	– studying the bureaucracy (Warren)[71]
	– school principals define themselves (Ketelle)[72]
	Cell seven: PE as method
	– overview (4, Harper, Clark-Ibanez, Caufield, Grady)[73]
	– graphic illustration (Crilly)[74]
	– how the interviews work, children
	– monks in Sri Lanka (Samuels)[75]
	– collaborative interaction, military identity (Jenkings)[76]
	– PE interviews and narrative (Robinson)[77]
	– studying food, overview of potential (Power)[78]
	– how people experience the world, Scandinavia (Carlsson)[79]
	– digital photography and research relationships (Woodward)[80]
	– overview of transnational research (Van Auken)[81]
	– what makes photos memorable? (Stones)[82]
	– class, habitus in Buenos Aires (Meo)[83]
	– history of the interview in sociology (Lee)[84]
	– PE and feminist methods (Smart)[85]

prostate cancer, which includes photos men made of their experience of the disease, including wearing bags to collect leaking urine, photos of graveyards and other images that held considerable meaning to those struggling with an often fatal illness. None of these research reports was a photo essay per se. The most novel use of PE was Smith and her colleague's interview study with three addicted heroin users, based on reflections on Larry Clark's documentary photo book on heroin and methamphetamine users.

Barnidge and her colleagues adopted a method used by the Dutch students discussed above, in which a professional photographer made images, but was guided by the study participants. He made seventy photos from which fourteen were used in the interviews.

The research articles on health brought to mind two book-length visual/ autobiographical studies of health and disease. These were written by Jo Spence, an English photographer/writer, and writer Dorothea Lynch, who collaborated on the project with her partner, photographer Eugene Richards.[86] Both projects use photography and self-reflection to explore identity, disease, disfigurement and death. They are not formal research projects and the photographs are not used in a conventional research format, but the images structure the stories that challenged and then ended their lives. These essays can be called photo elicitation because both authors reflected upon the meaning of the images that they made (or, in Lynch's case, those made by her partner Richards) as part of their autobiographical narratives.

Clearly photo elicitation, in conventional or experimental form, has become an important part of health studies. As we will show, it is even more prevalent in the form of photovoice studies.

Cell two: Educational research and photo elicitation

Photo elicitation is a natural method for studies of education, as these pioneering studies show. The studies listed in cell two use photo elicitation to study how people learn to teach and to reach across the culture of adults to the culture of children. Researchers use photo elicitation to study how students are involved in governing schools in the UK, and British researchers use it to study inclusiveness in education, especially among those typically excluded (such as those with AIDs) in Africa and Indonesia. Researchers put cameras into the hands of first-year university students in the US, who explore their experience via their photos. Photo elicitation has thus been a way to study how teaching works. It has been a tool that allows students of several ages, many circumstances and from many national backgrounds, to explore the actual process of education.

As was the case in studies of health-related topics, the published articles talked about photography much more than they published photos. Only one article, by Taylor and his associates, included many of the photos used in the study, alongside the excerpts of interviews. While educational researchers are beginning to use images, they are still cautious about including them in the research reports. What does this say about pedagogy, as well as research about teaching?

Cells three, four and five: Studying culture with photo elicitation

Photo elicitation has been commonly used to study different forms of culture. Of course "culture" is a broad term and thus part of what we've seen reflects how many categories can be subsumed under the umbrella the term provides. It is also true, as we've said in Chapter 1, that culture is often visual and that it can be studied visually.

Cell three identifies six studies of cultural consumption using photo elicitation. In general they are evaluations of how consumers make decisions about what to purchase, or how they evaluate what they have purchased and consumed. Several of these studies address the consumption of imagery as the cultural activity: tourists go on holidays to make photos, for example, so having tourists analyze their pictures is actually having them analyze one of the central aspects of the tourism experience. Erika Andersson Cederholm's study of the backpacker experience is the most theoretically satisfying of these studies, as it is grounded in phenomenology and Simmelian sociology. Croghan and her assistants study how young teens identify with specific products.

It is likely that methods related to photo elicitation are commonplace in studies of product placement and other marketing strategies but they did not appear as academic publications aside from those cited. It was, however, especially interesting to contemplate the meaning of consuming nature in leisure activities, or to see how social discrimination affects who can buy certain products.

While I used several strategies to search for applied studies, I found only a few, and I've noted that I think if we scratch the surface differently we might find a great deal more. For example, in leisure research a method called VEP (visitor employed photography) could be considered a form of photo elicitation, though I have not included some of the studies using this method because they appear to have become their own mini-tradition.

Photo elicitation in the non-applied categories (beginning with cell four) include cultural studies of family, gender and ethnicity; identification with place and things, cultures of work and PE as a research method.

In cell four, France Winddance Twine's study of interracial family dynamics uses family photographs to study the presentation of what might be called the "family self," using a single photo to guide her work. Her work draws upon the pioneering work of visual anthropologist Richard Chalfen, who was the first and remains the most important scholar in the area of family photography studies.[87] Ricabeth Steiger's study of family dynamics in Switzerland draws upon her skill as a professional photographer as well as her training as an anthropologist. Faccioli and I studied how Italian and American women interpreted gender narratives in public display ads in Italy (see Chapter 6), and it is one of the few studies to use the same imagery to interview subjects in different cultures. Payne's previously discussed study uses PE to redefine an official archive, to repatriate visual memory among the Inuit of northern Canada. Hethorn and Kaiser's study of youth style among young teenagers in a multicultural setting explores self and ethnic definition and conflict through apparel. Megan Stiebling used photo elicitation to understand how kids in sports define and experience gender difference.

In the past two years there have been several very interesting studies in this category. They include Vassenden and Andersson's study of how a multicultural population in inner city Oslo explores the meaning of two images: one of the Bible and the other of the Quran. Steven Farough's study of whiteness and masculinity draws upon poststructuralist theory to ponder what the author calls "the matrix of vision" in several contexts. This is one of the most ambitious and theoretically interesting examples of PE research and it is derived from Farough's Ph.D. dissertation, indicating that at least one more scholar has successfully defended collaborative methods to a graduate committee.

The cross-disciplinary potential of the collaborative model is shown in landscape architects Clare Rishbeth and Nissa Finney's research, which used photo elicitation to assess how refugees and asylum seekers defined and used urban greenspaces in Sheffield, UK. Their funded research was entitled "Walking Voices" (a previous iteration was called "Viewfinder"), which included many of the participant-produced photos and a website where the participants speak about their experience in negotiating the urban realities of a new society.

Thompson and Gunter worked with students in a school in the UK to define bullying from the perspective of those who experienced it. As is the case in several of these studies, the research was in-depth and extended over several stages of photo making, consultation, interviewing and analysis. Their study was similar to Azzarito and Katzew's analysis of created gendered identities in physical education classes. Their study recalled Farough's analysis of race and gender. Bignante's study of how the Maasai perceive and use natural resources is one of the strongest examples of crossing culture with the aid of photo elicitation; one gets the sense that the study could not have been accomplished otherwise. Bignante takes particular advantage of the web publication of her research; her article includes fifteen photos (several times more than most article publications) and they are reproduced in large format and in color online.

In these studies, the researchers used found photos, such as Twine's reflections on the meanings of photos found in the home, or they produced images that presented the subjects with a compelling portrait of their own lives. My photos of Italian display ads were mostly photos of photos in the form of posters or billboards, but the way I framed the images influenced their messages. For example, in one instance I juxtaposed an image of a transvestite advertising her sexual services next to a photo of a model in a swimsuit ad, to encourage people to think of the messages of each image in relationship to each other (see Chapter 6). Several of these studies depended on subjects to make photos, often as a result of a training exercise. We are left with several very excellent studies that make a strong case for studying culture via elicitation. That goes for both looking at taken for granted aspects of one's own culture, such as Farough's study of race and gender, and several examples where researchers reached across age, national culture and subcultural differences.

In cell five we examine how researchers have used PE to study the connections people experience to places and things. In that places and things are material, they can usually be portrayed visually. They range from neighborhoods to landscapes to objects to the urban and rural experience. They include the study of place meanings; kids' worlds in Denmark; Fijians' sense of place in the face of increased tourism; and routine objects in the lives of those whose worlds are shrinking due to aging. Those interviewed with imagery from these settings include members of ethnic groups, children, old people, residents of particular places and consumers of touristic leisure.

Marisol Clark-Ibanez shows how PE interviews allow children from Hispanic neighborhoods to explain their life experience. In addition to the two studies of neighborhood identification that have been previously discussed, Dona Schwartz explained how she used PE to study a rural community, a theme taken up by Mitchell Stewart and his colleagues' study of involving the community in landscape planning processes in Chicago. Matthew Fitzjohn's study of how the inhabitants of Troina, Sicily construct images of the places they live in uses PE interviews in combination with Geographic Information Systems (GIS) software. Van Auken explores the interesting issue of what he calls landscape fetishism in Norway and rural America. Others study the meaning of place at an agricultural fair. Finally, Whitmore uses PE interviews to investigate how the elderly find meaning in treasured objects.

What I found curious was that in the non-applied articles photos were more apt to be published. In the applied studies, most researchers described projects using photography, but usually only included a photo or two as an example, if any were included at all. In the non-applied cells (four and five) nearly all articles included photos, and often many.

Cell six: Work

The cultural study of work is ripe for PE study. Work is, after all, generally visual, either actually or in the imagination of workers and the people or things workers serve. I used PE to study the work of a rural mechanic and to understand how the work of farming changed with mechanization, discussed earlier. Perhaps photo elicitation is best suited for detailed studies where a small number of subjects can ferret out the nuances of a complicated topic, but the articles listed in this cell also demonstrate how PE works with larger groups and in a wide range of work situations. Some studies, such as my study of Willie's work, focus on the material aspects of work: that is, jobs where hands and bodies form, fix or otherwise modify the material world. Similar projects include Rieger's study of logging and Belin's study of how farmers identify conservation practices. But PE is not limited to these rather obvious choices, where work by its nature is visual. One of the most interesting applications is Leticia Gonzalez and her colleagues' use of PE methods to study how people attributed success as baseball players to racial background; here the PE becomes part of a survey. Phil Mizen's use of elicitation interviews reaches across the barriers of age and class to study how teen workers in the informal economy in the UK experience and define their work. Mizen's study uncovers meanings attributed to work, and in so doing describes political and economic structures that define the teen workers' lives. Samantha Warren explores the huge potential of studying the bureaucratic organization of non-hand work in her groundbreaking study. Finally, Diane Ketelle photographed eight school principals and asked them to write their reactions to their portraits on the photos, an approach used by photographer Goldberg on several projects.[88] Ketelle's project is one of the most successful adaptations of a method from the documentary tradition to visual sociology.

Many of these studies are of visually vivid work: hand work; work with machines or tools; or work that is part of specific landscapes. While this is a natural use for PE (the details of the actions, objects and settings can inspire explanation) it is also natural to imagine PE used in studies of service work, intellectual work or other forms where the work is more abstract, and where images could be symbolic as well as specific. Ketelle's project on school principals is an excellent example; we see how those inside the portrait offer cheery, optimistic views of the stressful job they hold.

Cell seven: Method

Sociologists spend a great deal of time discussing, developing, working at and arguing about how they do their studies. There are several examples in cell seven. These include Jeffrey Samuels' study of how what are called auto-driven interviews engage subjects (in this case, young Buddhist monks in Sri Lanka), and Elaine Power's argument for visual methods, including PE, in the study of food.

Two studies stand out; one is Lee's discussion of photo elicitation in his interesting history of the interview in sociology and the other is Carol Smart's thoughtful essay on qualitative methods that sees collaborative visual sociology as an example of creating data in new ways. Her reflections remind us that the collective search involves active listening and creative constructions of new understandings.

It is inspiring and occasionally numbing to read eighty-four articles on photo elicitation. PE research now investigates nearly the full spectrum of sociology, as well as appearing more frequently in psychology research (it is, after all, a projective test and in this way similar to both the Rorschach and the TAT), and visual anthropology. The method has been used to study topics in health, consumer behavior and education. While the method has begun to crack mainstream sociology journals, the trickle has yet to become a torrent.

A final comment: a great change in the past ten years is the increasing opportunity to publish visuals afforded by web publication. Many articles cited above de-emphasized their visual dimension. Web publication, where images can appear large, crisp and in the color they were created with, makes it possible to expand the role of imagery and I'd suggest we take advantage of it!

Chapter 9

Photovoice

As I noted in the previous chapter, collaborative visual research can be dated to Sol Worth and John Adair's project "Navajo Film Themselves," though surely earlier examples exist. Worth and Adair (with the assistance of Richard Chalfen, then a graduate student) trained several Navajo Native Americans to operate wind-up silent 16 mm film cameras, and to edit their footage into several films, most about twenty minutes long. The films are remarkable in part because they introduce the viewer to the Navajo experience of time, the organization of tasks and, perhaps, an appreciation for a different relationship between ends and means. For example filmmaker Susie Benally's Navajo weaver spends most of the time in the film walking slowly through the terrain, looking for natural elements to use as dyes, and taking care of sheep which she will eventually shear for the wool for the rugs. It is fifteen minutes into the twenty-minute film before she begins to weave, and then cutaways return to the care of the sheep, now the responsibility of her little brother. The film embodies the importance of process in which many small steps are each respectfully presented.[1] The film is a remarkable teaching tool because it locks the viewer into a reality that is structured in a way that most middle-class North Americans have not experienced, and this is very different than reading about the cultural definition of time and task management.

While the Navajo project was influential, it was likely the 1985 publication of Wendy Ewald's *Portrait and Dreams*[2] that had the most impact on those who were contemplating putting cameras into the hands of those being studied. At the time Ewald was a college graduate from the Northeast who had done post-graduate studies in photography at MIT under Minor White, and she was to become a teacher in the Appalachian region of Kentucky. Modest grants allowed her to build darkrooms in several schools, and over time she developed a curriculum where children photographed, developed and printed their photos, and reflected on what they had photographed. Eventually Ewald and those who subsequently developed her method at Duke University's Center for Documentary Studies[3] devised assignments instructing children to photograph such topics as their dreams; their understandings of nature and the environment; and the closeness of their families (the list of topics explored in typical assignments is now much larger). The process is known as Literacy Through Photography and will be reviewed in the discussion of teaching. The photographs made by the Appalachian children confirm common stereotypes of Appalachian poverty, including social isolation and material deprivation. The photos in context with the students' thoughts and words, however, describe deep connections to the physical environment, vivid imaginations, strong connections to family and poetic story telling. They often seemed to contradict the messages of the photos, or one could say they completed them in a surprising way. In the meantime Ewald completed similar projects in several settings that she regards as art rather than sociology, and as such are beyond the purview of our discussion. The inspiration to put cameras in the hands of subject-collaborators, however, had taken form, and continues to grow.[4]

The emergence of photovoice

While Worth and Adair and Wendy Ewald were both important inspirations, Caroline Wang first defined the photovoice method. For Wang, as we shall see, the issue of empowerment is central, and it is not surprising that she traces her inspiration to Brazilian educator Paulo Freire, as expressed in his 1968 book, *Pedagogy of the Oppressed*. Freire encouraged education for what he termed critical consciousness: that is, developing an understanding and willingness to act on the economic, social and political forces that affect one's life. While not about visual methods per se, Freire's theories of education provide a justification and rationale for much that has become photovoice.

The first use of photovoice was Wang and Burris' 1992 (published in 1994) participatory action research project that was intended to encourage Chinese village women to identify aspects of their community and public health that they wanted to change. The project was described in several publications, as listed in the following tables. In this initial work, Wang and Burris defined photovoice as a method through which knowledge would be generated by people who were normally passive objects in the research process. Their work drew its theory from feminism and the then common critiques of documentary photography. In Wang and Burris' words, photovoice was intended to motivate people to "record and reflect their community's strengths and concerns ... to promote critical dialogue and knowledge about important issues through large and small group discussion of photographs, and ... to reach policymakers."[5] In the eighteen years since their first project, the use of photovoice has skyrocketed.

As the following will make clear, for a long time photovoice has been primarily used by researchers interested in subjects such as public health promotion or community organizing, and it is now becoming more common in visual sociology and anthropology per se. Perhaps the most distinctive feature of photovoice as it had been practiced for many years was its progressive agenda, and that may change when photovoice begins to be used more for the primary goal of creating knowledge.

Photovoice research is being published widely, but until recently it has been even more distant from sociology than photo elicitation. I located just under ninety journal articles and dissertations using photovoice-type methods, published in fifty-seven journals, few if any from the mainstream of sociology or anthropology. Several photovoice studies have been published in *Visual Studies* recently, though they are absent or very rare in the seven or eight best-known journals of qualitative sociology, anthropology, or visual anthropology. Photovoice research has appeared in professional journals on AIDs education, public health, nursing, community psychology, disability, health education, adolescent mental health, interprofessional care, human services, special needs, dementia, various aspects of education and management. A recent publication in *Cultural Studies Critical Methodologies* shows that the divide between theory and practice has been bridged. Most of the authors of these publications teach and research in medical or public health schools, social work graduate programs or graduate studies of education. I analyzed the citations from just under ninety articles and noted that about a third included references to visual sociology or anthropology, and these tended to be among the most recent photovoice publications; the large majority had no references to visual sociology or anthropology. This suggests that the gulf between photovoice and visual sociology is now narrowing.

In Table 9.1 I map photovoice research by topic and then examine each category in more depth. I've undoubtedly missed some papers, and clearly there are several ways to categorize these publications. While there is no single way to create a report of ninety publications that is light and breezy, I have attempted to design a means through which readers can quickly trace their way to the original source by including the last name of the first author on all references below, and an endnote that indicates the full citation.

Cell one: Empowerment

Most photovoice studies involve empowerment, though the term is used in many ways. The line between these studies and others listed in the table is not firm; the papers listed in cell one could arguably be placed in other cells, or many of the studies in other cells could be inserted here. Nevertheless, these are examples in which empowerment is the central theme and included is Wang and Burris' definition of the method in 1994, which they then called the photo novella, in their description of research designed to inspire sixty-two Chinese women to increased consciousness and political involvement. It is here that Wang and Burris first trace their method to Paulo Freire's education for a critical consciousness, and connect it to feminist theory and a critique of documentary photography. Other reports from these studies show how Chinese village women influenced social policy through their photovoice activism, and how the researchers collaborated with those they worked with. We learn what specific changes were made in the lives of Chinese village women due to photovoice research; we understand collaboration as a complicated phenomenon that changes at different stages of the research. There are reflections on the limitations of photovoice or missteps taken along the way. For example, while the authors felt that the photovoice project in China did empower village women, it left them in a political system that was otherwise dominated by men. It may have had an important impact on a local power structure but it did not lead to significant or lasting social change.

There are primarily two groups served and studied in the research included in this category. The first group is made up of members of desperately poor communities in the US and abroad, where daily life means confronting problems that are largely outside the experience of middle-class researchers. The second population consists of students, including children with autism, fifth graders and university students. Reading these studies makes it clear that the knowledge of outside researchers, no matter how involved they might have been with the community, could never approximate to the understanding reflected in the research images made by the subject-collaborators.

Carnahan uses photovoice to study the education of children with autism. The study was intended to help teachers identify ways to become more sensitive to the needs of autistic children, and to help autistic children overcome their impaired use of language, to increase their involvement with group activities and to stimulate their interest in education. Wilson and her colleagues used PV as an aspect of an afterschool program called YES, and they showed that photovoice allowed students to work in teams, to engage in dialogue about school problems and issues, and to suggest solutions by performing skits, creating posters and initiating letter-writing campaigns. In other studies, fifth grade students used photovoice as part of a comprehensive, months-long afterschool program, and university students used the process to identify what they perceived as significant problems in their environments.

While empowerment remains the central theme of these studies, the term is used in several ways. Some researchers suggest that making photos of community or institutional problems is empowering without saying why or how. Others apply Freire's ideas about changing the consciousness of the oppressed from what he calls the magical, where the poor remain helpless, through a second level where the poor perceive the world as rational but corrupt, to a third level of consciousness where they become aware of their choices to accept or to try to change reality. Carlson and her colleagues acknowledged the narratives of "despair and anger" that permeated the stories and photos written by their impoverished community members, and the "apathy, dependency thinking . . . and intense distrust of themselves, their neighbors, and the larger community . . ."[6] that had to be overcome to move community members beyond Freire's first level of consciousness. Carlson was also the only researcher to call upon visual anthropology and sociology in the analysis of photos; other researchers generally took the meanings of the photos for granted.

Table 9.1 Research publication using photovoice (numbers in parentheses indicate the number of research articles; author listed is first author only; all articles are listed in endnotes)

Cell One: Empowerment
– first use of photovoice as photo novella; Chinese village women (3, Wang, all)[7]
– youth from poor inner cities identify problems in their communities (Strack)[8]
– community members from inner city neighborhoods make photos and write stories to identify problems in their communities (2, Carlson, Kramer)[9]
– PV is used in afterschool program to engage students to school improvement (Wilson)[10]
– students define healthy and unhealthy practices (Necheles)[11]
– college students use PV to identify issues of health and safety (Goodhart)[12]
– teachers and kids with autism use PV (Carnahan)[13]
– definition and review of studies that stress empowerment (4, Wang, Wang, Wang, Molloy)[14]

Cell two: Community health
– factors that influence the health of African-American men (Ornelas)[15]
– health needs assessments in an Appalachian community (Downey)[16]
– family planning services for Hispanic immigrants in Midwest (Schwartz)[17]
– Canadian single mothers struggling with poverty (Duffy)[18]
– exhibit of portraits of the mentally ill with photovoice narratives (Fleming)[19]
– evaluation of home visitation for at risk mothers (Vaughn)[20]
– review of thirty-one articles using PV (Hergenrather)[21]

Cell three: Adapting to illness and recovery, living with AIDs/HIV; mental illness and disability, defining involvement with non-healthy activities

Pain
– understanding chronic pain (Baker)[22]
– quality of life among Huntington's Disease caregivers (Aubeeluck)[23]
– life with kidney disease (Allen)[24]
– living with spinal cord injury (Newman)[25]
– life after brain injury (Lorenz)[26]
– chronic disease management with teens; visual storytelling (Drew)[27]

Cancer
– breast cancer survivors (Lopez)[28]
– Aboriginal women with breast cancer (Brooks)[29]
– youth experience and evaluate camp for kids with cancer (Epstein)[30]
– women with cancer make art to redefine themselves (Reynolds)[31]

AIDs
– studying employment-seeking behavior of those with AIDs (Hergenrather)[32]
– in South Africa, an overview of a study of HIV/AIDs for youth (2, Mitchell, both)[33]
– risk of HIV/AIDs among non-gay African-American men who have sex with men (Mamary)[34]
– creating visual stories to bridge gap between people with AIDs and health care providers (Schrader)[35]
– stigmatizing of those with HIV/AIDs in South African school (Moletsane)[36]

Disability
– people with long-term mental illness express, Sweden (Erdner)[37]
– adolescent adjustment among those with mild intellectual disability (O'Grady)[38]
– mothers with learning disabilities (Booth)[39]
– Latinos living with intellectual disabilities (Jurkowski)[40]

Cell four: Community; class; poverty
– homeless take photos and reach policy makers, Ann Arbor (Wang)[41]
– ethics of photovoice as community empowerment project (Wang)[42]
– documenting community assets and concerns, Flint (Wang)[43]
– young homeless women and elderly women plan co-housing (Wang)[44]
– ten newly arrived Latino adolescents discuss adjustment (Streng)[45]
– Eskimo health, women (Vollman)[46]
– community health assessment (Wang)[47]
– women in Belfast, community, relationships and politics (Mcintyre)[48]
– indigenous communities, injustice, inequality and exploitation (Castleden)[49]
– Canadian prairie women and poverty (Willson)[50]
– community problems in rural Hungary (Harper)[51]

Continued

Table 9.1 Continued

Cell five: Education; youth
- seven Latina girls, voices and needs (Vaughn)[52]
- making management education collaborative (Chio)[53]
- teaching writing to urban youth (Zenkov)[54]
- fifth graders, farm-to-school program (Sands)[55]
- views of grade school students in the age of AIDs, southern Africa (Mitchell)[56]
- young teens mummify Barbie (Wagner)[57]

Cell six: Culture; identity; work
- older women talk about aging (Wiggs)[58]
- female athletes talk about muscularity and leanness (Mosewich)[59]
- juveniles in prison photograph their world (Arendt)[60]
- kids talk about being refugees (Guerrero)[61]
- how grazing farmers in Australia view ecological crisis (Sherman)[62]
- reactions to living near oyster farms (Pierce)[63]
- how immigrant women in Finland define everyday life (Jangibeb-Abryqyagm)[64]
- how people of different nationalities respond to IKEA (Burt)[65]

Cell seven: Reviews of literature; analyses of effectiveness of PV; ethics
- evaluating PV to study Hispanic women with health issues (Keller)[66]
- evaluation of visual methods in study of young moms in SA (Liebenberg)[67]
- comparing PV and non-visually based interviews in study of health in rural Guatemala (Cooper)[68]
- how well do image elicitation techniques work in health projects with young people? (Guillemin)[69]
- ethical concerns generated by visual methods; children in Lima (Joanou)[70]
- overview of PV in nutritional and dietetic research (Martin)[71]
- review of lit., thirty-seven health-related arts, before 2008 (Catalani)[72]
- non-photo image elicitation: diagrams and drawings (Varga-Atkins)[73]

Several of these projects culminated with exhibitions of photos that were attended by policy makers, peers of students and community members. In several cases the exhibitions were alluded to as an important part of the empowerment process.

The issue of empowerment is very complex, as many of the researchers note. Determining whether an activity has been empowering may be easier to claim than to prove. Photovoice methods may be easy to use superficially, but they are also a potent method when used well. This was shown in many presentations in the 2011 IVSA annual meetings in Vancouver, BC, where the theme of the entire meeting was participatory visual methods, but especially in the research presented by Franziska Meyer of the University of Bern, who, along with an interdisciplinary team, developed a photovoice method to study the visual–spatial abilities of adolescents with Down Syndrome.[74]

The research was presented as a documentary film that both explained the goals of the research and its unfolding. The adolescents (a study group of less than five) were first asked to draw a map of their route from their homes several streets and bus rides from their school. We saw them struggle to do so. One child asked for three sets of large paper on which he drew a straight line, parallel to the long side of the paper, to indicate the length of his walk down a particular street. We were led to conclude from these efforts that the students had a very minimal mental map. Similarly, their written or verbal descriptions of their routes were minimal at best.

The children were then given cameras and were instructed on how to use them, covering essentials such as not putting one's fingers across the lens. They were asked to photograph their route, which they did in a long sequence of photos, which they then laid out on a large table, duplicating the actual route they took. They had photographed key landmarks that signaled where they were to turn, get on a bus and so forth. What the project showed was that the adolescents had mental maps, but they were not easily communicated in drawings or words. However, they could be very easily communicated with photos laid into a grid. Photography had been the means to express this knowledge and to communicate it to others.

The empowerment that resulted was evident in the adolescents' pleasure at their success and their newly found ability to express themselves. Their parents also expressed the idea that the process had made their children more open, happy and confident. In this case the empowerment was made very convincingly.

Cell two: Community health

Community health refers to efforts to encourage the public to adopt lifestyles that promote health, or to confront conditions that deter healthy living. Lisa Schwartz (et al.) used photovoice to inspire consideration of family planning services for Hispanic immigrants in the American Midwest. Others studied African-American men's health and factors influencing the participation of mothers in home visit programs. Fleming reports on a study in which a professional photographer made portraits of people suffering from mental illness who then narrated the photos. The researchers used what is referred to as an iconographic technique that understands photographs on increasing levels of abstraction. This was first identified by Theo van Leeuwen in an influential text[75] on visual analysis. Finally, Lynne Duffy used a photovoice method to encourage mothers living alone to identify aspects of their communities that were important to their "health, health promotion, and quality of life." Themes included "finances, stress, support, personal development, violence and abuse, place and transportation."[76]

The common thread in these studies is health in the community context, in circumstances where communities are challenged by racism, poverty and other social problems. Hergenrather and his colleagues reviewed thirty-one photovoice studies that examine research that is intended to promote community change. Their overview compares community concerns addressed, organizational challenges posed by the projects and the range of outcomes they produced.

Cell three: Adapting to illness and recovery; living with AIDs/HIV; mental illness; reacting to and defining non-healthy activities

With twenty-one studies published in this category, it is clearly an important use of photovoice research, and well it should be. Photovoice is designed to encourage people to engage their worlds in order to have a stronger, more capable relationship with it. Most of the people who participated in these studies face serious challenges to their previously taken-for-granted states of being. For people suffering from disability the conditions may have been lifelong. Clearly these studies could have been included in the discussion of empowerment, but the specific foci of these studies justifies their separate treatment.

I summarize four subtopics separately: living with pain, disease and injury; responding to cancer; living with HIV/AIDs; dealing with mental disabilities, and defining one's willingness to engage in non-healthy behavior.

Pain, disease and injury

Tamara Baker and Caroline Wang evaluated, in this study, whether photovoice could be used to measure the pain experience of adults past fifty years of age. Their attempt was to offer an alternative to quantitative measures of pain. For example, one participant photographed a knife and wrote:

> My everyday pain feels like someone is stabbing me with a knife. The pain would stop for a bit and then I will get a surprise attack (of pain) again. Sometimes the pain is so bad that I feel like taking that sharp knife and chopping both hands off . . . and what is so disappointing is that there is not one pill that I have taken that has helped.[77]

Other adults created visual metaphors, including roses and thorns, to describe the condition of their pain.

Aubeeluck and Buchanan focused on the experience of spouses who were long-term caregivers of Huntington's Disease patients. Photos made by the participants were coded into categories including "care and security," "small pleasures," "loneliness," "escape," "support," and "daily hassles," to name some of the most important. The study is not of pain itself, but the emotional toil of being a caregiver. What is particularly powerful in this study is how images and short excerpts of narratives combine to create a pointed, incisive statement, certainly more powerful than either could achieve alone. This was also the case with studies of the patient experience, especially Aubeeluck's (et al.) study of living with kidney disease.

In that study, patients were asked to visualize the challenges of living well with renal disease, and possible solutions to those challenges. In the case of Allen's study of kidney failure, several people cited the sense of empowerment gained by having someone listen or pay attention to their medically challenged lives. Many of the people in the studies were living in difficult circumstances, facing disease itself, stigmas against their disease, poverty, isolation and loneliness. Still, the act of imagining an image and producing it appears to have had transformative effects in all studies reported upon.

Most researchers worked with a small sample; that is, fewer than ten. Laura Lorenz concentrated her efforts on a single participant, and approached the lengthy interviews she completed with her subject in several ways. As a result we understand much about the process of living with brain injury nearly two decades after a tumor operation redefined the subject's life. Lorenz's study shows that photovoice as well as photo elicitation is well suited for a sociological biography, which I certainly felt when studying the social world of an auto mechanic, Willie (see Chapter 8). Drew and her associates, however, demonstrate that photovoice also works well with a large sample. Their study of how teens manage chronic disease coded the stories of sixty-eight participants to produce a broad picture of disease management.

Cancer

In these studies people were asked to visualize sources of strength when facing breast cancer (the only photo published in Lopez's study was of an opened Bible) and to do the study they had to overcome the norms of silence that surround speaking about cancer among African-Americans in the rural South of the US. Carolyn Brooks and her associates used photovoice to cross cultural boundaries to work with Canadian Native women who had breast cancer. The sense from the study is that those involved became a community that advocated for policy changes. Their work is similar to many of these projects, where researchers and subjects used collaborative visual methods to overcome gulfs of misunderstanding between those who had experienced disease and those who had not; and to overcome cultural divides of ethnicity, social class and other poverty.

HIV/AIDs; living with disabilities

The studies of HIV included two overviews in South Africa geared toward youth activism and understanding the process of stigmatizing those with HIV/AIDs. Hergenrather and his colleagues' study shows factors that affect how people living with HIV/AIDs seek employment. Edward Mamary and his colleagues used photovoice to study factors that affect how non-gay male sex workers engage in risky behavior from their sexual encounters.

Four studies of living with disability explore themes that include dependence on medication and allegories of growth and maturation. Researchers were challenged by working with subjects with mild intellectual disability (specialized, one-on-one training was required, and people involved forgot to bring cameras back and so forth), yet they reported that the experience had fostered pride and confidence among those who were able to master the assignments and photograph abstract concepts such as "health." O'Grady's dissertation was a gentle reminder of the difficulties of adolescence, in this case made more complicated by mild intellectual disability. The dissertation included thirty-four color photos made by the adolescents that were integrated with their stories and comments. O'Grady's research showed how well the method adapted to a larger and longer format than a research article, including images and the interview data they generated.

Cell four: Community; class; poverty

Photovoice research is almost always focused on community, in one form or another. In the decades before photovoice, Community Based Participatory Research (referred to by its acronym CBPR in public health research) emphasized research that began with and located itself in the community. The studies included in cell four look at community per se, or artwork as a part of community.

The studies focus on people whose research task is to identify and photograph assets and challenges in troubled communities (for example, Californian communities that rank low in all measurable indexes; communities of women in politically troubled Belfast; citizens of de-industrializing Flint; and poor communities in the Canadian prairies or people who are on the periphery of community, such as the homeless. Killion and Wang's pilot study links a small number of elderly women with young single mothers to steer them toward sharing housing. The photos show the aspirations of each and explore the meaning of home and housing.

Mcintyre's study of Catholic women in Belfast shows how one works through the contested politics of an embattled place by turning to the comforts of local institutions and family. Wang and her colleagues analyze the ethics of photography as employed in their study of Flint by comparing how they train their researchers to take photos on the street in line with the current legal definitions of allowable photographic activity. In several instances they assert a higher standard for photovoice photographers.

Researchers interested in communities of recent immigrants (Latino adolescents in the US), indigenous communities in Canada or communities who suffer discrimination (the Roma of Hungary) found photovoice to be a window into experiences and perceptions that defined marginality as well as hope and social location.

It was frustrating that aside from Krista Harper's photo essay on the Roma in a Hungarian neighborhood, these publications, like most in the photovoice tradition, included few photos. It has unfortunately been the case that the understanding of how well photos communicate has not broken the tradition of a word-heavy (visual!) social science!

Cell five: Education; youth

One can say that photovoice is about education as much as it is about empowerment, given the focus on educating collaborator/participants and the connection, cited by most, to the theories of education for critical consciousness, made popular by Paulo Freire. Most reports of studies include descriptions of the training that photovoice researchers make mandatory for those to whom they give cameras. At the core is a commitment to the understanding of the ethics of making a photo of another. The six studies of education/youth included in cell five involve using the photovoice method to understand pre-adolescent Latina girls' views of health, to develop a better classroom of diverse students, as a means to invigorate the curriculum of troubled schools in difficult socio-economic settings (including one in southern Africa), and to provide an overview of integrating gardening into the curriculum of fifth grade students in Massachusetts. The researchers in these studies are often looking for ways to teach more effectively; that is, they desire student voice and involvement, and students respond with images and writing that opens their worlds and shows their concerns and their sources of strength and self-confidence. From the handful of photos published and the excerpts of student writing, it appears that the goal of seeing from the inside out has been achieved.

In other examples, especially Laura Azzarito and Jennifer Sterling, and Darlene DeMarie's examples, various categories of kids in school were given the opportunity to define the school experience. Jane Jorgenson and Tracy Sullivan used photovoice to explore kids' relationship to household technologies such as cell phones and computers. Finally, Jon Wagner's study of his daughter and her friend's mummification of their Barbie dolls tells a gentle tale about how young girls manage tasks, engage themselves in collective projects and create their separate social worlds.

Cell six: Culture; identity; work

Of the eight publications included in this category, all but one has been published in the past two years (speaking in mid-2011), and the remaining article was published in 2007. This indicates that photovoice has evolved from a singular focus on empowerment, community, health and other social activist orientations to the more generic themes of sociology. Some of these are in the sociology of work; Pierce's study is on how a community responds to oyster industry expansion and Burt's study is very close to marketing research, as it assesses how people from different countries define the IKEA experience. Sherman's study of Australian farmers' regard for the environment recalls studies cited in Chapter 7 on similar themes. Finally, several studies study identity and the impact of institutions. These include Arendt's study of juveniles in prison and their experience of incarceration; the challenged identities of young people in the US and Colombia who are refugees; Wiggs' study of shifting identities of aging older women; and Janhonen-Abruquah's dissertation on the experience of recent immigrants to Finland.

These studies are, for most sociologists who regularly focus on identity and aging, covering familiar ground: the immigrant experience; the sociology of work;

and the experience of prison. Assigning the task of photographing the scene to the study participants probably made studying IKEA more interesting; perhaps even fun. For aging women it was likely a means to come to terms with transitions in one's identity that are complex and contradictory. Likewise Mosewich and her colleagues explored the contradictions between being a muscular female athlete and the ideals of feminine beauty that stress leanness. The authors noted that attitudes toward muscularity have been studied before but that their in-depth interviewing and the participant photography provided a fuller account than questionnaire studies. The three photos published in the paper are metaphors of display, difference and development and they amplify the lengthy interview segments included in the analysis. Arendt's study of incarcerated juveniles sought to reverse, at least temporarily and partially, the surveillance system that the youth were "hyper aware" of. Given the rules of the facility, the researcher was required to be with the prisoners when they photographed. Their tours of the facilities, even under these circumstances, produced remarkable images and explanations. For example, BamBam, an incarcerated juvenile, photographed Crystal, a terribly abused dog he was responsible for in a pet therapy program. He spoke in reference to his portrait of the dog:

> How would I wanna be treated if I was a dog? I mean, I know if I was a dog I wouldn't wanna be beat, I wouldn't wanna be abused, I wouldn't wanna be yelled at—I don't wanna be yelled at or nothing . . . You gotta keep it in a sweet calm and gentle voice. And if you get frustrated with a dog or with any dog, take a minute—take a break, calm down you know. Say, wait a minute—put yourself in that place and you're—how you're speaking to 'em and change the way you speak to 'em. Umm . . . in this picture—this dog—she does look, I mean, you can see for yourself she does look kinda [scared], sad, depressed, down.[78]

Arendt refers to the images made by the imprisoned youth "snapshots into their lived experience" and the photos show how an institution that is made up of bare walls and small rooms can become a canvas on which people express and interpret their own experience.

Cell seven: Overviews; reviews of literature; methods and ethics

These publications show the maturing of photovoice because they review literature in specific areas of photovoice; they ask questions about ethical implications that may not have been addressed in the studies themselves; and they venture into visualization beyond photography. Clearly these are all indications of research energy, refining of methods, and innovation. Let's take a look.

One of the most thoughtful discussions of the potentials of photovoice is Linda Liebenberg's description of her work with a small number of mothers who parent alone in South Africa. The photos made by the young mothers don't seem remarkable in and of themselves, but they lead the participants to thoughtful embrace with the complexity of their lives and, in Liebenberg's words, "perceptions of the enormity of the task that lies ahead, the impact this will have on her life, and to explore these tensions further . . ." One of the mothers, Brenda offers the following in response to her photos:

> At first I thought it must be this way, this is my life, this is how it must be, and I must just go with the flow. But now that I have taken the photos, now it is different for me. I *see* things in a different way. [My life] isn't going to stay this way. It is going to change.[79]

Her experience leads Liebenberg to conclude:

> we cannot understand the meaning of an image in isolation of the context from which it emerged . . . the field work process demonstrated how meaningless participants' images are to researchers prior to interviews. Similarly, interviews on their own would possibly have missed some of the richness and clarity that images brought with them. The combination of the two, however, provided for a fascinating, rich data set where visual representation of lived experiences "allow communication to occur in the worlds we study".[80]

Cheryl Cooper and Susan Yarbrough offer one of the few comparisons between conventional and photovoice interviews to gather information about "health-related conditions in rural Guatemala" in relationship to the views and perceptions of traditional birth attendants. Their paper is useful precisely because of their evaluation of photovoice:

> The photovoice project gave them [*comadronas*–birth attendants] creative control and the freedom to tell us—and later to show us—other issues that concerned them. In addition, it provided a stimulus for a broader discussion and to introduce new questions, thus offering the potential for new approaches for solving problems that concerned them. These findings reflect similar observations by others about the empowerment benefit of photography and visual stimuli . . .[81]

These discussions are a variation of the ethical considerations of all field work, except that the asymmetry of the researcher–subject relationship in photovoice research is often extreme and the involvement of all participants is more intense, making the ethical issues more pronounced. That is especially the case in Jamie Joanou's report on "the bad and the ugly" sides of photovoice research done with street kids in Lima, Peru. Joanou considers many ethical issues: setting expectations higher than the results can achieve, inadvertently invading people's privacy, facilitating photography that may get people into trouble, or even endangering people by giving them cameras that other people in marginalized communities consider worth stealing. Joanou's report is particularly helpful in setting the terms for future considerations of photovoice/field-work ethics.

The term 'photovoice' indicates the central role of cameras and photography in the method but perhaps it is time for a new term to describe the expanding scope of image elicitation research. Tünde Varga-Atkins and Mark O'Brien's research explores how people make drawings or diagrams (and the comparison between the two) in elicitation exercises. Their research specifically explored how school administrators understood the formal and informal networks that included their schools, and they were encouraged to draw pictures or make diagrams to "focus the interviewee on the given topic or gain extra meaning not covered verbally as part of the interview . . ." They came to see the two forms of representation as essentially different, with drawings more capable of capturing "a salient feature" of what is being studied, and diagrams "more suited to the simplification of complex ideas."[82] Their research is helpful in part because it studies not only how diagrams and drawings communicate, but also what factors seem to influence how well the participants will do on their assigned tasks. Their work is a demonstration of expanding research in what has come to be known as "graphic elicitation",[83] which may represent some of the most interesting exploration of how people actually put their ideas into visual form.

Summary

Photovoice has emerged like a summer thunderstorm over the past two decades. Until recently the visual sociology and anthropology community has largely watched from the sidelines, since photovoice research has been primarily the work of scientists or educators, and published primarily in the specialized journals of, or in the areas of, health, education, community organization and social services. As noted previously, the central figure of the movement, Caroline Wang, often cites photographer Jo Spence and arts educator Wendy Ewald as inspirations for the photographic aspect of the movement. She also cites a research tradition in public health dating to the 1950s that stressed community involvement. Photovoice has succeeded because it has proved itself to be effective for the researchers it serves. Photovoice researchers have developed an effective pedagogy and ethical principles for field work, and have remained committed to putting the insights gained to use in the real world.

The published photovoice research reflects the interests and backgrounds of the researchers, and the values, traditions and orientations of the journals, but it also demonstrates an orientation toward imagery. Photovoice is based on the assumption that photographing one's world is empowering because it leads to greater awareness of both assets and problems of communities or research situations. This perspective reflects an unstated assumption that a photograph of a surface reality—what the camera sees—reveals its structural underpinnings, and it will lead to an enlarged understanding, a kind of sociological decoding of the world pictured. The idea of empowerment also assumes that to photograph one's world is to advance one's mastery of it. The participants in photovoice projects are usually identified as having been passive victims; the collective work including the teaching of the method and the photography itself is assumed to wake people up to a will to create social change.

It is clear that in photovoice the photographs are not important by themselves, but they are important for their role in the lives of those who make them. For this reason photos may not be relevant to research publications. Seen another way, however, not being able to examine images limits how and what the articles communicate. Until recently, the articles also seldom included much of the interview text generated by the photos. Instead they followed the typical scientific research publication mode: introduction with backgrounds of previous research cited; overview of projects; discussion of findings and implications. About 10 per cent of the total number of articles located (which was most of the articles) broke with these traditions to show several images and to include lengthy text excerpts, but these exceptions were usually not published in the scientific journals concerning public health, education and similar outlets.

Photovoice requires that study participants learn to photograph and analyze the photos made. Because of the cameras used in most studies—that is, inexpensive "point and shoot" film cameras—learning to make photos is normally straightforward. But what about teaching where to aim the camera, and what questions to ask about the images made? Most of the researchers instructed participants to follow a sequence of questions referred to by the acronym SHOWeD (briefly stated: What do you SEE here; what is really HAPPENING here; how does this relate to OUR lives; WHY does this situation exist; how can we become EMPOWERED by our new social understanding; what can we DO to address these issues?) that have become part of the photovoice canon. All but one author accepted the usefulness of these questions uncritically. Alice Mcintyre, who studied Catholic women in Northern Ireland, noted that the Irish women she worked with over several months were frustrated by the SHOWeD protocol. One participant, Lucy, is quoted as saying: "The questions are preventin' me from thinkin' about the photos without havin' to have an answer to them." Winnie agreed, stating that she just wanted to "write and not have to stop and see if it all fits into those questions 'cause I don't think my photos do really. Not the way the questions are listed there."[84] In other words, while SHOWeD emphasizes the activist orientation of photovoice, it is seen by some as overly directive and inimical to more natural discussions of images.

Two researchers used what Theo van Leeuwen termed the iconographic approach to analyze photos made during the research, which begins with a question of representation ("What do the images represent and how?") and proceeds to the "hidden meanings" of images ("What ideas and values do the people, places and things represented in the images stand for?)".[85] Van Leeuwen's interest is in imagery found throughout society (popular culture, fine arts, scientific documentation and others) so the point of the research is less in making images to deconstruct the world as deconstructing the world as it is represented in images.

Lengthy discussions of ethics and practical issues of photography are typically followed up by discussion of photo assignments. Images are developed, sorted and analyzed, usually with the SHOWeD sequence, and stories and reflections are written. For some, this produces a research experience that happens too quickly and is one-dimensional. For example, Heather Castleden and her colleagues adapted the photovoice process to an in-depth study of community concerns among First Nation people in Western Canada:

> Wang's approach to PV was initially planned for the Huu-ay-aht study. However, it quickly became apparent that the "classic" Photovoice approach was similar to the academic trend of doing "parachute" research in Indigenous communities. In previous Photovoice studies, data were often collected in a few short weeks, whereas the data collection for this study extended for six months. This prolonged immersion in the field served to establish rapport and build trust.[86]

Their research model included a feedback loop that produced a more grounded theory approach. Photography continued over time; discussions about photos influenced the next rounds of image making. Their criticism makes the point that the photovoice model is usually a single intervention into the lives of the subjects; once the research is over the process is complete. In some instances (particularly photovoice projects integrated into classroom teaching or afterschool programs) research is drawn out, developed over time and integrated into the lives and circumstances of those involved in an ongoing way.

Leading figures of the photovoice movement voiced their dissatisfaction with documentary photography because in their view it represented a view from the outside looking in, rather than a view from the inside looking out. In reference to the first photovoice project in China, Wang notes that documentary photographers in China were nearly all male, which compounded the difficulty of seeing through the eyes of the village women.

Several photovoice researchers cited Martha Rosler's well-known criticism of documentary photography; an allegation that documentary exploits the poor and the weak, turning their misery into art and thus, into their privilege. In short, photovoice positions itself against documentary or ethnographic photography.

The rejection of documentary, however, is not universal in photovoice. In one study (Fleming, et al.), people with mental disability were photographed by documentary photographer Michael Nye; subsequently they wrote about the portraits as a way to explore their experience with mental illness. These images were still available on the website of the photographer at the time of this writing (http://michaelnye.org/fineline/about.html) and they suggest a model for photovoice that could include the skills and insights of a professional photographer. This example, however, was an exception to the general rule of putting cameras into the hands of those studied.

Photovoice researchers often cite their connection to and inspiration from feminist theory and methods; for example Wang, Burris and Xiang identify feminist methods as "an appreciation of women's subjective experience; a recognition of the significance of that experience, and political commitment."[87] Feminist methods are defined in several ways; most suggest that feminist methods are a key to understanding how women should photograph other women, but the ideas also led researchers to increased sensitivity toward the portrayal of disabled men, immigrant children and the homeless of both sexes that were the focus of other studies. Carol Smart's consideration of new methods that draw on the insights of feminism[88] focuses on "giving greater priority to hearing and understanding the ways in which ordinary people interpret and define social interaction . . ." which she takes to include the understanding of emotions and feelings. Recognizing that people often do not express themselves in a straightforward way leads her to consider elicitation methods grounded in the understanding of the material world. Smart's article is an invitation to open ourselves up to learning more in research, in part through the visual method. The essay itself is a model for expressing ourselves in a different way; almost literary in quality and admitting to complexity and even contradiction.

The range and nature of photos made

The organizers of most photovoice studies gave disposable film cameras to subjects, who were then instructed on the rudiments of camera operation. The disposable cameras make reasonable images in bright light and most even have a flash for low light situations. Given their cheapness the quality of their images can be poor (but, as noted in my discussion of the Diana camera in Chapter 10, cheap cameras can and do make interesting photos). The disposable camera does make photography available at a low cost; that is its obvious advantage. Some photovoice projects end with an exhibition, intended for researchers, peers and policy makers, and enlarging the disposable camera images for exhibitions requires skilled work to produce results of medium visual quality.

There was an intriguing exception to the disposable camera model; in two studies researchers gave their participant-collaborators plastic Holga cameras. These are delicate cameras with a limited number of controls that are distinctive because they use 120 medium-format film, which produces a negative that is several times the size of the standard 35 mm negative. Holgas are used by art students because the large negative, even with a plastic lens, can produce images of subtle quality, with fine-arts rendering of shadow gradation and high resolution. However, they have no light meter and to be used correctly require that the photographer has an advanced understanding of the practical aspects of photography. The researchers write:

> We selected the Holga camera for its simple design and operation, its affordability at US $20 per camera, and its appealing and creative format. ... A unique feature of the Holga camera is that it permits double and multiple exposures of images, thus allowing the photographer to literally layer his or her meanings. Participants used black and white film, which is particularly well suited to the Holga.[89]

Unfortunately, aside from one blurry photo in one of the several articles associated with these studies, the images were not published, nor available on a website, so we have no idea of whether the subjects-collaborators were able to take advantage of the expressive capabilities of the Holga. This is the only mention of teaching participants to think like photographers and it would have been interesting to see the effect; that is, whether participants understood the language of black and white photography and the possibilities afforded by manual aperture and shutter speeds, and even experimented with multiple exposures. It is possible that the experiment did not work; that the images were over- or under-exposed, inadvertently double exposed, or that the plastic cameras (whose film doors are prone to opening without warning) didn't hold up. Unfortunately there is no way to tell!

There seem to be two types of photos made by participants. Most are images of mundane objects that are special because of their role in the lives being documented. An aisle in a drugstore too narrow for a wheelchair is important if you are wheelchair bound. An empty lot turned into a trash heap is important to those identifying the assets and needs of their communities. A photo of paint peeling from the ceiling of a school shows the neglect of the community that students are reminded of as their gazes drift upward. Photos made by children of signs in grocery store windows reading "food stamps welcome" or of a homeless veteran carrying a sign, "job wanted", are important for their literal meanings.

The photographers also visualized metaphors, sentiments and emotions in their images. A tree bare of leaves might represent a state of dormancy, part of a healing process. Images of friends might represent a secure social existence. Parents holding hands may represent hope for the future. A photo of a flower bud may indicate the state of unfolding in a young athlete's life, and so on.

Even from the small number of published images in the articles, it seems that images made in the photovoice process could be instructive and interesting to view. Perhaps the image elicitation tradition will lead researchers to experiment more with presenting findings that include the images that are at the center of the work.

Photovoice is becoming more a part of the visual sociology and visual anthropology mainstream, as noted in the quickly increasing pace of research publications. The method has led to new knowledge and has become an activist method that has changed lives and communities. The method continues to develop in new and interesting ways, moving from a singular focus on empowerment to the generic themes of sociology itself.

It is fitting to conclude this part of the book on this note because collaborating with study participants to understand the meaning of an image, no matter who made it or for what purpose, is a dynamic, exciting proposition. I was an early convert and once I experienced the joys of becoming a student in the process of being a researcher, I never looked back.

Chapter 10

Teaching sociology visually

In the following I describe lectures, assignments, workshops and courses that use a visual approach. These are examples that can be developed in several ways. The two themes in the background are teaching visual sociology as a stand-alone topic, and bringing a visual approach to otherwise conventional teaching in the social sciences and in qualitative methods classes in health, education, community development and other professional programs. This chapter can be supplemented with the Appendix, which includes examples of several assignments.

Lectures

It is quite easy to add a visual component to most lectures in sociology but to do this well requires more than slapping some eye candy from Flickr into a PowerPoint presentation that repeats obvious themes from lecture notes. In fact, Edward Tufte and many others (and I include myself in this group) bemoan the general PowerPoint lecture model, where information is reduced to a few entries on bulleted slides that the speaker repeats, often pointing at the board with her or his back to the audience. Clearly, whether using presentation software like PowerPoint or any other multimedia aids, adding visuals to lectures can be illuminating or pointless and dull. The key is that visuals, whether photos, drawings, paintings, film clips, graphs or tables, should say something that cannot be communicated with words. I'll explain by way of illustration.

For a lecture on social stratification several years ago I developed a visual presentation that compared the lives in the US of the very wealthy, the suburban middle class and the very poor, as represented by urban homeless and migrant agricultural workers. I researched how documentary photographers had pictured similar objects and events in the lives of the members of these three strata of society, made slides from their books and organized the slides to be projected by three projectors on to three large screens.[1] Because the images were wall-sized, and the resolution of slide projectors was far sharper than any technology that has replaced it, the presentation was very strong visually.

I began with *housing*, comparing an image looking down at a city block in East Harlem from Bruce Davidson's *E100 Street*[2] to an image from Bill Owens' *Suburbia*, which looked down upon a suburban cul-de-sac. The third image was through the gates of the manor-like home of a wealthy family in a Chicago suburb, from Mary Lloyd Estrin's *To the Manor Born*. In all three images the viewer saw the community from the outside, and although the points of view were different there was enough in common to encourage comparison and contrast: What was the density of families in a particular neighborhood setting? How did neighborhood designs encourage or discourage social interaction with neighbors? What was the estimated square footage of housing per person in each situation? And how did the location of the housing in the United States influence where people of different social classes lived? A series on *sleeping* compared an image of a palatial bedroom from one of Estrin's wealthy family homes, furnished with antiques, to a bed in a suburban box-like bedroom in Owens' suburbia. To picture sleeping arrangements for the poor I showed a room of empty beds, a foot or two apart, in a homeless shelter and a second image of a room in a camp of migrant workers shared by an entire family. I illustrated the category of *water* by showing trim, young adults in elegant clothes on a sailboat in Nantucket (an image from Barbara Norfleet's *All the Right People*) to middle-class suburbanites enjoying an above-ground swimming pool. The image of water in the life of the poor showed a migrant farmworker washing her five-year old child in a river from LeRoy Emmet's book *Fruit Tramps*.[3] The mother is holding the child with one arm wrapped around her and the other grasping a tree branch in a rushing river. I created about twenty-five similar visual comparisons, and I found that the more simple the concept or the phenomena (transportation, dwellings, parties, schools, rites of passage, for example), the more visually provocative the comparison.

The visual information leads to class discussions in which students question virtually all aspects of social stratification; often finding lines of inquiry that I'd never imagined. Often the images lead to second level questions. For example, it is straightforward to portray the work of a migrant apple picker, or a clerk in a bureaucracy, but what about the work of an executive? What is the most socially useful basis for social stratification? Income or assets? Job responsibilities? Honorific status? Ownership of the means of production? Seeing images of housing, transportation and luxury or privation may lead to more meaningful understandings of stratification than do numbers in a table, or they may work with graphic display to build a bigger and better understanding.

The examples cited above are now a few decades old but make the point that while styles of clothes and interior design evolve, very likely the material realities behind the surfaces do not. I ask students to conceptualize earlier manifestations of social class, based on photos, portraits and fine arts paintings (and the web makes it very easy to study these questions). Seeing class differences in the US leads students to investigate social class in other countries or eras. I have, for years, photographed extremes of poverty and wealth in many countries, and I use these images as an introduction. Students are often startled to discover that the slums of Iceland (etc.) are very nice, indeed.

This exercise allows us to connect images of migrant workers to the inexpensive food we take for granted (and this is pretty easy to visualize with photos of tomatoes in a supermarket, with the prices indexed to the typical incomes of various social strata), while other relationships between social location and activity may be more abstract and hard to visualize. I've developed visual essays for several introductory textbooks in the area, including socialization, rituals, liminality, organic and mechanical solidarity, techniques of neutralization, labeling theory, total institutions and stigma, to name a few. Very often one of the most useful strategies is to ask students to compare visual with other data, numerical or otherwise. Doing so leads to the question of what can be visualized and how visualization changes how we think about a concept.

There remains the issue of where to find images to use in these exercises. The easiest answer is that images are everywhere and increasingly easy to get access to, given the web and the numerous sites where free images can be downloaded. But the serious visual sociologist should become a serious student of imagery. For me that has included collecting and studying a few thousand photo books over the years; mainly documentary studies, visual anthropology, history and sociology, historical archives, single artist collections and the like, and of course there are wonderful collections of such books in most large libraries. Images from these studies can be accessed in many ways, though copyright must be respected, but scanning images for lectures has become an acceptable practice. Very often there are website sources for famous photographs and projects from which images may be downloaded. Some of the most useful archives are held by the American government and are easily accessed; the FSA collection is but one example. Clearly the challenge is not in finding visual resources, but keeping all of the data in order and organizing them in a coherent way.

There are different points of view regarding whether one needs to have extensive background on the photographer and other contexts of the photo; my view is that such information helps (for example, you can't really appreciate images from Robert Frank's *The Americans* unless you understand how the book came into being) but free-floating images that you have little information about can also be useful in some circumstances.

One of the best ways to obtain images is to make them oneself. On a recent trip to Turkey I asked a wedding party in downtown Istanbul if I might photograph them to show my students in America and they happily obliged. I later asked permission to photograph two young boys being paraded as sultans on a throne as part of their circumcision ritual. Both were proudly experienced rites of passage that compare nicely with images of more familiar ceremonies in our own society. I simply asked (once through a translator) if I might make the photo, explaining that I was a

Figure 10.1
Social structure, poverty and immigration: in the past twenty years there has been a sizeable immigration to Iceland, primarily from Eastern Europe. Many work in the fish processing plants and live in neighborhoods (pictured) that are regarded as less desirable than normal, middle-class equivalents. In other words, this is as close as one gets to an urban ghetto in Iceland. My guide on this excursion into the class structure of Iceland noted the relative deterioration of the building and the poorly integrated green spaces in front of the building.

professor from the US. If approached politely most would agree to be photographed, but there is moral complexity in this, however. I have to assume that their agreement extends to allowing me to show the photos to my students, but I do not feel comfortable reproducing them here.

It is also useful to photograph material reality sans people. My friends in Iceland recently took me to Polish neighborhoods in Reykjavik, and the images I took in that urban space provide new visual grist for my social stratification image bank. Thor, an architect, was sensitive to urban design issues and he pointed out things I would have missed about the neighborhood of high-rises that made them different, including the allocation of green spaces, the haphazard organization of social spaces and the deteriorated infrastructure (hardly visible to an American used to cities that seem close to falling apart!) that set the immigrant neighborhood apart from the working-class neighborhoods of native Icelanders. In the grocery store I photographed rows of imported Polish pickles, beets and cabbage, and fast food that Thor indicated would not suit Icelandic tastes. In other words, visual clues were everywhere, if you knew how to see them, about new ethnic habitations of a previous homogeneous society.

Of course you don't have to journey to Iceland or Turkey to make interesting sociological photos. In an ongoing project on the Mon Valley river communities (adjacent to Pittsburgh), which exemplify the deteriorated rust belt perhaps more

Figure 10.2

Social structure and poverty, the rust belt: Main street, Clairton, Pennsylvania. Clairton, like many of the former steel towns, has all but collapsed economically. The old main street (pictured) has almost no functioning businesses. Just off what was the main drag, abandoned and deteriorating houses stand among the well-kept housing of those who have found a place in the post-steel economy. This photo shows systemic poverty; the effect of decisions made by steel executives, politicians and urban planners.

than any region in the US, photos of churches, high-rise parking lots at midday, expanding regions of towns given over to fallen-in housing and, eventually, urban wildernesses of weeds and refuse give face to numbers citing population decline, economic collapse and social survival.

The point is that a visual sociologist sees the world in an active way, and since it is now so easy to make photographs, that seeing can be preserved. In fact one of the most important tools for a person using visual imagery in this way is a program like Lightroom (there are several comparable programs), that allows images to be classified in several ways and then retrieved on the basis of multiple term searches. Since I label photos in my Lightroom catalogue on the basis of location and sociological themes (in the example of a Polish neighborhood in Iceland these include *immigrant community; social stratification; Iceland; stores; housing; European cities*—as well as the dates they were made and a rating of their quality) I can later ask to see all images of a certain rating level that pertain to any one or a combination of key words. For example, to prepare a recent lecture on the social significance of death memorials a Lightroom search based on several key words produced more than 100 quality images on cemeteries in several countries, churchyards in the UK, statues of dead politicians, tattoos remembering slain gang members, fascist glorifications of war, Mussolini's family tomb, roadside crosses in the US, impromptu memorials in Rome, and gangland graffiti memorials, to mention a few.

Before Lightroom it would have taken hours to remember and locate all images relevant to such a search, and it would have been easy to forget many along the way. Gathering images on a theme such as death memorials can become a free-floating search for ideas; in this case the question "how do we remember death, and what are its various social functions?" produces answers that we would not have anticipated when we made the photographs. A quaint churchyard in rural England makes a pretty photo but its significance regarding social control in a pre-industrial society may only emerge when it is viewed in the context of a wide variety of other images on a similar topic.

Assignments

Visually based assignments work in many courses, in addition to those dedicated to visual sociology. I often teach a basic sociology course to freshmen students, many of whom are away from home for the first time. I show images in lectures throughout the semester, but usually reserve a fully developed assignment for their Thanksgiving vacation. Often this is their first visit home and they are both excited to be home and feeling something of a stranger to their old sense of the familiar. To encourage them to exercise their sociological eye, I ask them to photograph the social organization of their Thanksgiving feast. I instruct them on the ethics of photographing other people and the need to explain carefully what they're up to; getting permission and making it clear where and how the photos will be shown. I define social organization to include the division of labor, organized by gender, family role and age. I remind them that the division of labor also includes the issue of who labors and who does not. Social organization also includes the organization of consumption, and the norms that guide leisure activities that surround the event. The assignment instructs students to

> photograph as much of the labor that led to the Thanksgiving dinner as you are able to. This includes planning the meal, shopping for the food, preparing dishes and silverware, organizing and cleaning the house, buying wine or other beverages, cooking various dishes, cleaning the kitchen during and after cooking, setting the table, making table decorations, serving the food, replenishing the food, removing and storing left-over food.

Regarding the organization of the meal itself, I ask students to photograph the spatial layout of the table to identify symbolic dimensions such as the head of the table, and to note who serves food and where they sit. They are asked to photograph the rituals, including prayer, carving the turkey and pouring the wine. Even the order of serving has sociological significance: who is served first and allowed to choose the choicest cuts of meat?

Students are to record special clothes or outfits worn for the event, and any rituals unique to their family. Are there special stories told, actions performed, or other events that indicate the special status of the day? They are to record the organization of the dinner itself; the order of dishes served and the combination of specific foods in courses. What would happen if someone violated the rules of food combinations; covering pumpkin pie with gravy or turkey with whipped cream? Or what if Uncle Ned insisted on having his pumpkin pie before the main course? The larger question is to what extent are norm violations visual?

Some things consumed are both dangerous and desired. Who is allowed to consume alcohol and under what circumstances? For example, do those who are cooking begin drinking before dinner? How about those who are not? If you are watching football games, can you drink wine or liquor, or only beer? Are kids or people below legal drinking age allowed to consume alcohol, and under what circumstances? What governs how it is consumed at the dinner? Are there special wines or other drinks that have ritual significance?

Students are required to describe the assignment to their families, to enlist their cooperation. People who do not want to be photographed should, of course, be excluded. A firm understanding must be made as to whether students are gaining the right to show the images exclusively to their professor, or whether those involved would mind the images being shown in public. Often the images are made available to the family members, increasingly easy packaged as a family album, commercially produced by many web-based companies.

Proper certification by Institutional Review Boards can be required for student projects involving human subjects, though most universities exempt student projects from requiring full review.

The Thanksgiving project is a natural for visual sociology because it involves studying people doing things together in an organized way. There are social roles based on gender, age, family membership, and relatives and guests; there are patterns of cooperation that are learned, modified over time and taught to others; and there are outcomes defined by traditions which change as people age and generations replace each other. There are expected emotions and perhaps quasi-sacred objects such as old photo albums that are viewed and spoken about. Other forms of memory are likely evident in specific dishes, glasses or silverware that are reused each time the event is repeated, and it may be that special foods are only served in specific dishes that are otherwise stored away in the china cabinet. People may act in special ways; maybe a toast of thanks performed by the grandfather or reigning adult. There are norms that knit the event together and deviant actions that challenge the normal flow of the script. All of these elements are visible and photographable.

When students return from their field-work projects they have often seen a taken-for-granted reality with new eyes. It can be exciting or disarming to see one's often cherished world performed in a way that closely resembles those described by other students. There are usually discussions as to what constitutes rituals or deviance. Aunt Martha is hitting the sauce, but she did last year and the year before, so is that deviant? Sis's new boyfriend is a chef and disdains football, so he wants to spend the day in the kitchen with the women instead of in the living room with the men, swilling beer and watching game after game . . . can the family survive this deviant display of gender non-conformity?

The feast is made up of things, people and actions, and that makes it a good candidate for visual analysis. Not all sociological scenes are equally prone to visualization, though there is no list of what concepts work and which do not. In the following I describe some of the sociological topics that have worked well.

For a two-week workshop in Italy I once assigned us all to photograph social control. I defined the assignment broadly and we focused on both formal rules and informal norms, as well as norms that guided how rules were broken (for example, under what circumstances is it OK to ignore a red light in traffic?). Later, with Patrizia Faccioli, I elaborated on an aspect of the classroom work with a paper that discussed the norms of urban bicycling in Italy[4] where we explored a large number of norms that guide how bicyclists negotiate urban streets; how they interact with pedestrians, other bicyclists and drivers of cars, buses, scooters and motorcycles, and how, in fact, bicyclists follow some rules and break others. At first the Italian students felt that social control was in fact obvious but soon realized it was not. It was everywhere but hard to see. What I especially recall from this workshop was the transformation of student skepticism into enthusiasm; a topic they treated mostly as unworthy of serious attention became a great puzzle to solve.

I often ask students to imagine how a space becomes social: that is, how it gains its definition through human actions. This is an assignment that is easily adapted to workshops. For example, for a several day IVSA workshop in the city of Antwerp, I asked participants to photograph what I called dualisms in the central city plaza. I identified these as paired opposites such as insider/outsider; above ground/underground; woman/man; young/old; rich/poor; tourist/resident; day/night; conformist/non-conformist. I asked participants to identify how people acted within the norms of the space, and how the opposites in the pairs interacted with each other. The plaza was oddly shaped, with nooks and crannies at ground level and below, where different groups staked out their places at different times of the day or night. The results of the IVSA workshops, which take place at many annual meetings, are shown and discussed at the conclusion of the conference, which allow the participants to compare and contrast their work, and also demonstrates how quickly and efficiently dedicated visual sociologists can produce interesting results.

Students also discover that not all physical spaces are social in the same way. For example, I ask students to study the boundary areas between regions in cities referred to as liminal, or in-between. In natural environments, such as the boundary between a field and a forest, these are areas where species from adjoining environments interact with each other. Liminal urban spaces also combine qualities from their bordering regions to produce a unique environment. An example is the Damstraat in Amsterdam, a street between the university area and the red-light district. The Damstraat is a point of entry into both regions and a buffer between them. The establishments, people and interactions on that street have a distinctive social identity; the norms that guide interaction in that region are different from those in either adjoining area. These differences are visual and can be recorded as a photo, a painting or a graphic representation like a map.

The idea of photographing dualisms is part of an approach I often use in beginning assignments, which is to ask students to make photographs that have more than one topic. There can be any way to describe this: they can be conceptual (like *latent* and *manifest*) or substantive (*ancient* and *modern*). I ask students to find a way to portray the two themes to explore whether they are harmonious or in tension; whether they derive meaning from each other; whether the two themes are a lead into a more detailed sociological investigation; or whether they are restatements of the obvious, or at least the taken-for-granted. Once students begin photographing in this way they often become transformed into sociological seers; visual ideas are everywhere!

Rules, norms, and norm violation can be easy or difficult to represent visually. For example, it is hard to portray highways in the US as social spaces, even though they are full of rules, norms and violations of both. In Italy, however, this was much easier to do because the differences they presented to a North American driver are so dramatic. I made the following photographs as a passenger, holding my camera outside the car window. The photos show (Figure 10.3) how cars edge into the street before they pass into it, trying to force oncoming traffic to slow sufficiently so they can enter, which is very annoying to an American driver but expected by an Italian; (Figure 10.4) the transformation of two lanes to three lanes, a process that allows traffic to actually move more efficiently, though maddening to a driver not used it; and (Figure 10.5) the haphazard merging that takes place at unregulated intersections, where a driver has to become something like a member of an impromptu team made up of strangers organizing to survive the moment and, in fact, advance the interests of all.

Social life can also be inferred from material artifacts distributed through a landscape. For example, a student photographed bus stops throughout Pittsburgh to discover that while the bus stops were the same, other visual clues (unobtrusive measures)[5] suggested the economics of the surrounding region, or the social class, race or ethnicity, age or other statuses of the people who used those sites. Here was a social landscape embedded in unnoticed details.

Geographic Information Systems (GIS), increasingly common, have opened up the potential of this way of thinking. GIS refers to the study of the spatial distribution of information, usually including the statistical analysis of the relations between elements. These could be elements such as trees or green spaces, economic data such as income levels in specific neighborhoods, records of behavior such as violent crime, uses of public transportation or other factors. GIS allows a researcher to see several of these data in relationship to each other. For example, a recent *New York Times* website showed the location of all murders in a

Figure 10.3
Nudging into traffic, Rome.

Figure 10.4
The transformation of two lanes to three, Rome.

Figure 10.5
Creative merging, Rome.

twelve-month period. Moving the cursor over the site of the murder revealed the age, ethnic or racial background of the perpetrator and victim, the average incomes of the neighborhood where the event took place and the date of the event. Of course it was possible to assemble these kinds of data before there was GIS software, but it was cumbersome, tedious and inefficient, limited by the practicalities of drawing maps on transparent material and stacking them on each other. Most use of GIS in sociology draws upon pre-existing data from censuses, government data sources or other data banks. Students can, of course, create their own data to be integrated with those existing in public banks. For example a student recently combined projects in visual sociology and urban ecology courses to qualitatively assess different Pittsburgh neighborhoods. Her approach was to photograph Starbucks coffee shops in various locations through the city. The distribution of Starbucks coffee shops is by itself a sociologically interesting phenomenon, more so when combined with economic or crime data relevant to various neighborhoods. The student attempted to show how similar environments—the coffee shops—took on different character-istics, moods, and qualities in different settings. The student found it difficult to get strangers to cooperate, but asking permission to photograph allowed her to encounter groups of friends who met at the corner shop regularly, some of whom eventually agreed to participate. While it would be difficult to gain permission to photograph the interiors of fast food restaurants, one could record observed information on charts and graphs that would specify who (by gender, age and clothing cues) uses the spaces, what they purchase and how long they stay. Speaking locally, a downtown Pittsburgh McDonald's is a haven for the homeless (especially in the winter); others in the suburbs are filled with teens on dates. The way these different crowds fill up the same space makes them into different social realities. It is also important to teach students that their work can be used to unanticipated ends, and we must face the fact that some projects will produce knowledge that we may not want to make public. Is it in the interest of the homeless to publicize their use of fast food restaurants as refuges from the cold of winter?

Assignments that draw on semiotics allow students to see commonplace realities in new ways. For example, a student recently photographed a high school football game to highlight the symbolic dimensions of the event. She first realized that almost everyone in the stadium identified their position in the social drama through the clothes or objects they wore. Team players, of course, wore exact replicas of color-coded uniforms, usually with images of totems that identified with the town and school. The colors were repeated on clothes worn by fans, band members, cheerleaders and others, and they adorned signs, flags and other objects in the stadium. Students spoke about how strongly they were still attached to the colors of their high schools (noting that only certain colors were acceptable for school colors; no pastels!). The officials of the game were dressed in white pants and striped shirts, but the most highly ranked official wore a white hat and others wore black hats. Cheerleader uniforms had a muted sexy quality from the styles of many years ago; the uniforms of band members also had not changed in decades. The uniforms of the players were both utilitarian and stylized, and they mimicked the uniforms worn by professional teams. There were no modifications to any of the uniforms and no one wore the wrong uniform for the wrong activity, except that a muddy football player joined the school band to play for the half time show. The reverse—that is, a band member playing in his band uniform on the football team—is impossible to imagine, for practical and symbolic reasons.

The student photographed the rituals performed throughout the game, including audience participation in singing, standing and placing one's hand over one's heart to sing sacred songs. At the beginning of the game the team, led by the team captain (indicated by special markings on his uniform), ran through a long tunnel of cheerleaders on to the field, bursting a huge paper barrier that sealed off the end of the tunnel. Other rituals involved synchronized or spontaneous cheering, but only for certain events or plays. It is sarcastic to cheer for routine plays, but it is done when a team or a player is doing poorly.

Many symbols are obvious but students must be reminded that what is obvious to them would not be to their counterparts in Indonesia. They might note that the jeans they purchase are hip, not because of their cut, but because of the advertised image that goes along with them. Other symbols work for reasons that cannot be explained. Colors of clothes mean a great deal to gang or sorority members; sports logos and colors can also have a wide range of meanings. I've been surprised by how important professional team symbols are for college students, both male and female, and at times these meanings escalate to a larger universe. In Chicago recently I observed that African-American men wear White Sox hats and shirts and Caucasian men wear the symbols and colors of the Cubs. I observed carefully and saw no exceptions, though I have no idea how and why this pattern exists. Students now photograph American flags made into clothes, which they define as vaguely patriotic, and they are surprised to learn that the same symbols worn in the 1960s led to arrest. In any case, assigning students to photograph and try to explain symbols they and their friends consume is a good way to begin to explain semiotics.

Just as I have listed several sociological ideas that I've successfully made visual, I could list topics that students have explored successfully. But I think it would be better simply to say that assignments of these sorts usually create dialogue that explores root definitions of sociology. We tend to assume we understand the meanings of complex ideas but we are often sloppier in our thinking than we think. And there is no final visual verification of a given idea or concept, precisely because the point of viewing and interpreting it is forever changing. Visual exploration has a role in all this. I know that my own understanding of sociological ideas changes when I see the ideas represented in images made by my students. I have also learned from students' photos how poorly they have sometimes understood my teaching. In short, visual expressions of sociological ideas express the discipline in a way that words and numbers will never do.

Courses in visual sociology

There are now visual sociology courses in many departments in the US, Europe and other parts of the world. They vary a great deal and participants in the IVSA listserv often exchange syllabi and discuss assignments, approaches and challenges.

Most people who taught visual sociology in the 1970s and 1980s, when these courses first emerged, were knowledgeable about documentary photography, experienced in field methods and interested in symbolic interaction or other theories of micro interaction. In the early 1980s at SUNY Potsdam, I designed a semester-length course, team-taught with a photography professor, Steve Sumner, and we sought an equal number of sociology and art students to make teams with a member from each discipline. Our idea, and it worked well, was that art students could teach sociology students about photography and vice versa. We taught students to develop film and print photos in darkrooms that were then common in colleges and universities. Given the amount of work and money that was required to make a photographic print, there were only two photo assignments in a course, and these resembled assignments in field-work courses; visual studies of institutions, popular culture social movements (a successful project was a study of the Deadheads, the tribe that then followed the band The Grateful Dead), cultures of occupations (a memorable project came from a student who rode with the police in their cruiser for several nights a week for a month and photographed the routines of their work), studies of social change (students found historical photos in local museums or other sources and rephotographed them), the norms of dating (a team of two so attached itself to a high school senior that they photographed her prom date; and, coincidentally, the team members, who had not known each other prior to the assignment, got married a few years later). We tended to assign longer projects based on a standard field-methods course, often having students photograph the same institution or setting several times. In these instances it was the development of more complex understandings that often resulted from re-visualizing the same setting over time. Students were pleased to learn to develop film and print photos in a darkroom, and we usually had an exhibition of the final projects in a gallery or an art department hallway.[6]

We adopted the idea of in-class critique from fine arts courses as we encouraged students to ask their peers "What sociological idea are you exploring? What elements in these photos present the idea well and which do not? How could you explore the idea better?" In other words, the quest was not for a "good photo" but for photos with convincing sociological content. It is often said, however, that photos that engage viewers are perfectly OK, just like well-written sociology is better than turgid, jargon-laden prose. In other words, a sociological photo could be artful, engaging and moving if that increases its sociological power. If it detracts from the sociology, artiness is a problem. For readings we mostly worked from field-methods texts and documentary photography, as well as the handful of articles being written by sociologists interested in the visual approach.

The digital revolution has required some rethinking. At first many of us clung to the old ways, assuming that processing film and making prints was an indispensable part of visual sociology, even a rite of passage (and, correspondingly, that making photographs so easily in the digital world would somehow cheapen the process). Early digital cameras were not very good, so it was easy to remain committed to the higher quality images created by film, and there was the unstated assumption that we would work in black and white, like serious documentary photographers did, whether it suited the topic or not. But as darkrooms went dark and digital cameras improved it was clear that for visual sociology to survive it had to adapt to the digital world, and to do so would offer real benefits.

As digital cameras improved so did presentation software and hardware. Photos could be made instantly (forget about development and printing!) and viewed immediately by plugging memory cards into the computers and projectors that are now part of most classrooms. But like so many advances this has come at a cost. Making black and white photos or color transparencies was expensive and time consuming, so students took each photo seriously. The least expensive SLR (the old faithful Pentax K1000!) to the fanciest Nikon had the same manual controls and so we easily taught how aperture, shutter speed, lens choice, film type, artificial light and other technical aspects of photography created a visual grammar. As a result we collectively became better photographers. It is often difficult to teach these same basics on inexpensive digital cameras because the controls are generally automated or reduced to generic settings; for example, a "nighttime" setting on a consumer digital camera generally boosts ISA, opens apertures and turns on flashes. This produces an image that makes sense to the computer inside the camera but may have nothing to do with a photographer's intentions. For example, if you want to represent movement by blur, and freeze the background information at night, you use a long exposure, a tripod, a low ISO and a small aperture; simple to do with a manual camera and often very hard to do on a typical consumer level digital camera with programmed settings.

As digital cameras have become easier to control manually it has been easier to teach the craft of photography. Now even moderately priced small sensor digital cameras produce remarkable photos in all but the lowest light, and professional quality digital cameras now make better images than are possible with 35 mm film, with the possible exception of rendering extreme shades in the highlights and shadows. Because it has become so easy to make photos, it has become possible to design increasingly elaborate assignments, and to expect students to concentrate their energies on visual thinking rather than mastering film development and printing.

Learning to read photos

Most visual sociology courses begin by teaching students to see photographs in a sociological way. I ask students to deconstruct a single image for several minutes

Figure 10.6
Vietnam war protest, St. Paul, Minnesota, 1970.

or by writing two or three pages, cataloguing the details that are normally overlooked in the glance that one usually gives a photo. Because most students, as well as the rest of us, generally glance at photos and move on, this way of looking requires instruction. Earlier in the book I offered an example; here is another I often share with students.

After giving students two or three minutes to record their interpretations, I first ask them to imagine the factual/historical context of the photo, which might be the text you'd find attached to the photo if you found it in an archive. In this case it would read:

This was one of the largest demonstrations against the Vietnam war in Minnesota, about a month after the Kent State demonstrations in May, 1970, in which the National Guard opened fire on demonstrators, killing four. The result was a national moratorium against the war, and universities went on strike. This demonstration took place on Summit Avenue, a stately boulevard that runs between St. Paul and Minneapolis.

Secondly, we examine the photograph to read its sociological meaning. In this case the themes include:

The photograph shows a social movement that had come into existence to oppose the war in Vietnam. This demonstration was led by returned veterans, some gravely wounded. For years it had been assumed that soldiers and anti-war protestors were cultural poles apart, and this photo shows that as the war continued, this divide had been broached, at least for some. This demonstration, like all large events, required planning and compromise, the expenditure of money, and the mobilization of volunteers that is evident in the visual aspects of the orderly event.

The photo also records a wide range of socially constructed identities:

The veterans wear parts of their old uniforms, including worn fatigue jackets and floppy hats. Some wear uniform jackets with insignias and medals. Every veteran wears his military boots. Most of the uniforms are worn casually and are startling in the context of long hair, beards and anti-war insignias that connect the vets to the non-military anti-war demonstrators. The identities seem to be full of contradiction; the returned soldiers look more like hippies, who were defined as unpatriotic dopeheads by the political right. The expectation was that soldiers were to look like soldiers, only appearing in public in crisp, clean, uniforms, hair recently shorn, standing at attention.

There is much symbolism in the photo:

The signs and symbols the soldiers and protesters wear and carry combine familiar anti-war slogans: "Bring the troops home NOW," with an unusual banner that carries the message: "Death wins all wars." Some protestors carry American flags (this is notable since many politicians and citizens linked anti-war demonstrators with lack of patriotism), and others carry drawings of the peace dove, which was the symbol of anti-war candidate Eugene McCarthy's presidential campaign two years before. The leaders of the march carry a crude coffin with an American flag painted onto its surface and they march alongside the figure of Death. None of these symbols were unusual in and of themselves, but their combination was unusual.

Finally, there is the subjectivity of the photographer to consider:

I was a college senior and since my college had been on strike I had not graduated. After years of constant worry about the war, a lucky number in the first draft lottery had suddenly lifted me like a bird above the politics of the moment. It was a heady, almost impossible feeling to define. Yet the war persisted, with no end in sight. My feelings about the future were highly confused.

I was inspired by the demonstration and I did not like being one of many photographers on the edge of the action. As the demonstration approached I walked off the sidewalk toward the center of the street; framed the image and released the shutter of the camera.

Deconstructing photos takes some imagination and patience. There is often much information waiting to be interpreted but it is possible to overreach, especially when we have only minimal knowledge about the situation portrayed or the photographer.

John Berger and Jean Mohr's experimental ethnography of modern European peasant life, *Another Way of Telling*[7] is an invitation to engage in the process of photo deconstruction. The book begins with short essays about how photos communicate, the politics and ethics of making images and a brief descriptive background on peasant life in twentieth-century Europe. When this was published in 1982 Berger was already famous for his commentaries on photography and art history, and he had moved from London to a small village in the Alps to write novels. The book represents a new direction in his work with photographer Mohr (with whom he had done several books),[8] as they encouraged people to engage photos differently. Berger introduces a gallery of 150 of Mohr's uncaptioned photos: "We are far from wanting to mystify. Yet it is impossible for us to give a verbal key or storyline to this sequence of photographs . . ."[9] The photos suggest the story of an elderly peasant woman in the Alps who has lived through two world wars, spent part of her life as a domestic servant in the capital and returned as an elderly woman to the village, where she works on her farm during the day and knits in the evening. The photos appear to recall memories assembled over a lifetime; Berger asks us to imagine the narrative they imply. I have asked students to write a story from the woman's point of view and since they usually know little about European peasants this exercise requires that they do some background research before taking the plunge. The goal of narrating the photos becomes a kind of sociological puzzle set in a historical context. Practically speaking it is a path into a mystery that has no final resolution, yet has the potential for new insights.

As we learn to look carefully at photos we question who has the right to photograph whom, and under what circumstances. Increasingly, visual sociology assignments must pass Institutional Review Board purview, but the larger question raises the question of whether a signed consent form really covers the issues. Are those who sign the consent form aware of what they are giving away? It is necessary to assess potential harm in each assignment, and to avoid assignments that may inadvertently lead to harm (which are remarkably common). We also remind ourselves that once we place a photo into the public eye (increasingly easy in social media such as Facebook) we cannot control its future life or the impact it may have on the people pictured.

Additionally, I remind students that photos made by documentary photographers and photojournalists show people who can be identified, and that visual sociologists, photographing in public or with the permission of those they meet in private spaces, can be reasonably expected to work in the same way.

Teaching how photos communicate

I also teach students how the construction of a photo contributes to its meaning. I compare identically framed photographs made with different lenses, shutter speeds, aperture settings and ISOs to show how these choices define what a photo looks like and thus what it means (see the Appendix for a handout that explains this information). We discuss points of view, framing (and lens choice) and the treatment of light, either natural or supplemental. A photographer such as Robert Frank, who did not use a strobe, can be compared to one who did, such as Jacob Riis, and the messages and meanings of their images can be compared on the basis of the simple matter of adding light or not.

I make the point that photography is about light and ideas, and that each camera sees differently and is thus able to make different kinds of statements. A good example is shown in the portraits made by Milton Rogovin, discussed in Chapter 5 and easily found on a quick web search. Rogovin looked down into his double lens Rolleiflex to photograph his subjects, who were mostly the urban poor. The position of Rogovin's camera in relation to his subjects elevated them and lent them an aura of dignity. Rogovin didn't thrust the camera into their faces, and with his head lowered he assumed a posture of submission and respect. They would have to be patient as Rogovin set the controls of the manual camera, and as a result they looked relaxed and yet serious. The perspective captured by the Rolleiflex does not include a lot of sideways context, so the subjects are generally centered in the frame. The overwhelming sense of the photos is dignity, calm and respect. Had Rogovin approached his subjects quickly and photographed them at eye level with a modern reflex camera the portraits would have communicated an entirely different reality.

Though expensive cameras do certain things well, they are not necessary, and their superior resolution and clarity may even get in the way of making certain kinds of visual statements. For example, during the 1970s several artists used plastic Diana cameras, which then sold for $1.98. Nancy Rexroth was one of these photographers, and she used the soft focus, inconsistent lenses to communicate the feelings of dreams and faded memories of childhood visits from the East Coast back to the Midwest. She writes that "The Diana's made for feelings. Diana images are often something you might see faintly in the background of a photograph . . ."[10] Mark Power asserted that the Diana images

> describe subjective feelings, not facts. They are autobiographical vignettes, not environments, social landscapes, or documents. They deal with the interior reality of a little girl's memories, not with the exterior appearance of things in time and space in front of a lens.[11]

In this case, it was the camera reduced to a plastic version of its essentials that made a certain visual statement possible, and students should take Rexroth's example as an inspiration to use whatever camera they have to its particular potential. In fact there are apps on iPhone cameras and controls in Lightroom that produce almost exactly same effect.

In another example of how modest cameras affect what sociological messages an essay communicates, Jacob Holdt documented his trips through the American underclass with a cheap, half-frame camera.[12] Holdt, a Dane, traveled for several years on the $40 he had arrived in the States with and he sold his blood to pay for film and the printing of the photos that became the book. His photos are an artless mix of black and white and color, framed without regard, lit with the glare of a cheap strobe or the faded light of underexposed film: the result is a vivid portrait of the politics and experiences of American poverty. The directness of the vision is a result of the lack of concern about photography itself: the photos are a glance into an otherwise unseen world. An expensive camera would never have survived the life Holdt lived on the road, and attempting to make artful photographs of the world he saw would contradict what he was saying.

This reminds us that it is necessary to understand how a camera works to record an idea successfully. The greatest challenge posed by inexpensive digital cameras may not be the quality of their lenses or their small sensors, but in overcoming their automatic features.

Learning to read a photo, and understanding how the technological aspects of photography influence what photos look like, leads students to understand how the meaning of all imagery is constructed. A tidy way to tie this up is with Howard Becker's question of whether visual sociology, documentary photography and photojournalism are actually different, or only images seen differently because of their contexts.[13] Because many students hope to work as image-makers this discussion can be extremely useful, if sometimes demystifying.

Assignments in a visual sociology course

The first photo assignment in my current visual sociology course is to create a self-portrait without self. I suggest ways to render the personal into the sociological via images of objects, places, activities; and ideas, values, emotions and dreams. I ask them to make photos to investigate how they are socially rooted, and also how they are challenged by unresolved issues and disappointments. The projects are shown in class and submitted with written essays (again, see the Appendix for the exact assignment).

Many recent examples stand out. One student, Russian by birth and adopted as a baby by American parents, made a small physical shrine that featured her only photograph of her mother, whom she had never met, as an attractive young woman in St Petersburg. The portrait was surrounded by objects her mother had left for her, and in the foreground she had placed an egg. The photograph was lit by the slanting rays of the late afternoon sun and had a feeling of melancholy and yearning; a startlingly powerful image.

Recently a student from the first class I taught in Amsterdam contacted me to ask about restarting her work in photography after a two-decade layoff. I sent the assignment on self-portraiture and she sent her images and text a week later. I include them here because they show how a small number of photographs and paragraphs can explore major life themes, including death and parenthood.

Self-portraiture without self, by Jasmijn Antonisse

My first struggle in life was the fact that I had to face my dyslexia. I was seven or eight years old and still could not read or write, which made me insecure, and it still does. I became shy, introverted and timid. After a while I stopped talking altogether.

My mother brought me to a dance school where I found my love of dance, a way of expressing myself without words. This gave me confidence and determination and I became more positive in life. This power of seeing things, although at first seeming negative, can make you search for your own qualities and strong points.

Words in motion

My mother was a powerful woman who had a big influence on me. If I had to make a decision I would ask her for advice. Our love of art, dance and opera linked us together. This very close relationship had also a down side, as I would experience later on in life.

The sudden death of my mother had a big emotional impact on me. I was with her when she went in a septic shock. My life fell apart and

Figure 10.7
Trapped in words.
(Photographs in Figures
10.7–10.15 by Jasimijn
Antonisse.)

Figures 10.8–10.10
Son dancing.

Figure 10.11 (near right)
Portrait in leaves.

Figure 10.12 (far right)
Light beyond.

Figure 10.13 (below)
Perseverance: artificial
insemination.

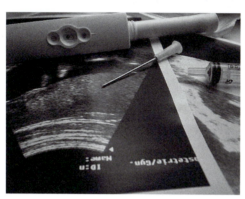

stopped. The struggle to get over the guilty feeling of the death of my mother is horrible and it will never totally be gone.

I had to make my own decisions now and had to learn to cope on my own. This was something I never had done before. I started relying on the wrong people and made a lot of mistakes. Luckily I started to believe in myself again and found myself in all the pain, sorrow and loneliness. It made me a stronger person.

A child was one of the wishes I had, but how? I waited for the right partner but they never came. So I had to make the biggest decision of my life and to do this on my own, because I was not getting any younger.

The road to pregnancy was hard and an emotional rollercoaster. Every attempt hoping that this time it will work, and when it didn't, trying to get over the loss. But not giving up is what I learned in my life so perseverance gave me a healthy baby boy. Now I had not only to make decisions for myself but also for another living person.

I became a Mom.

Again the struggle of hoping and trying to believe in myself paid off. I tried for a second child but had to make my second hardest decision in my life to stop pursuing that wish and let it go. At my age the chance that my second child would have medical problems made me think it was not fair to my son if his life would be put upside down. With pain in my heart I decided to give up my dream.

Sometimes in life you have to let go and find love in the things you already have.

Jasmijn described her work on the essay:

Figure 10.14
Becoming Mom.

My goal as a photographer was to show my transformation during my life, especially the things I learned. To embrace the positive things, learn and reflect on the bad things but to not let them ruin your life.

The photos tell the story of change and metamorphosis. I try to link words and emotions, and in other photos places and emotion to tell this story.

I decided to shoot the first photos in black and white, because that is the part of the history of my youth that I will never be getting back. After my mom died there aren't people any more who can tell me about my childhood. The second series is in color and resembles the period of growing up, and starting my own life.

It was difficult not to make the photos too sentimental and stay close to the emotions objectively.

I have to say that it was an intense voyage for me. It brought me to places I have not gone to for a long time, and I looked at pictures I did not see in a long while.

The cemetery is a place I visit every week. Now I had to walk the long road once more to this silent place. But this time it was different. It brought back memories of loneliness and pain but also let me see beyond that sorrow.

Also the pictures of my mum in her younger years gave me an opening to start thinking of the relationship we had and the one that is now growing and developing with my own son.

This assignment gave me the opportunity to see how I have developed into what I am today.

Figure 10.15
Transformation of past to present.

The exploration of self, powerfully demonstrated by Jasmijn, is followed up by a discussion of visual ethnography. Students are to study and photograph a location, an institution, or an event. I ask students to photograph behavior that is guided by rules and norms, and to understand how to separate the two. I ask students to identify groups based on age, gender or other visual markers and to record how groups do things with each other and with members of other groups. The material settings have actual or symbolic boundaries that are usually visible. Places become social when they contain symbols that influence what and how things take place, and I encourage students to photograph small details as well as overviews and layouts of spaces.

I ask students to draw a map of the space and add elements they can see but not photograph. One student spent several afternoons observing trials in a city courtroom, and since photography is not allowed, she used her skill as an artist to visualize the social processes she observed.

The assignment includes a written essay that defines the project's goals and describes methods used, including the number of shooting sessions, the number of photos made, and the editing process that produced the final essay. An important element in the essays is self-criticism: I ask students to judge what went well, and aspects of the project that did not live up to their expectations.

The sociology of the subjective

The third assignment is introduced with a short review of fine arts photography, including the work of Alfred Stieglitz and Minor White, after which I show images and read passages from sociologist Richard Quinney's meditative and visual essays. The goal is to use photography to express feelings and thoughts within a sociological framework. This assignment can produce work that is closer to the fine arts than to sociology but when we ask the question of what self-expressions are permissible in a society at a given moment, and by whom, our quest becomes more sociological.

To encourage students to photograph freely and creatively I show the work of Russian photographer Alexander Rodchenko, who in the early twentieth century photographed Russian society in a way intended to embody the reality of the revolutionary moment. He photographed the mundane aspects of the new social world from odd angles and in strong patterns of light and shadow to claim *A society is reborn!* Rodchenko's and others' experiments awaken in students a freer regard for the camera as a means to explore their own subjectivities. It is radical to aim the camera straight up or down for the first time. Doing so makes students aware that they are trapped in a commonplace (visual) apprehension of the world, a level universe seen at eye level and represented in a rectangular format, with objects at appropriate distances from each other.

I also ask students to photograph aspects of the mundane world that take their meanings from human design. They are to become a fish and see the water they swim in. For this assignment one student who was an athlete discovered *grass* and set about to photograph its manifestations on athletic fields (in plastic); manicured and chemically treated on suburban lawns; as a neglected surface on forgotten urban parks; as a harvested feed for farm animals; and pictured in landscapes. Suddenly, she reported, the whole world was grass but in each case it was socially constructed in a different way. This is a fairly easy assignment to get wrong; it requires students who can muster an ethnomethodological imagination to deconstruct the mundane meanings of their lives.

Finally, still speaking of the subjective, I assign students to photograph what they imagine to be the world seen through the eyes of another. One of the more interesting examples was a student who photographed his dog's perspective on their typical walk through the park. He fastened his camera to a monopod that he held upside down at the dog's level, firing images with a long cable release. He used a lens that approximated the perspective of a dog's vision, which he determined from veterinary textbooks. Because dogs see monochromatically he photographed in black and white. He followed along with his dog and photographed the objects, other dogs and people that the dog interacted with, including fire hydrants. With this example, the class began to see how they took for granted their visual perception of the world—which was created by their height, a level horizon and the routine things they looked at—and began to see the world as seen by a dog. The student also regaled the class with the interesting conversations he had with strangers who wondered what he was up to.

Three to four assignments can be completed in a single semester when one does not have to develop or print film. Because a big part of the class is student commentary it is necessary to limit class size to about fifteen students, or what a typical field-work course would enroll. Time limits of student presentations need to be strictly enforced so that rambling presentations do not take over the class. Generally, not all students can present all assignments and the opportunity to share one's work must be fairly distributed. Typically the classes develop a strong identity as students learn to critique each other's work and to offer support to those who are intimidated (or terrified!) by the thought of showing their work.

There are, of course, many other strategies for assignments in a contemporary visual sociology course, some of which are listed in the Appendix. The assignments presented here move from self and identity to social organization to various forms of subjectivity. Other logics may guide other assignment logics. As noted, a visual sociology course can also be based on a semester-long project focused on a single setting or institution, essentially adding a visual dimension to a field-methods course.

Teaching visual sociology through documentary film

Teaching sociology through non-fiction films has been expensive and difficult until recently. For example, when I taught courses on documentary film in the 1980s I had to locate a 16 mm print via (then expensive!) daytime long distance phone calls and letters (there was no internet of course), pay a stiff rental fee, have the film shipped from a venue such as the Museum of Modern Art, secure a 16 mm projector (and learn how to run it), project the film and then ship it immediately back to the distributer. The film was easy to scratch, break or otherwise ruin and the projectors were finicky. Nevertheless I taught the course several times. I raised funds from a sympathetic dean and scheduled an evening showing of the films to the community as well as the students. In the pre-Netflix world there was interest in unusual films, and the evening showings for the community were almost always full.

My course asked two questions: How did we understand society through non-fiction film as compared to written texts? And, how did the evolving technology of film, audiences and social contexts affect statements made by documentary filmmakers? We began with Robert Flaherty's 1922 *Nanook of the North* to study how the non-European native was seen, understood and portrayed when much of the world was colonized by Europe and North America. We studied how the then-current technology affected what could be filmed, and how the relationship between the filmmaker and the filmed subjects was implied by the film.[14] We looked at film as an aspect of social revolution in Russian filmmaker Dziga Vertov's *Man with a Movie Camera* (1929) and *Three Songs for Lenin* (1934), as we studied how film had become an aspect of social revolution. The Russian "agit-trains" that took news of the revolution into the vast expanses of Russia included cars with equipment that allowed film to be developed, edited and projected. Films were made on location and shown to peasants who had hardly experienced electricity. I compared the Russian films to American films of the same era, such as Pare Lorentz's *Plow That Broke the Plains* (1936), which was artful propaganda for the 1930s Roosevelt administration.

Interesting case studies reside in films made by Hollywood director John Ford during World War Two. His *Battle of San Pietro* presented the routine violence of war so convincingly that it was only used as a training film (and was protested by many in the military) until several decades later. His 1946 film *Let There Be Light* was intended to assure the public that soldiers could be easily cured of the stress and trauma of battle (now called post-traumatic stress syndrome), yet it was seen as so damning by the military that it was not released until the late 1960s. In fact the film suggests that it is relatively easy to heal the psychological wounds of war, and it has a decidedly hokey ending. It certainly makes the case that what we are willing to accept as a filmic representation of reality has changed mightily in the past decades, and the very idea of documentary has evolved almost beyond recognition. That these and other classic films are easily viewed on YouTube makes their use almost unimaginably easy, given how difficult it was to locate and rent them in the recent past.

I used George Stoney's 1952 *All My Babies: A Midwife's Own Story*, to show how a midwife training film has become in hindsight a visual ethnography of southern African-American life. We moved to the question of how documentary film was revolutionized by hand-held cameras and portable sound synchronization, developed about 1960 at MIT. One of the films I showed from this era was Albert and David Maysles' *The Salesman*, which describes four Bible salesmen who ply their wares door to door in poor neighborhoods, but there are several of that era that are equally powerful. The course ended with contemporary documentaries by Frederick Wiseman, which examined several specific American institutions.[15] At times developments in non-fiction filmmaking were so influential that they constituted an avant-garde art movement; for example, *cinéma-vérité*, a product of portable sound sync cameras and recorders, became a worldwide artistic movement that influenced feature films, writing and journalism. This in and of itself becomes an interesting sociological theme.

Video revolutionized both documentary and the use of film in teaching, making it possible to make non-fiction films much more cheaply, and with the arrival of VHS it became possible to show videos in class. Instead of a bulky and expensive 16 mm system, suddenly one could buy or rent a VHS recorder and hook it to a normal television. But there was a huge downside: films transferred to video were degraded in quality and cropped to fit a TV. The experience of watching film also changed; a 16 mm film could fill a large screen in a moderate sized room, simulating a small movie theatre. A TV of the first generation video era was typically about 30 inches from corner to corner, the color was washed out and the non-HD resolution was poor. For those who had worked with 16 mm films, video of this era was a big step backwards.

VHS eventually evolved to HD DVDs, which recaptured much of the quality of film. Most modern classrooms include a computer tethered to a ceiling mounted projector, so showing any visual display, whether PowerPoint, still images, or film or video, is now very easy. Programs such as YouTube have made previously large numbers of non-fiction film available, mostly for free, though often at a compromised level of quality.

One would have thought all this availability would have led to increasing sophistication among sociologists regarding the use of film in teaching. Yet it may even work against its use; there may be too much available and no simple way to sift through for the best material. For example, the website Topdocumentary[16] (chosen arbitrarily from several documentary distributors) offers several hundred non-fiction films on topics including 9/11, comedy, drugs, economics, the environment, health, history, media, nature and wildlife, philosophy, politics, psychology, sexuality, sports, technology, arts and artists, biography, conspiracy, military and war, music and performing arts, mystery, religion, science and society. The most respected repository of documentary and ethnographic film, Documentary Educational Resources, now has a catalogue with several thousand titles. It is not simple to separate the wheat from the chaff.

Documentary film, however, continues to have a strong presence in culture and equally strong relevance for sociology. For example, Michael Moore's movies about gun violence, healthcare, 9/11 and other topics[17] seem to have returned documentary to the critical, ironic posture it took in the 1960s and 1970s. Documentaries by Frederick Wiseman, now more than thirty in number, explore a wide range of important sociological themes and have been shown to audiences in the many millions. The distribution company Appalshop, which describes itself as "a non-profit multi-disciplinary arts and education center" supports filmmaking and audio production focused mostly on Appalachia, and the ninety-nine films that they currently distribute are a specific canon with a consistent quality and point of view. Sociological filmmakers David Redman and Ashley Sabin created the distribution company Carnivalesque Films[18] inspired by Mikhail Bakhtin, which "curates stories united by the raw and startling sensibilities of transgression, spectacle, and variations of truth and falseness." The ten films currently on their distribution list include studies of globalization, the Mexican dream, homelessness after Katrina and other similarly contemporary social issues. Clearly documentary film has become a vital resource and it is available rather cheaply. For many sociology departments its use is now common.

It would be natural, of course, to teach visual sociology by teaching students to make films. Why is this still rare? Near professional quality cameras now cost a small fraction of what they did just a few years ago. Most students carry smart phones that are film cameras and recording devices, which is hardly believable when one remembers the difficulty of making movies with synchronized sound just a few decades ago. Inexpensive point and shoot cameras have credible video capability and several digital SLRs now shoot in high definition movie mode; their large sensors and excellent lenses produce high quality results. Some of the most influential films have been made with some of the most modest equipment, so available technology is no longer the limiting factor. But where is the instruction and inspiration to make these films? I do not know of a single sociological qualitative methods text that includes a serious discussion of film or video making, and the topic is largely missing from the standard texts on visual methods. Decades ago the sociologist Roy Francis began teaching students to make 8 mm films[19] and there have been courses taught in more experimental curricula that include filmmaking. There are texts on filmmaking that are appropriate for teaching sociology students to make films[20] but they are largely unread by sociologists.

Another reason so few sociologists produce and teach non-fiction film is because there is virtually no training in graduate schools in filmmaking and film is not considered equal to written scholarship in most evaluations of scholarly work. This is partly because the distribution networks are not peer-reviewed. But it also reflects a mistrust of film as a legitimate way to express sociological ideas. As a result there are only a handful of sociologists who produce professional films. These include Jim Ault, whose 1987 film with Michael Camerini, *Born Again*, examines fundamentalist Christianity, and John Grady, who made six documentary films between 1982 and 1995 as a member of Cine Associates. David Redmon, who has a Ph.D. in sociology, directed several non-fiction films and is currently working full time as a filmmaker. Finally, DePaul University sociologist Greg Scott teaches filmmaking in a sociology department, and makes films as well as written research. These rare examples (and I have surely missed others) make the point that film works as sociological research. It is also extraordinary to realize that in the US alone there are many thousand members of the ASA (American Sociological Association) and likely fewer than ten who are professional-level filmmakers.

The newness of the digital revolution is part of the explanation. In the early 1980s, Steve Papson and I made a twenty-two-minute 16 mm documentary, *Ernie's Sawmill*. It was an arduous affair practically; not to mention the challenges presented by the filmmaking itself. We had to drive 350 miles to New York to rent a 16 mm camera, and more than that distance to work on a borrowed flatbed editor in Buffalo. This was a huge effort and expense, absorbing several months, for a project that had a brief life in a handful of film festivals and university showings, and was not considered seriously in my annual report or tenure file. I recall realizing that every time we started film rolling through our rented CP 16, we were spending about what it cost to feed my family for a week.

The natural connection between documentary film and sociology cannot, however, be ignored forever. Surely costs having dropped so dramatically, visual sociology will soon be able to encourage the institutionalization of non-fiction filmmaking in sociology curricula as part of its own canon. I am currently finishing off a one-hour documentary film produced by a small collective of two professors and five journalism and sociology graduate students. The factors that have thus far contributed to the success of our experience include:

- a feeder course that identified a small number of students who were highly motivated to make the film;
- a sympathetic dean who allowed two senior professors to team-teach a two-semester course with five students;
- a group of students willing and able to spend a great deal of time in the field, and a field setting (a halfway house for ex-incarcerated drug addicts) which became an enthusiastic partner in the project;
- a funding source to cover a minimal budget of about $4,000;
- the development of a filming and editing process that resembled sociological field work. This included in-depth interviews, full transcription of all footage, coding that resembled typical qualitative research procedures and cutting the raw footage to reflect coding decisions. While the final edit is in process, the quality seems sound and the learning experience for all involved has been intense, valuable and productive.

At this moment there are four professors in different departments (psychology, sociology and journalism) at my university who are teaching via the production of documentary films. With more and more students learning the rudiments of film editing via free software programs such as iMovie (that is, if you use a Mac!) and competent with fairly daunting software programs like Final Cut, it will certainly be natural for sociology to take advantage of this extraordinary version of visual sociology.

Teaching visual sociology with feature films

It has become common to show feature films in sociology classes, sometimes in a thoughtful way, and surely, sometimes, unfortunately, as a way for lazy professors to get out of their lecture responsibilities. At Duquesne University, for example, for several years our course in Social Theory has been organized around feature films. This was the creation of retired professor Eleanor Fails, who used films including *Casablanca* (1942), *Breaker Morant* (1979) and *Death of a Salesman* (1951) to explore classics of Marx, Durkheim and Weber.[21] When I taught the course I adopted Fails' model, and had students view Chaplin's *Modern Times* (1936) to accompany my discussion of Marx's critique of capitalism; Ridley Scott's *Gladiator* (2000) to explore Weber's analysis of traditional, charismatic and bureaucratic authority; and Peter Weir's *Witness* (1985), to explore Durkheimian ideas about mechanical and organic solidarity and the division of labor.

Like Fails, I found that using films to teach social theory allowed students to transform abstract and distant concepts into examples they could make more real in a viewed universe. For example, students compared the social interaction among Amish building a barn in the police drama *Witness* to the bureaucracy of the police station; two worlds a few miles apart in the same society. In *Gladiator*, the Russell Crowe character, Maximus Decimus Meridius, operated within traditional, bureaucratic and charismatic authority in different moments throughout the drama; organizing a well-coordinated army attack, acting within the accepted norms of power in the Roman political structure and becoming a charismatic hero in the gladiatorial ring. Careful viewing of the film shows how these forms of authority overlap and evolve. Finally, *Modern Times* presents a comic analysis of the contradictions of industrial capitalism, and the Charlie Chaplin character becomes an everyman for the otherwise faceless working class. The class experience suggests that core ideas in sociology have sufficient relevance to the human experience that they can be found in themes of internationally acclaimed cinema.

I have also offered an evening film series as part of a freshman course, Global Sociology. In past years this five-film festival has included films such as *Nói Albinói* (2003), an Icelandic film that explores the rites of passage to adulthood in an isolated Icelandic village; Mira Nair's *Monsoon Wedding* (2001), which shows how love and betrayal emerge in the complexities of an arranged marriage; Hany Abu-Assad's *Paradise Now* (2005), which examines how two young Palestinian men chose or reject the decision to become suicide bombers; and Florian Henckel von Donnersmarck's *The Lives of Others* (2006), which investigates the operation of the East German Stasi secret police. The course studies five countries spread throughout the world and the films are roughly keyed to those societies, though not exactly. They have made excellent adjuncts to texts and lectures, though they are presented in non-class times (I offer strong incentives to stimulate attendance). The freshmen students often have never seen a foreign, subtitled film, and often have never regarded film as anything but entertainment. Even when the assigned films test their patience, or explore topics beyond their comfort zone, the experience has been extremely positive. The example shows the potential for visual sociology to become a part of normal sociology courses, though convincing students to attend films out of class time is not always easy.

Using excerpts of film to illustrate sociological ideas

It has been technically challenging to isolate film passages to explore sociological concepts until recently. It is now much easier, though it resides in the realm of the quasi-legal. Herein lies a great potential for linking up visual passages and sociological ideas, however. Short passages may be cut from films and projected at a specific moment in a lecture. For example, in a scene from the 1988 movie, *Bull Durham*, starring Kevin Costner and Susan Sarandon, Costner plays an over the hill Triple-A baseball catcher who is retained to teach pitchers on the way to the majors the informal norms of the big leagues. A skilled but egotistical pitcher, played by Tim Robbins, continually shakes off (rejects the signals of) the catcher. Finally Costner, in view of the pitcher, tells the batter: "inside heat"—the pitch the pitcher has finally agreed to throw. Informed, the batter laces a hit. Costner trots to the mound where the pitcher says to him, incredulously: "You told him what I was going to pitch." "Yep," says Costner, and returns to his position. This three or four minute segment is a brilliant example of informal socialization in a profession, and it leads students to find parallels and comparisons in jobs they have had or observed. Because the film sequence is limited to five or six minutes the illustration does not take up an inordinate amount of time. Since most modern classrooms are now equipped with projectors and computers, film clips can be easily projected. What remains is to plumb the tens of thousands of hours of commercial cinema to cut these segments, and to gain the right to do this legally.

Using feature films as texts

It is also possible to teach courses that use feature films primarily as texts. An example was a course "Italian Society Through Film" I designed for a curriculum taught to North American students studying in Rome. This was relatively straightforward because many Italian post-World War Two films were strongly related to the social contexts in which they emerged. Beginning with the Neorealist movement, they were morality tales about a society struggling to overcome its fascist past. Themes of Catholicism, family, migration, poverty and wealth, and love and sex permeated films of this era. Bertolucci's *1900* (1976) tells the story of the rise and fall of fascism from the experiences of several characters who each represent peasants, futurists, fascists, landlords, partisans and a host of others. Rossellini's *Rome, Open City* (1946) casts partisans as heroes pitched against their Nazi occupiers in the last winter of the war. Fellini's *La Dolce Vita* (1960) portrays the decadence of the rapidly modernizing 1950s. Pasolini's *Mamma Roma* (1962) shows the deviant extremes of motherly love and Pietro Germi's *Divorce, Italian Style* (1961) mocks Italy's double standards surrounding sex, crime and religion. Recent Italian films such as Matteo Garrone's *Gomorrah* (2008) brings Roberto Saviano's undercover journalism on contemporary organized crime in Naples to life in a way that critiques the Hollywood glorification of organized crime. Several other modern Italian films are equally insightful regarding other aspects of Italian society.

Italian culture is well represented in film, but so are many others. To teach a sociological course on film requires that professors master film analysis and develop a nuanced understanding of the historical and sociological contexts in which the particular film tradition developed. However, modern technology allows for repeated viewings, isolating passages for analysis, and the viewing of single frames or slow motion examination of film passages, and sociologists are adept at understanding the relationship between culture and society, so the opportunity is there.

Teaching collaborative methods

Chapters 8 and 9 describe the range of topics that have been studied with collaborative methods, which are sufficiently distinctive to justify a separate discussion. It is also true that collaborative visual methods are more complex, more time consuming and more demanding than other projects described, and might be best suited for graduate education. Recent undergraduates in my courses have used photo elicitation to study topics like youth clothing style, the consumption of popular culture such as advertisements and the meanings of home photography. One student used family photographs to interview family members about a divorce. My daughter Molly interviewed our four family members to study our relocation from northern New York to Florida, using photos that depicted our typical family activities in New York: self-provisioning, partying and working with neighbors. Another student photographed how she made herself up in the morning (the camera positioned as the mirror) and used the photos to interview her peers about the construction of female identity. In these examples the students are familiar with the worlds and themes they are photographing and making photos is not in and of itself a problem.

Many of the topics covered by professional PE researchers imply an understanding of social processes. These include perceptions of landscape, consumer decision-making, analysis of the teaching process and community or individual self-definition. One of the most interesting recent examples was a student's elicitation interview study of his urban girlfriend and his small town father, using photos of the father and son's many deer hunting experiences. These were significant and important rituals and the basis of his connection to the male members of his family, which his girlfriend did not at first understand. The project provided a way to do so.

The interview

The ideal student who takes on an elicitation project has experience in social science interviewing. Typically the biggest challenge is to move from the indexical questions—such as *Who is in the photo?* or *What are people doing?*—to conversations where subjects reflect on the meaning of the images. In my study of farming modernization, I encouraged farmers to discuss their relationships with draft animals; to reflect on the unseen costs and benefits of less efficient farming; to compare the challenges, pleasures and monotony of different kinds of work; and to talk about the kinds of social relationships that farmers had with neighbors who were using these technologies. To get to these themes I asked farmers to tell a story about a memory, which often seemed to encourage deeper reflections.

There is no standard procedure for PE interviews. In many studies (such as the study described above) several farmers analyzed the same photos, so there was an opportunity to fine-tune interviews. This approach was also used in Colter Harper's interviews on the social history of jazz using the photos of Teenie Harris,[22] where he tailored each interview to a subset of his images, but remained flexible during the interview to substitute or eliminate images. In studies such as Payne's work with the Inuit, most subject-collaborators discussed specific photos in which they knew the people in the photos. The Dutch study of Schilderswijk produced five photo collections, one per researcher–informant pair, and these were then circulated to the others for further reflection. This was, in my view, a brilliant opportunity to understand and share the multiple realities that the neighborhood represented. To teach photo elicitation successfully one needs to think creatively about every project. Probably most important is to teach student researchers patience and to remind them of the need to pursue follow-up questions, the way one teaches students in any qualitative research course to actively listen.

Most of us who teach photo elicitation are committed to the full transcription of interviews. This is a tedious process but students quickly learn that transcription teaches them what was said; what was left out; and what issues remain. Listening to a tape during transcription also teaches the researcher about whether their own interruptions and pacing were effective.

When photo elicitation was first used in the 1950s, John Collier mentions printing 200 8 by 10 inch prints to prepare for a single interview. Until recently that was the model: a researcher exposed and printed black and white photos that would be printed in a darkroom for subsequent interviewing. The digital revolution has offered new possibilities; Carol Payne's project with the Inuit involved digitizing photos, and then having researchers take laptops into the interviews, clicking on one photo after another as the Elders looked and spoke. I wonder about the effect of not having an actual photo to hold, look at closely and to examine, but it is clear that having the images on the computer worked. No matter the technique it is crucial for the interview to be keyed to specific images. It has been my experience that a large photo (at least a full page) holds people's attention and encourages the close examination of details. The way photos are made available to the person being interviewed also affects what is said. Colter Harper noted that if he left a stack of photos on the table an informant would often grab the stack in order to get through them as quickly as possible. It was more productive to give photos to the informant one at a time, allowing for a long discussion when an image stimulated it. Advanced students will create their own versions of PE interviews, especially if they are aware of approaches used in prior studies.

Coding and writing up the results

The PE interview, as a variation of a qualitative methods interview, produces material that is coded, analyzed and presented as a formal paper. This is really a separate topic covered in any qualitative methods text; the PE interview is simply a variation of an old research standard.

Photos take a lot of space in a research publication and if a researcher wants to stress the visual dimension of the study it is necessary to find a journal that will publish a sufficient amount of the visuals. Journals such as *Visual Studies* are ideal but most conventional journals are less so. More journals are willing to publish visual material, but images are usually published in small format and with muddy reproduction. On the other hand, more and more journal articles are available on the web, and web-based publication can and does more easily accommodate much improved image reproduction, including color.

Because photo elicitation connects images to text it resembles a film. It is necessary to edit the text so that it flows through the visual presentation, the way one weaves images and words together in a film. When I was designing the book *Working Knowledge*, I remember that on some pages I included as many as nine photos that were discussed briefly, and in other instances a single photo lead to several pages of discussion. In my own development as a visual sociologist, the opportunity to design my books using PageMaker or InDesign has been invaluable. As more and more students arrive with experience in multimedia, discussions of design become more natural. Teaching photo elicitation thus becomes a way to teach photography, interviewing, conceptualizing, coding and design.

Teaching photovoice

Much of what has been said about teaching photo elicitation is relevant to teaching photovoice. As was pointed out in Chapter 9, typical participants in photovoice projects are members of communities or groups who are at some disadvantage. Doing a photovoice project usually means crossing cultural barriers to inspire community members to examine themselves and their surroundings in a newly critical way by making photographs of some aspect of their world.

As noted above, photo elicitation and photovoice research is often done by graduate students or professional researchers. My review is directed to an experienced researcher teaching a graduate student, another researcher who wants to know how to do photovoice, and the researcher in the field teaching research participants who will, in fact, be making photographs.

Teaching participants in a photovoice project can be an elaborate process. Strack (see Chapter 9), working with youth in an after school program, used twenty two-hour sessions over twelve weeks to teach photography, ethics, power relationships, consent, safety, cataloguing and exhibition preparation. Nance Wilson and her colleagues describe meeting subjects for twenty-five ninety-minute sessions, focused on participatory education techniques, youth development and the management of projects. In most projects the training was more limited, usually limited to a few sessions of a few hours each. Often the people involved were paid for the training; homeless people in Michigan received $20 per training session; others received cash, free food or coupons.

The training focuses on ethics and the responsibility of photographing people in public, and de-emphasizes the technical aspects of making photos. Wang comments

> . . . I have been working with photovoice since 1992, and we have never started by teaching people how to use a camera. Instead, the first workshop is a group discussion. We talk about ethics and power. We talk about how cameras can confer authority on the user, and how they also confer responsibility. We discuss the responsibilities one has when one uses a technology, and what it means to introduce a tool, even one as commonplace as a camera, into a neighborhood, a clinic, or a community group.[23]

Aside from the teaching of photography as a technical practice, there is the matter of teaching participants where to aim the camera. Often settling these issues was itself a collaborative process. On a project on employment-seeking among people with AIDs, for example, the group brainstormed to identify the following themes to explore through photovoice:

- When you think about the word employment, what comes to mind?
- Are there advantages to employment?
- If you became employed, would there be disadvantages?
- Persons or groups who influenced your decision to become employed?
- What would help you return to employment?
- What would stop you from becoming employed?[24]

This was a typical example. Researchers helped Latina girls identify themes to photograph, including their perceptions of health, and things that they thought impacted on their health. In PV studies on education researchers encouraged students to identify factors that were helping or hindering their education. Teaching this aspect of photovoice was largely an effort to awaken critical consciousness among the people in the project, and to help them collectively and democratically define the goals of the photo project.

Photovoice projects usually (but not always, note earlier comments about using Holga cameras in two studies) depend on auto-everything amateur cameras. Disposable 35 mm color cameras have become almost standard in the photovoice projects reviewed; only one or two projects used digital cameras. As a result there is little teaching about photography per se, but a lot about *looking.*

As noted earlier, the analysis of photos was often based on asking the questions represented by the SHOWeD acronym, (*What do you see here, what is really happening here, how does this relate to our lives, why does this situation exist, what can be done?*). This was so common among photovoice projects that it appears to have become part of the standard research tool kit. And while this procedure would give the teaching of photovoice a recognizable form, and participants could have a fairly concrete list of questions on which to base their interrogation of the photos, some quiet voices wondered if this was the only way to analyze photovoice photos.

While there is a great deal of writing by participants in the photovoice projects, little of that text was included in the published research reports. Published articles tend to be technical reports of completed projects.

In the twelve months between the first and final draft of this chapter, much has changed in the photovoice world. The number of photovoice publications in sociology journals has increased and the specific focus has widened. Finally, as mentioned in several places in this discussion, the line between photovoice and elicitation has blurred. It appears that the influence and impact of all collaborative visual methods is on a rapid ascent, and may carry visual sociology writ large along for the ride.

Finally, as mentioned previously, an approach called Literacy Through Photography[25] resembles photovoice but is sufficiently distinctive to warrant separate comment. LTP places cameras in the hands of participants, but generally in schools or other educational situations. LTP has become influential among those dedicated to educational reform and the redefinition of documentary photography. While LTP, like photovoice, stands somewhat apart from visual sociology, because it is less about the generation of knowledge and more about empowerment, they draw from the same theoretical wells and have much to do with each other.

The core purpose of LTP is typically to train teachers who will apply LTP principles to their own needs and uses. The approach has a kind of living character in this way; rather than a doctrine, it is an invitation to teach from a perspective in which students are creative authors of their learning through photography. LTP workshops and training sessions have led to the introduction of the visual method in English, science, math, history, the arts and, in fact, in most courses in a normal curriculum.

The LTP experience places students in charge of finding visual solutions to academic assignments. Working together to think through image making, students figure out how to visualize a mathematical concept; how to use imagery to learn simple vocabulary; how to use photography to link specifics to general ideas. For example, grade school students in Tanzania photographed farm animals in a simulated moment of slaughter to communicate principles of economy. Through LTP students learn to use photographs to explore their own expressions and feelings: how they touch, experience and define the world, including their dreams. In these ways LTP assignments are very much like assignments in a visual sociology course.

Photography is combined with several forms of writing. This includes freewriting to brainstorm ways of approaching the visualization of a concept, and essays about identity, self, community and dreams that accompany photos. Both photography and writing are approached with concepts of framing, point of view, timing and the use of symbols. Very often students write on photos with ink makers, creating a dialogue with the image, or mount photos on posters and caption them with texts written in the borders.

Literacy Through Photography has been developed in workshops, university courses and training centers, and demonstrates perhaps more than any comparative program how seeing can create a dialogue about culture that empowers those involved. The method draws upon photo elicitation because it takes the meaning of the photo as rooted in conversation, and photovoice because it places the camera in the hands of those who are less powerful. It has the capability of reforming whole educational systems (as is possibly taking place in school systems in Africa where it is currently taught) and as such is a vital part of the visual sociology movement.

Clearly, teaching photovoice and its variants charts new ground for sociology. Typical considerations of ethics become more complicated when people are making images. There is yet to be a "best practices" understanding for this activity and I don't think there can ever be. The ethics are situational; researchers rely much on their judgment as well as the dictates of IRB committees. That being said, some of the most considered views of ethics and visual representation in field-work situations appears in the articles cited here.

The photovoice/LTP model brings sociology back to an activist posture, but the methods are appropriate for a wide range of topics, as this review makes clear. Collaborative models including elicitation and photovoice will have an increasing influence on sociology and will make the argument for visual sociology in the process.

Chapter 11

Final words

I end with some thoughts about why visual sociology, so long a small footnote to sociology, has suddenly found its stride. I think there are several answers.

The best answer is that visual approaches do sociology in new, creative and interesting ways. The visual approach can be applied pretty much across the discipline. For example, John Grady's work on ads and attitudes toward racial integration shows that visual data work as well, if not better, than other forms of data for testing hypotheses. It is reasonable to say that a visual approach can expand the meaning of data itself; the aerial photos that I triangulated with numerical data offer an example. Recall: I'm not a narrow empiricist! I've roamed widely among methods in this discussion to show how what we see can be part of how we know in sociology.

Visual approaches also cover most topics in sociology. I have discussed some but certainly not all of them. For example, one could easily add a long chapter on the visual study of institutions, starting with the family. Families create their own histories through visual records, and as family albums give way to digital forms of visual record keeping, the forms of visual history change but don't disappear. Family images have profound meaning for those involved yet they are also a record of only what is acceptable to record (no fights or divorces! Only births, celebrations and happiness!). Institutions such as corporations have for a long time employed skilled photographers to argue their case in annual reports and, increasingly, television advertising. And, with huge budgets and talented PR departments, the visual arguments become very persuasive indeed. For example, I live in western Pennsylvania which is on the edge of the Marcellus Shale natural gas reservoir, and extracting natural gas from these reserves is a controversial environmental process. But the companies that are involved blanket the evening television audiences, with one family after another telling the world how their lives have improved since they sold their natural gas rights to Range Resources. It is not so much the stories themselves, which boil down to family X getting X amount of royalty. But the ads are persuasive because of the way the people look; their postures and earnest expressions, and the unspoiled nature which surrounds them. In other words, the persuasion is based on what is largely a visual construction. So there are two chapters that could have been added, and there are several more.

I think that visual sociology is also coming of age because sociologists are visually hungry and a little weary of nuanced statistics and abstracted arguments. But the meaning of this visual hunger is not agreed upon. In the nineteenth century Charles Baudelaire called the urban stroller the *flâneur* and since then the debate has raged: is it voyeurism that draws this interest in looking? Or is it a passionate immersion in the new forms of anonymous urbanity? (Susan Sontag, in the chapter "Melancholy Objects" in *On Photography* puts it this way: "The photographer is an armed version of the solitary walker reconnoitering, stalking, cruising the urban inferno, the voyeuristic stroller who discovers the city as a landscape of voluptuous extremes.") But I'll not engage the argument because there is no way to resolve it; one's view boils down to one's ideology. Simply I repeat that this visual hunger has been present at least since cave painters began making images more than 30,000 years ago,[1] and maybe sociology is finally getting on board.

Visual sociology is also coming of age because it is a global movement. Evidence is everywhere: the meetings of the IVSA are mostly held outside the US and they always produce new recruits. The International Sociology Association (ISA) has a growing visual interest group, as do national organizations in several countries. Workshops are more and more common; in the past year or two I've been invited to Russia, Italy, the UK, Germany, Sweden and Switzerland to do workshops or teach visual sociology; others are in Africa changing how teachers transform a memory-based pedagogy with image-driven methods. The movement is broad and deep, with interesting variations in different settings. Quite probably the global expansion has something to do with the notion that the image-interest is pan-human and image-driven sociology is a natural way to communicate across cultures and national boundaries.

Visual sociology is also growing because it is useful to researchers in many disciplines. This includes public and community health, communication, cultural geography, education, leisure studies, rural sociology, cultural studies, ethnomusicology, disability studies, epidemiology and criminal justice, to name a few. Sociology studies group life, community, the social construction of meaning, inequality and social status, the symbolic basis of communication; and the activist orientation of sociology is consistent with collaborative methods used in community health and related areas. In other words the work done in many disciplines is sociological in nature whether it is recognized as such or not. This is especially true in the case of visual studies of social life.

I finish with an image rather than words, or, I should say, an image with words. Gordon Parks took this photo in the late 1940s in upstate New York. It is a curious image; three men sitting in and out of the sun in front of a rough-hewn building. Parks was part of the team employed by the Standard Oil Company of New Jersey to record the importance of petroleum in the US during World War Two but he was

Figure 11.1
Three farmers. (Photograph by Gordon Parks.)

under the nominal direction of Roy Stryker, director of the FSA and later, SONJ. Stryker sent his photographers out to record not what was important then, but what might become important later. So, what is important about this image? The farmers seem remarkably similar: their postures; their clothes; even their bodies seem cut from a cookie cutter; their hands enlarged from years of manual work, pulling on the teats of their cows for the milk that made their living. But there is something else; their gaze toward the photographer. And then we realize: the photographer was Gordon Parks, an African-American who became one of the most important photographers of the late twentieth century. They were looking at a black man, quite likely the first they had ever seen, and he was master of a machine none of them understood. There is respect in their eyes, bemusement and some suspicion. The photo is about the parts of their lives that make it to the visible surface, but it is also about how they saw and reacted to a moment they had never experienced before. This is, I believe, visual sociology.

Appendix I

Teaching overview and sample assignments

The following adds specifics to Chapter 10, which describes approaches to teaching visual sociology. I've listed assignments I've developed over several years and note that since the digital revolution it has seemed that students can complete about three assignments in a fourteen-week semester. If it is possible to limit the enrollment of the class to under twenty students they gain the opportunity to present much of their work to their peers, and to learn to critique each other. It is also possible and desirable to display student work, even if just for a brief exhibition, or to develop a website or other forms of digital distribution.

ASSIGNMENT EXAMPLE ONE: Self-portrait without self

The goal of this assignment is to render *the personal into a sociological context*; to reflect on aspects of your identity that can be visualized. Please expose images and then edit them into a series of not more than twenty-five photographs that represent you as a social being.

There are five basic approaches to this assignment:

*   *Photographs of objects* that define you. Cars, jewelry, tools, collections, photographs, books, guns, musical instruments, letters, make-up, toys, furniture. Anything.

    Find a way to photograph the objects or object to communicate how they tell us about your identity. Think about the distance to the subject; point of view; framing; focus; light. You might want to make photos of objects as they are being used, or you may want to make photos of parts of objects. Please do more than visually listing objects: try to interpret their meanings.

- *Spaces and places* where *you* are *you!*

  a   A place in a dwelling, neighborhood or community that you feel has defined you. That may be changing in this era of your lives.

  b   A place in a non-institutional place; a position at a table; in a room. Do you have implied "ownership" of that place?

  c   Is there a place in nature where you return normally? Is there a time in which this place is especially meaningful to your identity?

  d   Do you occupy a place in an institution in such a way that it creates your identity? (A place in a church where you pray; a seat in a stadium where you watch a sports event? A stool in a restaurant or bar that is "yours?" The TV show *Cheers* got much mileage from this concept.) Karl Marx wrote at the same desk in the same chair for years at the British Museum; I sat there once; ghosts!

  e   A place in your family's home that is "yours?" Does your family occupy space in some collective way that you are a part of? What happens there that defines you? Do other people occupy this space when you are absent?

- *People who make you who you are.* How do you pose them to communicate their importance to your identity? What gestures, expressions, props do you assign to them? How do you assign them a place in an environment?

- *Ideas/values/emotions.* This may be the most complex thing to photograph: you are trying to tell us about yourself by expressing your subjectivity in visual metaphors, narratives and reflections.

- *Activities* in which you become who you see yourself being. Can you find a way to photograph these activities looking from the inside out?

  You may wish to combine several of these themes, or to work with one. Or, you may find an entirely different strategy for this assignment.

  The photos should be turned in on a disk or memory stick so I can view them to evaluate your project.

  The photos must be accompanied with a typed essay, which should tell us what your goals were as a photographer and what you think worked and what did not. Do you use color or black and white? Did you link images into a sequence to tell your story? Reflect on your struggles and what you think were your successes; describe specific photographs and whether or not they communicated the ideas you hoped they would.

ASSIGNMENT EXAMPLE TWO: Interaction in a social space

A *social space is* where people interact in regular ways. The interaction is guided by norms (unwritten rules) and often by official rules. These are, of course, often at odds with each other.

What are some examples of a social space?

- *A neighborhood.* What constitutes a neighborhood? How is it understood by people living there; how it is defined legally; how is it defined by tourists? What are different institutions that neighborhoods share; how are different purposes achieved in different neighborhoods? You might define this simply as "ways to be social," or "places to catch buses. . ."
- *A public square.* What was the original purpose of the square? How did this change as political definitions and technologies, such as transportation systems, changed?
- *An institution* where the public meets, such as a bar, a court, a train station or an airport. It may or may not be possible to photograph some of these spaces. Please use your good judgment.
- *Social spaces* are sometimes inside larger shared spaces. For example, the inland sea in Holland is a social space; there are detailed norms to guide one how to sail in certain areas and even how to park one's boat in a crowded harbor. You could think of roads, highways, paths, bike paths, nature trails in similar terms.

Doing the assignment:

You just landed from Mars and despite the excellent Martian sociology classes that prepared you for this project, you're quite amazed by what you see. Thank goodness you've got your Steeler's (note for non-Pittsburgers, a famous American football team) jacket on, which hides several of your extra appendages and even allows you to tuck your Martian 2000 megapixel camera out of sight. You've done your homework, but it didn't begin to prepare you for what you're seeing.

Your crazy Martian professor sent you here to study and photograph how Earthlings "use their spaces." They go here and they go there. There seems to be some order to it, but it is hard to see. Are there rules to their wandering? Do Earthlings adorn themselves to identify themselves as part of one group or another? Do they follow their silly laws and rules, or do they make up their own ways of doing things? You want to tell your friends back on Mars what this scene is like, so you try to get the best of your excitement and get down to work. Some of the things you know your fellow Martians will want to know include:

What is the essence of particular spaces where Earthlings chill?
Do they contain contradictions, such as between categories like:

- insider/outsider;
- tourist/resident;
- female/male;
- night/day;
- morning/evening;
- young/old.

**What do Earthlings do in these spaces? How do they interact
with each other? Do they seem to agree completely on what
they are supposed to be doing? How do they mark
themselves to show they are supposed to be there? Do you
see people doing things that don't fit in?**

Write your paper as a letter home to Mars; your lousy spaceship broke so you'll be
here for a while, but you don't even care; you just got invited to the Steeler's game
and after a few beers nobody seems to mind the extra appendages . . .

ASSIGNMENT EXAMPLE THREE: The social organization of work

Suggestions for organizing themes:

- *The social interaction of work.* This might include the interaction between
  workers, or the interaction between workers and clients or the public. I am
  particularly interested in social interaction that moves across the lines of social
  class, gender and other sociological categories.
- *Rituals of work.* Think of rituals as repeated events that integrate groups.
- *The role of gender in work,* expressed in body language, status systems,
  comparative work spaces, deference, etc.
- *Human–machine* or *human–animal* aspects of work.
- *Skill and de-skilling* in hand work and other forms of visual work. What does
  this concept mean in the computer age?
- *Work and identity:* uniforms, gestures, postures, expressions.

Instructions:

- Select a work setting. Obtain permission to photograph in this setting, if
  necessary! Think about the moral and ethical issues as discussed in class.
- Observe the setting (somewhere between two and three hours and several
  days). Realize the difficulty in finding a role as observer that won't be disruptive,
  insensitive or get you arrested. Write field notes from your observations. These
  are informally written guides to your experience, written in a journal-like way.
  For this assignment they will probably be three to four pages.

     Plan your photographic strategy to explore an idea you have developed
  during your observations.
- Photograph the setting, probably exposing twenty to forty images. After
  finishing, describe what you did and what succeeded and failed in your photo
  sessions.
- Write the paper. Print eight to ten photographs, arranged in a sequence if
  relevant. Include captions for photos if they are particularly helpful.

ASSIGNMENT EXAMPLE FOUR: Visualization and re-imagination

The assignment is to re-imagine a taken-for-granted aspect of your normally perceived world.

As an example, in the film days I used to photograph exclusively in black and white. I had given a lecture in Bologna on the public life of the piazza, illustrated with my typical images. An audience member reacted: "Why do you reduce our beautiful city to these ugly shades of grey?" That was not the point of the talk, of course, but it raised a challenge.

I decided to try to see the urban environment in color and quickly realized that because I had spent decades reducing images to shades of grey this was not easy. I had a hand-held filter that took the color out of reality: you would hold it to your eye and, presto! a world in black and white; with the filter to my eye the world had become a black and white movie.

So my goal was to reverse this process. At first, I identified the larger world of "color." But that was far too huge a subject: I could imagine that any photo I would make would be a cliché of postcard prettiness. I was in a gorgeous city, where the colors of the external plaster walls are mandated by the city government to be painted a beautiful ochre color or a mild yellow, with window frames and other trim painted a medium green. So it was a temptation, but I sensed the canvas as too large: unmanageable.

So I narrowed my focus to a given color, in this case green. I walked for an hour without making any photos (I had purchased a single roll of color film and wanted to do this carefully; there was no room for experimentation). I framed several images with the camera but took no photos. Green trees; green windows; green neon on a few signs. I knew the images would be uninspired because I had not yet begun to "see" my new topic. I was crossing the street and suddenly, there he was, the *green man of Bologna* (the walk symbol on the traffic light). I had my subject!

I imposed rules: I only allowed myself to make one photo per green man appearance. I wanted to photograph him in his natural habitats, the various positions of traffic lights, creating a visual narrative of the city from the perspective of the green man. My camera didn't have automatic controls and I used a 35 mm lens, so I faced decisions regarding exposure, shutter speed and framing. The green man was elusive; appearing momentarily and then disappearing. Since I was using a wide-angle lens it was hard to get him close up. I would cross the street, typically in an Italian crowd, getting as close to the green man as possible before exposing the frame. I'd have to stop abruptly, still in the street, and often people walked into me. I hereby apologize for any inconvenience caused that day!

The result, however, was that I began to notice things I had never seen before, though I had seen green men instructing me to cross streets all my life. This reminded me that photography can be a way to reinvigorate seeing; to re-sort one's apprehension of the world, to become more appreciative of the visual universe and to become more aware of the normal.

The key is to perceive something normal, typical and common in a new way, which may lead you to understand the typical way you construct the world unconsciously.

You can chose a common or generic physical category. One student last year, who was an athlete, chose to photograph *grass*. Suddenly, she said, the whole world was grass. Grass she played on; grass she mowed; grass neglected in parks; grass made out of plastic; grass in paintings in a museum; grass in suburbia; grass cows ate. And there was more.

Because you are trying to re-imagine part of the world you experience in your normal life this is an elusive assignment. It involves becoming an observer of the obvious, and usually involves adopting an ironic tone. Try to find ways to photograph your topic in a fully new way.

ASSIGNMENT EXAMPLE FIVE: Semiotics

Symbols are all around us, at the simple level of denotation, and ranging in complexity toward the connotative. We can determine the meaning of symbols in our own lives, or use images of symbols to determine to what extent the symbols are perceived, understood or reacted to by others. Some questions that might guide your research:

- When do visual symbols direct you to act in a certain way? How do they do that? (Color, shape, words, proximity to lines of sight.) What visual symbols have you encountered in other countries or societies that have confused you?
- What visually symbolic messages are appealing to you? Do you find yourself acting on the basis of their appeal?
- When are sets of symbols internally contradictory?
- When are they ironic or critical?
- To what extent can we trace visual symbols to what Roland Barthes called "myths?" (How do they combine to create an entire ideological system?) To what extent can we perceive large-scale social, economic and political manipulation between symbolic messages?
- How are the visual symbols displayed? How much of their contextual environment is relevant to their message? Be sure to photograph the symbolic universe, not just the symbols.

When you write the paper please include as much of your experience as possible. If your views of the role of symbols change, please include that.

ASSIGNMENT EXAMPLE SIX: The collaborative method (please note that this has been described extensively in Chapter 10. The following is a template for a specific assignment)

Photo-elicitation: you can use virtually any photographs and you can interview more than a single person, but I'd advise that you choose about ten to twenty photos (maximum!) and interview one to three or four people. You can use photographs you have made or photos from another source. These might be from family albums, from the web, from a local historical association, or from mass media.

Some guidelines and ideas:

You need to number the photos so that when you transcribe your tape you know what comments belong to what photographs.

You have to develop an interview style that encourages people to tell stories, reflect on memories and remember in an active, complex way, rather than simply telling you literally what the photos depict. If you show a photo of a Christmas parade *circa* 1960 in an old steel town to an elderly person who lived through those times you'll get a more interesting response to the question: "Can you tell me a story or more about what you remember about these parades; anything will do." If you simply place the photo in front of the subject they will likely say: "That is a Christmas parade; it used to be a lively place!"

Please turn in copies of the photos and a full transcription of the interview (which should be about forty-five minutes in length; possibly a bit shorter). The paper is different, you need to introduce the topic, tell me how you proceeded, and then edit the transcription so that it has the essence you think important. The photos or images should be included and captioned.

Appendix II

Notes on photographic technology

A bird sits on a limb. It is a vain bird that does not mind being photographed! So, let's photograph it in several ways to achieve several effects.

Here are the variables you need to understand:

- *ISO: the sensitivity of the digital sensor.* The lower the number (usually 100 is the lowest) the more detail the sensor records, but the more light it needs. If you expose at over 600 to 1,000 there will be noticeable "noise": that is, you can see pixels in the image and the color will be less rich. Some modern cameras operate at very high ISO ratings, which means their sensors can record very low light with a minimum of pixelation.

- *Shutter and shutter speed.* Inside the camera is a light-sensitive digital chip or a piece of film. There is a window (the camera shutter) that opens and closes on command. The longer it is open, the more light falls on the sensor or film. The length of time is called "shutter speed." A camera shutter could be open, practically speaking, for several minutes, or for one four thousandths of a second. If you take a "long exposure"—shutter open for anything past 1/30 of a second, you need to make the camera steady by fastening it to a tripod unless you want a photo that will have a jerky, unsharp look. If you set the camera for a one-second exposure and our bird flies away it will just be a blur. If you set the camera for 1/4000 of a second you will stop the bird in mid-flight. Depending on what idea you are exploring, either strategy could give you the photo you want.

  Typical shutter speeds you'll probably be using are (in seconds and fractions of a second): 1, 1/2, 1/4, 1/8, 1/15, 1/30, 1/60, 1/125, 1/250, 1/500, 1/1000 (etc.). You can use much longer shutter speeds, especially if you are working at night. Note that each of these doubles the light being let through the lens or diminishes it by one half. That becomes relevant later.

- *Aperture.* There is a mechanism inside a camera lens that looks like a sphincter muscle. It makes the round hole in the lens larger or smaller. It has a series of "stops," (called "f-stops") which are usually indications of half or twice as much light being let through the lens as the aperture opens or closes. Typical lenses have the following f-stops: 1.4, 2.0, 2.8, 4, 5.6, 8, 11, 16, 22.

  You have to remember that the larger the number, the smaller the hole in the lens. Since each number is a doubling of the amount of light let in or not, this matches to shutter speeds.

  So to expose for a given amount of light; say outside light on a cloudy day in shadow with an ISO of 200, the choices of shutter speed and aperture might be as follows. The top row is the aperture and the lower row is the shutter speed. Think of each vertical grouping as a pair. Each one of these pairs will let exactly the same amount of light through the lens and camera to the sensor; each will thus be exactly the same in exposure but each photo made with each shutter speed/aperture combination will look different.

  Why will each of these combinations make different looking photos if they all let in the same amount of light? First, the larger the aperture (but the smaller the f-number; here it is f/1.4) the less the depth of field. If you take a close-up portrait of a person at f/1.4 their nose may be in focus and their ears will be completely blurry. If you take the same photo at f/16 their entire head will be in focus. Of course either strategy may get the image you want; it depends on what you desire. The second reason these will look different is that the slower the shutter speed, the more movement taking place in front of the camera will be blurred. If you let the shutter remain open for several minutes, a person walking by the camera will not appear at all. If you expose an image for 1/4000 of a second the flapping wings of a bird will be frozen.

  When you internalize how this simple variation of two variables works you will able to make images that emerge from your creative imagination. In inexpensive digital cameras these choices are automated and to be a photographer in the real sense you need to learn how to establish manual control over your camera, which can be daunting. Ironically, the more expensive the camera, the more manual its operation.
- *Framing.* A long "focal length" lens is like a telescope; a short focal length lens is referred to as a wide angle. Practically speaking, the lens that sees a view that is closest to a normal person's vision is a 28 mm; at about 150 mm you are really magnifying objects. A sports photographer may use a 1,000 mm lens to capture the details of action taking place a half a football field

Table A.1 Equivalent aperture/shutter speed combinations for a typical amount of light on a cloudy day

1.4	2.0	2.8	4.0	5.6	8	11	16	22	32
P1/4000	1/2000	1/1000	1/500	1/250	1/125	1/60	1/30	1/15	1/8

away. Zoom lenses may cover many focal lengths, but they are "slow" (most have a maximum aperture of f/4 or 5.6); they are physically large, and their optical quality is not as good as fixed focal length lenses unless you spend a great deal of money. The unique ability of the swing-lens panoramic camera was demonstrated in several photos published in this book.

Back to our patient bird. If you want the bird frozen in place and you want the background to be blurry, choose a wide aperture (f/1.4—big hole in the lens; lots of light coming through), which will require a very fast shutter speed (the window only open for an instant!) to make a proper exposure with the light of a normal day.

If you want the bird to disappear into the foliage by having everything in sharp focus you need to expose at f/16 or 22 (small hole, large depth of field). To get sufficient light to the sensor you need to leave the shutter open for a long time; about 1/15 of a second. Maybe the bird will move during that time, and will be blurry. Again, neither is the "right" decision but each combination makes a very different image.

There are other variables as well, including film or sensor size and format that strongly influence what your images will look like, but this covers the basics!

Appendix III

Sources

A. Photo documentaries

Adelman, Bob and Michael Harrington. 1981. *The Next America: The decline and rise of the United States*. New York: Holt, Rinehart and Winston.

Adelman, Bob and Susan Hall. 1970. *On and Off the Street*. New York: Viking.

Agee, James and Walker Evans. 1939. *Let us Now Praise Famous Men*. Boston: Houghton-Mifflin.

Alinder, James, ed. 1981. *Roy DeCarava, Photographs*. Carmen, CA: Friends of Photography.

Anderson, Robert, ed. 1973. *Voices from Wounded Knee*. Rooseveltown, New York: Akwesasne Notes.

Berger, John and Jean Mohr. 1967. *A Fortunate Man: The story of a country doctor*. New York: Holt, Rinehart and Winston.

Berger, John and Jean Mohr. 1975. *A Seventh Man: Migrant workers in Europe*. New York: Viking.

Berger, John and Jean Mohr. 1982. *Another Way of Telling*. New York: Pantheon.

Brandt, Bill. 1984. *London in the Thirties*. New York: Pantheon.

Burrows, Larry. 2002. *Larry Burrow's Vietnam*. New York: Alfred A. Knopf. Introduction by David Halberstam.

Cartier-Bresson, Henri. 1952. *The Decisive Moment*. New York: Simon & Schuster.

Cartier-Bresson, Henri. 1979. *Henri Cartier-Bresson: Photographer*. Boston: New York Graphic Society.

Cartier-Bresson, Henri. 1991. *America in Passing*. Boston: Bullfinch Press, Little, Brown and Company.

Clark, Larry. 1971. *Tulsa*. New York: Lustrum.

Clark, Larry. 1983. *Teenage Lust*. Larry Clark (self-published).

Coles, Robert and Alex Harris. 1973. *The Old Ones of New Mexico*. New York: New York Graphic Society.

Coles, Robert and Alex Harris. 1977. *Last and First Eskimos*. Boston: New York Graphic Society.

Coles, Robert and Nicholas Nixon. 1998. *School*. Boston: Little, Brown and Company.

Copeland, Alan, ed. 1969. *People's Park*. New York: Ballantine.

Couch, Stanley and Deborah Willis. 2002. *One Shot Harris: The photographs of Charles "Teenie" Harris*. New York: Abrams.

Couderc, Jean-Marie. 1996. *A Village in France: Louis Clergeau's photographic portrait of daily life in Pontlevoy, 1902–1938*. New York: Abrams, 1996.

Davidson, Bruce. 1970. *E100 Street*. Cambridge: Harvard University Press.

Davidson, Bruce. 1986. *Subway*. Aperture Foundation.

DeCarava, Roy and Langston Hughes. 1955. *The Sweet Flypaper of Life*. New York: Simon & Schuster.

Estrin, Mary Lloyd. 1979. *To the Manor Born*. New York: New York Graphic Society.

Ewald, Wendy. 1985. *Portraits and Dreams: Photographs and stories by children of the Appalachians*. New York: Writers and Readers.

Ewald, Wendy. 1992. *Magic Eyes: Scenes from an Andean girlhood*. Seattle, WA: Bay.

Ewald, Wendy. 1996. *I Dreamed I had a Girl in My Pocket: The story of an Indian village*. New York: DoubleTake.

Ewald, Wendy. 2005. *American Alphabets*. Zurich: Scalo.

Ewing, William, ed. 1989. *America Worked: The 1950s photographs of Dan Weiner*. New York: Abrams.

Fenton, David. 1971. *Shots: Photographs from the underground press*. New York: Douglas Book.

Fink, Larry. 1984. *Social Graces*. New York: Aperture.

Frank, Robert. 1969 (originally published 1959). *The Americans*. New York: Aperture.

Frazier, Danny Wilcox. 2009. *Driftless: Photographs from Iowa*. Chapel Hill: Duke University Press.

Fulton, Marianne. 1988. *Eyes of Time: Photojournalism in America*. Boston: New York Graphic Society.

Ganzel, Bill. 1984. *Dust Bowl Descent*. Lincoln: University of Nebraska Press.

Goldberg, Jim. 1985. *Rich and Poor*. New York: Random House.

Gowin, Emmet. 1992. *Changing the Earth*. New Haven: Yale University Press.

Greenfield, Lauren. 2002. *Girl Culture*. San Francisco: Chronicle.

Griffiths, Philip Jones. 1971. *Vietnam Inc*. New York: Collier.

Hansberry, Lorraine. 1964. *The Movement*. New York: Simon & Schuster.

Harrington, Michael and Aldeman, Bob. 1981. *The Next America: The decline and rise of the United States*. New York: Holt, Rinehart and Winston.

Heartfield, John. 1977. *Photomontages of the Nazi Period*. New York: Universe.

Hecke, Roswitha. 1982. *Love Life: Scenes with Irene*. New York: Grove.

Hedgepeth, William and Dennis Stock. 1970. *The Alternative: Communal life in new America*. New York: Collier.

Holdt, Jacob. 1985. *American Pictures*. Copenhagen: American Pictures Foundation.

Jackson, Bruce. 1977. *Killing Time*. Ithaca: Cornell University Press.

Jackson, Bruce. 2009. *Pictures from a Drawer: Prison and the art of portraiture*. Philadelphia: Temple University Press.

Jackson, Bruce and Diane Christian. 2011. *In This Timeless Time: Living and dying on Death Row in America*. Chapel Hill: University of North Carolina Press.

Jones, Michael Owen. 1975. *The Homemade Object and its Maker*. Berkeley: University of California Press.

Kerry, John and the Vietnam Veterans Against the War. 1971. *The New Soldier*. New York: Collier.

Klett, Mark, Ellen Manchester and JoAnn Verburg. 1984. *Second View: The Rephotographic Survey Project*. Albuquerque: University of New Mexico Press.

Klett, Mark, Kyle Bajakian, William Fox, Michael Marshall, Toshi Ueshina and Byron Wolfe. 2004.

Third Views, Second Sights: A rephotographic survey of the American West. Albuquerque: Museum of New Mexico Press.

Klich, Kent. 1989. *The Book of Beth.* Millertown, New York: Aperture.

Lange, Dorothea and Paul S. Taylor. 1969. *An American Exodus.* New Haven: Yale University Press.

Lesy, Micheal. 1973. *Wisconsin Death Trip.* New York: Pantheon.

Letinsky, L. 2000. *Venus Inferred.* Chicago: University of Chicago Press.

Lyman, Christopher M. 1982. *The Vanishing Race and Other Illusions: Photographs of Indians by Edward S. Curtis.* New York: Pantheon.

Lynch, Dorothea and Eugene Richards. 1986. *Exploding Into Life.* New York: Aperture.

Lyon, Danny. 1971. *Conversations with the Dead.* New York: Holt, Rinehart and Winston.

Lyon, Danny. 1988. *Merci Gonaives: A photographer's account of Haiti and the February Revolution.* New York: Bleak Beauty.

Maharidge, Dale and Michael Williamson. 1985. *Journey to Nowhere.* New York: Doubleday.

Maharidge, Dale and Michael Williamson. 1990. *And Their Children After Them: The legacy of Let Us Now Praise Famous Men.* New York: Pantheon.

Maharidge, Dale and Michael Williamson. 2008. *Denison, Iowa.* 2008. New York: Free Press.

Meiselas, Susan. 1975. *Carnival Strippers.* New York: Farrar, Straus and Giroux.

Meiselas, Susan. 1981. *Nicaragua: June 1978–July 1979.* New York: Pantheon.

Meiselas, Susan. 1997. *Kurdistan: In the shadow of history.* New York: Random House. (Second edition. 2009. University of Chicago Press.)

Newhall, Nancy. 1975. *P. H. Emerson.* Millertown, New York: Aperture.

Norfleet, Barbara. 1980. *Champion Pig: Great moments in everyday life.* New York: Penguin.

Norfleet, Barbara. 1986. *All the Right People.* Boston: New York Graphic Society.

Norfleet, Barbara. 1993. *Looking at Death.* Boston: Godine.

Norfleet, Barbara. 2001. *When We Liked Ike: Looking for postwar America.* New York: Norton.

Norman, Dorothy. 1960. *Alfred Stieglitz: An American seer.* New York: Aperture.

Owens, Bill. 1972. *Suburbia.* San Francisco: Straight Arrow Books.

Owens, Bill. 1975. *Our Kind of People.* New York: Simon & Schuster.

Rankin, Tom, ed. 1995. *"Deaf Maggie Lee Sayre": Photographs of a river life,* by Maggie Sayre. Jackson: University of Mississippi Press.

Riboud, Marc and Phjilippe Devillers. 1970. *Inside North Vietnam.* New York: Holt, Rinehart and Winston.

Richards, Eugene. 1978. *Dorchester Days.* Wollaston, Mass.: Many Voices.

Richards, Eugene. 1994. *Americans We.* New York: Aperture.

Richards, Eugene. 1994. *Cocaine True, Cocaine Blue.* New York: Aperture.

Richards, Eugene and Dorothea Lynch. 1986. *Exploding into Life.* New York: Aperture.

Riis, Jacob A. 1971 (1890). *How the Other Half Lives: Studies among the tenements of New York.* New York: Dover.

Rogovin, Milton. 1985. *The Forgotten Ones.* Seattle: University of Washington Press.

Salgado, Sebastião. 2000. *Migrations: Humanity in transitions.* Millertown: Aperture.

Shudakov, Grigory, Olga Suslova and Lilya Ukhtomskaya. 1983. *Pioneers of Soviet Photography.* London: Thames & Hudson.

Simon, Peter and Raymond Mungo. 1972. *Moving on Standing Still.* New York: Grossman.

Smith, Eugene and Aileen Smith. 1975. *Minamata.* New York: Holt, Rinehart and Winston.

Stehle, Bernard F. 1985. *Incurably Romantic.* Philadelphia: Temple University Press.

Stummer, Helen M. 1994. *No Easy Walk: Newark, 1980–1993*. Temple: Temple University Press.

Stryker, Roy Emerson and Nancy Wood. 1973. *In this Proud Land: America 1935–43 as seen in the FSA photographs*. Greenwich, CT: New York Graphic Society.

Waplington, Nick. 1991. *Living Room*. New York: Aperture.

Warburton, Nigel, ed. 1993. *Bill Brandt: Selected texts and bibliography*. Oxford, UK: Clio.

Whelan, Richard. 1985. *Robert Capa: A biography*. New York: Alfred A. Knopf.

Wilson, L. 2000. *Hutterites of Montana*. New Haven, CT: Yale University Press.

Winningham, Geoff. 1979. *Rites of Fall: High school football in Texas*. Austin: University of Texas Press.

Winogrand, Gary. 1977. *Public Relations*. Boston: New York Graphic Society.

Winogrand, Gary. 1980. *Stock Photographs: The Fort Worth fat stock show and rodeo*. Austin: University of Texas Press.

B. Theory and method

Banks, Marcus and Howard Morphy, eds. 1997. *Rethinking Visual Anthropology*. New Haven: Yale University Press.

Barthes, Roland. 1973. *Mythologies*. London: Paladin.

Barthes, Roland. 1981. *Camera Lucida*. New York: Hill & Wang.

Bolton, Richard, ed. 1989. *The Contest of Meaning: Critical histories of photography*. Cambridge: M.I.T. Press.

Collier, John, Jr. 1967. *Visual Anthropology: Photography as a research method*. New York: Holt, Rinehart and Winston. (Second edition. 1986. UNM Press.)

During, Simon, ed. 1993. *The Cultural Studies Reader*. London: Routledge.

Edwards, Elizabeth, ed. *Anthropology and Photography 1860–1920*. New Haven: Yale University Press, 1992.

Emmison, Michael and Philip Smith. 2000. *Researching the Visual*. Thousand Oaks, CA: Sage.

Evans, Jessica and Stuart Hall. 1999. *Visual Studies: The reader*. London: Sage.

Ewald, Wendy, Katherine Hyde and Lisa Lord. 2011. *Teaching Literacy and Justice with Photography: A classroom guide*. New York: College Teacher's Press.

Green, Jonathan, ed. 1974. *The Snapshot*. Millertown, New York: Aperture.

Grimshaw, Anna. 2001. *The Ethnographer's Eye: Ways of seeing in modern anthropology*. Cambridge: Cambridge University Press.

Hariman, Robert and John Louis Lucaites. 2007. *No Caption Needed: Iconic photographs, public culture, and liberal democracy*. Chicago: University of Chicago Press.

Hockings, Paul, ed. 1977. *Principles of Visual Anthropology*. The Hague: Mouton.

Knowles, Caroline and Paul Sweetman, eds. 2004. *Picturing the Social Landscape*. London: Routledge.

Maddow, Ben. 1977. *Faces: A narrative history of the portrait in photography*. Boston: New York Graphic Society.

Mukerji, Chandra and Michael Schudson. 1991. *Rethinking Popular Culture: Contemporary perspective in cultural studies*. Berkeley: University of California Press.

Nichols, Bill. 1981. *Ideology and the Image*. Bloomington: Indiana University Press.

Pink, Sarah. 2001. *Doing Visual Ethnography: Images, media and representation in research*. London: Sage.

Pink, Sarah. 2006. *The Future of Visual Anthropology: Engaging the senses*. London: Routledge.

Pink, Sarah. 2009. *Doing Sensory Ethnography*. London: Sage

Prosser, Jon, ed. 1998. *Image-based Research: A sourcebook for qualitative researchers*. London: Falmer.

Rose, Gillian. 2001. *Visual Methodologies*. London: Sage

Rony, S. 1996. *The Third Eye: Race, cinema, and ethnographic spectacle*. Durham: NC: Duke University Press.

Rosenblum, Naomi. 1989 [1984]. *A World History of Photography* (revised edition). New York: Abbeville.

Rosenblum, Walter, Naomi Trackenberg and Alan Trackenberg. 1977. *American and Lewis Hine*. Millerton, New York: Aperture.

Sekula, Alan. 1984. *Photography Against the Grain*. Halifax: Press of the Nova Scotia College of Art and Design.

Sobeiszek, Robert. 1988. *The Art of Persuasion: A history of advertising photography*. New York: Abrams.

Solomon-Godeau, Abigail. 1991. *Photography at the Dock*. Minneapolis: University of Minnesota Press.

Sontag, Susan. 1977. *On Photography*. New York: Hill & Wang.

Sontag, Susan. 2003. *Regarding the Pain of Others*. London: Hamish Hamilton.

Szarkowski, John. 1978. *Mirrors and Windows: American photography since 1960*. New York: Museum of Modern Art.

Szarkowski, John. 1988. *Winogrand: Figments from the real world*. New York: Museum of Modern Art.

Tagg, John. 1988. *The Burden of Representation: Essays on photographies and histories*. Basingstoke: Macmillan.

van Leeuwen, Theo and Carey Jewitt, eds. 2001. *Handbook of Visual Analysis*. Beverly Hills: Sage.

Wagner, Jon, ed. 1978. *Images of Information: Still photography in the social sciences*. Beverly Hills: Sage.

Wolf, Daniel, ed. 1983. *The American Space: Meaning in nineteenth century landscape photography*. Middletown, CT: Wesleyan University Press.

C. Case studies

Barndt, Deborah. 1980. *Education and Social Change: A photographic study of Peru*. Dubuque, Iowa: Kendall, Hunt.

Barndt, Deborah. 2002. *Tangled Routes: Women, work, and globalization of the tomato trail*. Lanham, MD: Rowman & Littlefield.

Bateson, Gregory and Margaret Mead. 1942. *Balinese Character: A photographic analysis*. New York: New York Academy of Sciences.

Becker, Howard S. 1982. *Art Worlds*. Berkeley: University of California Press.

Bourdieu, Pierre. 1990. *Photography: A middle-brow art*. Stanford, CA: Stanford University Press.

Bourgois, Philippe and Jeff Schonberg. 2009. *Righteous Dopefiend*. Berkeley: University of California Press.

Bunster, Ximena, Elsa Chaney and Ellan Young. 1989. *Sellers and Servants: Working women in Lima, Peru*. New York: Bergin & Garvey.

Chalfen, Richard. 1987. *Snapshot Versions of Life*. Bowling Green, Ohio: Bowling Green University Popular Press.

Chalfen, Richard. 1991. *Turning Leaves: The photograph collections of two Japanese American families*. Albuquerque: University of New Mexico Press.

Danforth, Loring and Alexander Tsiaras. 1982. *Death Rituals of Rural Greece*. Princeton: Princeton University Press.

Duneier, Mitchell and Ovie Carter. 1999. *Sidewalk*. New York: Farrar, Straus and Giroux.

Gardner, Robert and Karl Heider. 1968. *Gardens of War: Life and death in the New Guinea stone age*. New York: Random House.

Goldman, Robert and Stephen Papson. 1993. *Sign Wars: The cluttered landscapes of television advertising*. London: Guilford.

Goldman, Robert and Stephen Papson. 1998. *Nike Culture: The sign of the swoosh*. Beverly Hills: Sage

Hagaman, Dianne. 1996. *How I Learned not to be a Photojournalist*. Lexington: University Press of Kentucky.

Harper, Douglas. 1982. *Good Company*. Chicago: University of Chicago Press. (Third edition. 2006. *Good Company: A tramp life*. Paradigm.)

Harper, Douglas. 1987. *Working Knowledge: Skill and community in a small shop*. Chicago: University of Chicago Press.

Harper, Douglas, ed. 1994. *Cape Breton, 1952: The photographic vision of Timothy Asch*. University of Southern California: Ethnographics Press.

Harper, Douglas. 2001. *Changing Works: Visions of a lost agriculture*. Chicago: University of Chicago Press.

Harper, Douglas and Patrizia Faccioli. 2009. *The Italian Way: Food and social life*. Chicago: University of Chicago Press.

Keil, Charles and Angeliki and Dick Blau. 2002. *Bright Balkan Morning: Romani lives and the power of music in Greek Macedonia*. Middletown, CT: Wesleyan University Press.

Knowles, Caroline and Douglas Harper. 2009. *Hong Kong: Migrant lives, landscapes and journeys*. Chicago: University of Chicago Press.

Latour, Bruno and Emilie Hermant. 1998. *Paris ville invisible*. Paris: La Découverte.

Levine, Robert. 1990. *Images of History*. Durham, NC: Duke University Press.

Lutz, Catherine and Jane Collins. 1993. *Reading National Geographic*. Chicago: University of Chicago Press.

Nye, David. 1985. *Image Worlds: Corporate identities at General Electric*. Cambridge: M.I.T.

Quinney, Richard. 1991. *Journey to a Far Place*. Philadelphia: Temple University Press.

Quinney, Richard. 1998. *For the Time Being*. Albany: State University Press of New York.

Quinney, Richard. 2001. *Borderland: A Midwest journal*. Madison: University of Wisconsin Press.

Quinney, Richard. 2006. *Where Yet the Sweet Birds Sing*. Madison, WI: Borderland.

Quinney, Richard. 2008. *Things Once Seen*. Madison, WI: Borderland.

Schwalbe, Michael. 2011. *Smoke Damage*. Madison, WI: Borderland.

Spence, Jo. 1988. *Putting Myself in the Picture: A political, personal and photographic autobiography*. Seattle: Real Comet.

Schwartz, Dona. 1992. *Waucoma Twilight: Generations of the farm*. Washington: Smithsonian Institution Press.

Schwartz, Dona. 2009. *In the Kitchen*. Heidelberg: Verlag.

Swiderski, Richard M. 1995. *Eldoret: An African poetics of technology*. Tuscan: University of Arizona Press.

Vergara, Camilo José. 1999. *American Ruins*. New York: Monacelli.

Vergara, Camilo José. 2004. *Subway Memories*. New York: Monacelli.

Worth, Sol and John Adair. 1972. *Through Navajo Eyes*. Bloomington: Indiana University Press.

Notes

Introduction

1   Becker, Howard S. 1974. Photography and Sociology. *Studies in the Anthropology of Visual Communication* 1 (1): 3–26.

2   I described the early history of the IVSA in:
Harper, Douglas. 1996. Seeing Sociology. *American Sociologist* 27 (3): 69–76.

3   For thirteen years I edited, produced and distributed *Visual Sociology Review* and *Visual Sociology*. This was possible due to support from several deans and a string of exceptional graduate assistants. We pushed early versions of Photoshop and Pagemaker, and very modest Apple computers, to their limits to produce an 80 page journal with hundreds of images. In fact, the visual sociology movement emerged just when desktop publishing was becoming viable, and that made it possible to establish our own, image-based publication.

4   Harper, Douglas. 2001. *Changing Works: Visions of a lost agriculture*. Chicago: University of Chicago Press. And Harper, Douglas. 2004. Framing Photographic Ethnography: A case study. *Ethnography* 4 (2): 241–66.

Chapter 1: Visual ethnography

1   This is summarized from John Collier and Malcolm Collier. 1986 (originally published 1967. New York: Holt, Rinehart and Winston). *Visual Anthropology: Photography as a research method*. Alburquerque: University of New Mexico Press, pp. 199–201. Togashi's unpublished manuscript and photo project was called "Japanese Home Styles in San Francisco."

2   See Harper, Colter. 2011. The Crossroads of the World: A social and cultural history of jazz in Pittsburgh's Hill District, 1920–1970. Ph.D. dissertation, University of Pittsburgh, 2011.

3   See Harper, Douglas. 1987. *Working Knowledge: Skill and community in a small shop*. Chicago: University of Chicago Press.

4   Bourgois, Philippe and Jeff Schonberg. 2009. *Righteous Dopefiend*. Berkeley: University of California Press is a recent example; other examples will be referred to throughout the book.

5   Deborah Willis has published extensively and curated many exhibitions on African-American life and culture and her work shows the natural connection and overlap between cultural studies (her formal background), photography and visual sociology.

6   There are many excellent examples to choose from. One could begin with the work of Barbara Norfleet, 1986. *All the Right People*. Boston: New York Graphic Society; Bill Owens' most well-known contribution remains his 1972. *Suburbia*. San Francisco: Straight Arrow Books. Bill Brandt's photos are published in many collections; a place to start is Brandt, Bill. 1984. *London in the Thirties*. New York: Pantheon. These and other studies of social class will be discussed in detail later in this volume.

7   Mead, Margaret and Gregory Bateson. 1942. *Balinese Character: A photographic analysis*. New York: New York Academy of Sciences.

8   The racism at the basis of the Holocaust was argued in visual terms. Jews were made to look different by restricting their access to razors, soap and new clothes in Nazi-occupied lands, and were made to wear the yellow star that reminded all of their religion and culture. Reports of the times show how Parisians, for example, came to see Jews as different because they were made visually different through Nazi policies.

9   See Edwards, Elizabeth, ed. 1992. *Anthropology and Photography 1860–1920*. New Haven: Yale University Press.

10   Charlton, Noel. 2008. *Understanding Gregory Bateson: Mind, beauty, and the sacred earth*. Albany: SUNY Press, p. 79.

11   Mead, Margaret. 1995 (1972). *Blackberry Winter: My earlier years*. New York: Kodansha America, p. 234.

12   Mead and Bateson, ibid., p. 52. Bateson describes in detail how he and Mead photographed in the field, an interesting essay for photo field workers. Bateson used medium to long telephoto lenses to look at details, rather than wide angle lenses that contextualized social life.

13   Mead and Bateson, ibid., p. 50.

14   Mead and Bateson, ibid., p. 46.

15   Mead and Bateson, ibid., xv.

16   Collier, ibid., p. 210.

17   Murphy, Lois Barclay and Gardner Murphy. 1943. Reviewed work(s): *Balinese Character: A photographic analysis* by Gregory Bateson and Margaret Mead. *American Anthropologist*, New Series, 45 (4) Part 1 (Oct.–Dec.): 618.

18   Ibid, pp. 617–18.

19   An introduction to visual anthropology as embodied in ethnographic filmmaking is found in the work of Jay Ruby, especially his essay Better Straw than Concrete: A critique of Bill Nichols' view of ethnographic film, which is found on his website, http://astro.temple.edu/~ruby/ruby/ (accessed June 2011). Jay Ruby's ideas lead to an examination of standard texts such as:

Heider, Karl. 2006 [1976]. *Ethnographic Film* (revised edition). Austin: University of Texas Press.

Grimshaw, Anna. 2001. *The Ethnographer's Eye: Ways of seeing in modern anthropology*. Cambridge: Cambridge University Press.

MacDougall, David. 1998. *Transcultural Cinema*. Princeton: Princeton University Press. The postmodern critique, as voiced in:

Marcus, George and M. Fischer. 1986. *Anthropology as Cultural Critique*. Chicago: University of Chicago Press.

Marcus, George and James Clifford. 1986. *Writing Culture: The politics and poetics of ethnography*. Berkeley: University of California Press.

As Jay Ruby notes, the critique initiated in these and other of the first generation postmodern voices on ethnography had been around for decades. For example, Del Hymes' *Reinventing Anthropology*. 1999 [1976]. Ann Arbor: University of Michigan Press was crucial in helping me figure out how to do and write ethnography in graduate school and, in fact, Del Hymes was the outside reader for my dissertation. In any case, one can easily see that ethnographic film is a complex affair with a great deal of contrary intellectual energy driving it on.

20   Collier, ibid.

21   Sorenson, E. Richard. 1976. *The Edge of the Forest: Land, childhood and change in a New Guinea protoagricultural society*. Washington: Smithsonian Institute Press. Foreword by Margaret Mead.

22   Danforth, Loring M. and Alexander Tsiaras. 1982. *Death Rituals in Rural Greece*. Princeton: Princeton University Press.

23   Cancian, Frank. 1974. *Another Place*. San Francisco: Scrimshaw.

24   Keil, Charles and Angeliki and Dick Blau. 2002. *Bright Balkan Morning: Romani lives and the power of music in Greek Macedonia*. Middletown, CT: Wesleyan University Press.

Chapter 2: Documentary photography

1   Rosenblum, Naomi. 1989 [1984]. *A World History of Photography* (revised edition). New York: Abbeville, p. 341.

2   Smith, W. Eugene and Aileen Smith. 1975. *Minimata*. New York: Holt, Rinehart and Winston.

3   Frank, Robert. 1969 (originally published 1959). *The Americans*. New York: Aperture. The original has a short introductory essay by Jack Kerouac.

4   Rosenblum, ibid., p. 341.

5   Document: A publication of the Center for Documentary Studies at Duke University. Summer/Fall 2005, inside front cover.

6   This perspective is found in:

Rosler, Martha. 1989. In, Around and Afterthoughts (on documentary photography). In Bolton, Richard, ed. *The Contest of Meaning: Critical histories of photography*. Cambridge: MIT Press, pp. 303–42.

Solomon-Godeau, Abigail. 1991. *Photography at the Doc: Essays on photographic history, institutions and practices*. Minneapolis: University of Minnesota Press.

Sontag, Susan. 2003. *Regarding the Pain of Others*. London: Hamish Hamilton.

7   Rosler in Bolton, ibid., p. 307.

8   Rankin, Tom, ed. 1995. *"Deaf Maggie Lee Sayre": Photographs of a river life*, by Maggie Lee Sayre. Jackson: University of Mississippi Press.

9   Becker, Howard S. 1982. *Art Worlds*, University of California Press.

10   Becker, Howard S. 1995. Visual Sociology, Documentary Photography, and Photojournalism: It's (almost) all a matter of context. *Visual Sociology* 10 (1–2): 5–14.

11   Coles, Robert with photos by Alex Harris. 1978. *The Last and First Eskimos*. Boston: New York Graphic Society; and Coles, Robert, with photos by Alex Harris and Thomas Roma. 1997. *Old and On Their Own*. New York: Center for Documentary Studies/Norton.

12   Among Jackson's many books, several are squarely in the documentary mode. These include: Jackson, Bruce. 2009. *Pictures from a Drawer: Prison and the art of portraiture*.

Philadelphia: Temple University Press, which examines official portraits discovered in an administrator's office in a Texas prison; and Jackson, Bruce. 1977. *Killing Time: Life in the Arkansas penitentiary*. Cornell: Cornell University Press, a collection of Jackson's documentary photos and documentary observations.

13   Becker, Howard S. 1974. Photography and Sociology. *Studies in the Anthropology of Visual Communication* 1 (1): 3–26.

14   While it would be very nice to include several photos from each photographer or era in this book, the costs of rights are usually extreme. On the other hand the Web is an incredible resource that most readers have access to. To suggest the obvious, I recommend that interested readers Google or otherwise search for any and all of the photographers of interest who are discussed throughout the book. Most (certainly not all!) will be available for viewing.

15   See Newhall, Nancy. 1975. *P. H. Emerson*. Millertown: New York: Aperture.

16   Bunnell, Peter. 1989. The Pictorial Effect. In Weaver, Mike, ed. *The Art of Photography, 1839–1989*. New Haven: Yale University Press, p. 156.

17   The significant titles by Peter Emerson were *Idylls of the Norfolk Broads* (1886), *Life and Landscape on the Norfolk Broads* (1886) and *Pictures of East Anglian Life* (1888).

18   Newhall, ibid., p. 4.

19   Rosenblum, Naomi. 1989 [1984]. *A World History of Photography* (revised edition). New York: Abbeville, p. 361.

20   Several photographers had taken on the subject of London's poor, and other photographers had photographed other industrializing European cities, leaving behind photos that are often not even attributable to authorship. See Rosenblum, ibid., pp. 340–92 for an introduction.

21   Henry Mayhew's work was perhaps the most important early example. His book *London Labour and the London Poor* was published about 1860, and included images that originated as daguerreotypes but were transformed into wood engravings for the book because the halftone process had yet to be perfected.

22   Unpaged excerpt of *How the Other Half Lives*, found on http://www.spartacus. schoolnet.co.uk/USAriis.htm (accessed June 2011).

23   It would also be interesting to contemplate why there was not a comparable documentary tradition focusing on the Chinese revolution or the emergence of fascism in Japan.

24   Ricci, Steven. 2008. *Cinema and Fascism: Italian film and society, 1922–1943*. Berkeley: University of California Press, p. 71

25   See Ricci, ibid., pp. 135–39.

26   There is an extensive literature on newsreels in continental Europe, the UK and the US packaged as DVDs and available commercially. Overviews are common on the Web.

27   Brandt's *The English at Home* (1936) included an introduction by Raymond Mortimer, and was published by B.T. Batsford in London. The unpaginated book was only seventy-two pages long and included only sixty-three illustrations. His book, *A Night in London* (1938) was simultaneously published in London, Paris and New York and was also brief; sixty-eight pages with sixty-four illustrations.

28   Warburton, Nigel, ed. 1993. *Bill Brandt: Selected texts and bibliography*. Oxford, UK: Clio, p. 30.

29   This photo appears on p. 17 of Warburton, ibid. Discussion of the altering of photos appears on pp. 8–19.

30   Warburton, ibid., p. 32.

31 Most well-known were Dorothea Lange, Walker Evans, Gordon Parks, Russell Lee, John Vachon, Arthur Rothstein, Marion Post Wolcott, Jack Delano, Carl Mydans and Ben Shahn. Others who had a smaller role, but went on to the SONJ (Standard Oil (New Jersey)) documentary project and other careers in documentary and related photography included Charlotte Brooks, Esther Bubley and Sol Libsohn.

32 See Hurley, F. Jack in *The Family in America: An encyclopedia*, Volume 1, p. 650. This incomplete reference is due to the location of the reference on the web, where it appears without full citation.

33 Shooting scripts are described in Collier and Collier, ibid.

34 See Suchar, Charles. 1997. Grounding visual sociology research in shooting scripts. *Qualitative Sociology* 20 (1): 33–55.

35 The multimedia exhibit, which includes a lengthy catalogue entitled "Russie! Memoria mistificazione immaginario" displayed at the University of Venice in 2010 is an excellent discussion of these issues.

36 Frank, Robert. 1969. *The Americans*. New York: Aperture.

37 This review appeared in *Popular Photography* and is widely cited.

38 Davidson, Bruce. 1970. *E100 Street*. Cambridge: Harvard University Press.

39 Owens, Bill. 1972. *Suburbia*. San Francisco: Straight Arrow Press.

40 Owens, Bill. 1975. *Our Kind of People*. New York: Simon & Schuster.

41 Estrin, Mary Lloyd. 1979. *To the Manor Born*. Boston: New York Graphic Society.

42 Sanders, Norman. 1977. *At Home*. New York: Morgan & Morgan.

43 Clark's first book, *Tulsa*. New York: Lustrum Press, 1971 was based on photos Clark made of his teen friends in suburban Oklahoma, shooting speed, having sex and playing with guns; his subsequent work, *Teenage Lust*. Larry Clark (self-published), 1983, and several films were looking backward at these forms of life from middle age.

44 Simon, Peter (photographer) and writer Raymond Mungo. 1972. *Moving On Standing Still*. New York: Grossman.

45 Richards, Eugene. 1978. *Dorchester Days*. Wollaston, Mass.: Many Voices.

46 Riboud, Marc and Philippe Devillers. 1970. *Inside North Vietnam*. New York: Holt, Rinehart and Winston.

47 Griffiths, Philip Jones. 1971. *Vietnam Inc*. New York: Collier.

48 Burrows, Larry. 2002. *Larry Burrow's Vietnam*. New York: Alfred A. Knopf. Introduction by David Halberstam.

49 Halberstam, David in Burrows, ibid., p. 14.

50 Copeland, Alan, 1969. *People's Park*. New York, Ballantine.

51 Hansberry, Lorraine. 1964. *The Movement*. New York: Simon & Schuster.

52 Lyons, Danny. 1992. *Memories of the Southern Civil Rights Movement*. Durham: Duke University Press.

53 Fenton, David. 1971. *Shots*. New York: Douglas Book Corporation. Also see Ray Mungo's 1970 book *Famous Long Ago: My life and hard times with the Liberation News Service*. Boston: Beacon Press.

54 Anderson, Robert, ed. 1973. *Voices from Wounded Knee*. Rooseveltown, New York: Akwesasne Notes.

55 Mungo, Raymond. 1970. *Total Loss Farm: A year in the life*. New York: E.P. Dutton. See also Peter Simon's 1970 book of photos, *Moving On, Holding Still*. New York: Grossman.

56 Lyon, Danny. 2003 (originally published 1967). *Bikeriders*. New York: Chronicle.

57   Lyon, Danny. 1969. *Conversations with the Dead*. New York: Holt, Rinehart and Winston. See also Jackson, Bruce. 1977. *Killing Time: Life in the Arkansas penitentiary*. Ithaca, New York: Cornell University Press.

58   Hecke, Roswitha. 1982. *Love Life: Scenes with Irene*. New York: Grove.

59   Susan Meiselas's 1975 photo study *Carnival Strippers*. New York: Holt, Rinehart and Winston, was the first of her many important photo documentary projects.

60   Winogrand, Garry. 1977. *Public Relations*. Boston: New York Graphic Society.

61   Hare, Chauncey. 1984. *This Was Corporate America*. Boston: Institute of Contemporary Art.

62   In this vein, the Center for Documentary Studies at Duke University, which for twenty years awarded the Lang–Taylor Documentary Prize (named after Dorothea Lange and Paul Taylor), a $20,000 award for book projects combining documentary writing and photography, was temporarily suspended in 2011 as the prize committee considers how documentary expression is changing as the publishing environment itself is evolving through the digital revolution.

63   Of Richard's many documentary studies, see especially *Cocaine True, Cocaine Blue*, New York: Aperture, 1994, on the lives of people addicted to crack cocaine, and, most recently, Richards, Eugene. 2008. *A Procession of Them*. Austin: University of Texas Press, on the institutionalization of the mentally ill in several countries.

64   Greenfield, Lauren. 2002. *Girl Culture*. San Francisco: Chronicle.

65   Waplington, Nick. 1991. *Living Room*. New York: Aperture.

66   Maharidge, Dale and Michael Williamson. 2008. *Denison, Iowa*. New York: Free Press.

67   Peter Menzel organized and wrote *Material World: A global family portrait*. 1994. San Francisco: Sierra Club Books. In this project sixteen photographers from around the world including Menzel documented a representative family's possessions. Menzel's second project, with writer Faith D'Aluisio. *Hungry Planet: What the world eats*. 2005. New York: Random House, documents the complete weekly diet of typical families in twenty-four regions of the world.

68   Jackson, Bruce. 2009. *Pictures from a Drawer: Prison and the art of portraiture*. Philadelphia: Temple University Press.

69   Frazier, Danny Wilcox. 2009. *Driftless: Photographs from Iowa*. Chapel Hill: Duke University Press.

70   Couderc, Jean-Marie. 1996. *A Village in France: Louis Clergeau's photographic portrait of daily life in Pontlevoy, 1902–1938*. New York: Abrams, 1996.

71   Meiselas, Susan. 1997. *Kurdistan: In the shadow of history*. New York: Random House. (Second edition. 2009. University of Chicago Press.)

Chapter 3: Reflexivity

1   Spradley, James. 1970. *You Owe Yourself a Drunk: An ethnography of urban nomads*. Boston: Little, Brown and Company.

2   Harper, Douglas. 1982. *Good Company*. Chicago: University of Chicago Press. Revised second editions were published in France and Italy as *Good Company: Un sociologo tra I vagabondi*. Milan: FrancoAngeli, 1999, and *Les Vagabonds du Nord-Ouest Américain*. Paris: L'Harmattan, 1998. An updated third edition entitled *Good Company: A tramp life* was published by Paradigm in 2006.

3   Maharidge, Dale and Michael Williamson. 1985. *Journey to Nowhere: The saga of the new underclass*. New York: Doubleday.

4   For an extended discussion, see Harper, Douglas. 1993. On the Authority of the Image: Visual sociology at the crossroads. In Denzin, Norman and Yvonna Lincoln, eds. *Handbook of Qualitative Research*. Newbury Park, CA: Sage, pp. 403–12.

5   I was editor of a book series, *Visual Studies of Society and Culture*, for several years and attended several SPE meetings to solicit projects. I found much interesting photography, but very little visual ethnography or documentary.

6   Goodwin, Charles. 2001. Practices of Seeing Visual Analysis: An ethnomethodological approach. In van Leeuwen, Theo and Carey Jewitt, eds. *Handbook of Visual Analysis*. London: Sage.

7   Rose, Gillian. 2001. *Visual Methodologies*. London: Sage, p. 130.

8   Pink, Sarah. 2003. Interdisciplinary agendas in visual research: Re-situating visual anthropology. *Visual Studies* 18 (2): 187.

9   Loizos, Peter. 1997. First exits from observational realism: narrative experiments in recent ethnographic films. In Banks, Marcus and Howard Morphy, eds. *Rethinking Visual Anthropology*. New Haven: Yale University Press, p. 94.

10   Pink, ibid., p. 189.

11   Banks, Marcus and Howard Morphy. 1997. Introduction. In Banks, Marcus and Howard Morphy, eds. *Rethinking Visual Anthropology*. New Haven: Yale University Press, p. 11.

12   Bourgois, Philip and Jeff Schonberg. 2009. *Righteous Dopefiend*. Berkeley: University of California Press.

13   Bourgois and Schonberg, ibid., p. 11.

14   Duneier, Mitchell and Ovie Carter. 1999. *Sidewalk*. New York: Ferrar, Straus and Giroux.

Chapter 4: The visual sociology of space from above, inside and around

1   Wagner, Jon. 1979. *Images of Information: Still photography in the social sciences*. Beverly Hills: Sage.

2   Harper, Douglas. 2001. *Changing Works: Visions of a lost agriculture*. Chicago: University of Chicago Press.

3   Harper, Douglas. 1997. Visualizing Structure: Reading surfaces of social life. *Qualitative Sociology* 20 (1): 57–78.

4   After experimenting with several altitudes I discovered that photographing between 1,500 and 2,500 feet with a 200 mm lens produced farm portraits that balanced detail and coverage. The partially melted snow of late winter often highlighted topographical or architectural outlines that were of interest to me as a sociologist but the contrast provided by the patches of snow also made photos hard to read. In the summer months the foliage often hid the details of the farmsteads and the sun glinted brilliantly from the metal roofs of farm buildings, creating contrast extremes. The best light was a slight overcast in a season where the natural features did not obliterate the features of the built environment in which I was interested.

One of the most challenging parts of the project was simply keeping track of where I was, and finding an angle that allowed me to frame the farmsteads to the patterns of shadow and light. I'd ask the pilot, an elderly ex-World War Two fighter pilot, who I sometimes felt was having flashbacks to combat, to bank the plane sharply to allow me to use the 200 mm lens in the tight confines of the cabin, which would cause us to lose altitude rapidly. Of course the plane was bouncing in the air and I needed to change film after 36 exposures. All in all it was a lot of fun.

5   This important issue was first discussed in: Grady, John. 1996. The Scope of Visual Sociology. *Visual Sociology* 11 (2): 10–24, although Emmison and Smith do not acknowledge Grady's seminal definition of the issue. Jon Wagner's review essay on Emmison and Smith and other books is the best recent discussion of the relationship between sight, visual images and visual sociology: Wagner, Jon. 2002. Contrasting Images, Complementary Trajectories: Sociology, visual sociology and visual research. *Visual Studies* 17 (2): 160–71.

6   Emmison, Michael and Philip Smith. 2000. *Researching the Visual*. London: Sage, p. 9.

7   Gowin, Emmet. 1992. *Changing the Earth*. New Haven: Yale University Press.

8   Moore, Gemma, Ben Croxford, Mags Adams, Mohamed Refaee, Trevor Cox and Steve Sharples. 2008. The Photo-Survey Research Method: Capturing life in the city. *Visual Studies* 23 (1): 50–62.

9   OPEN/CLOSED: Public Spaces in Modern Cities, by Lilia Voronkova and Oleg Pachenkov, a website that summarizes an exhibition. http://www.cisr.ru/files/publ/Katalog_OPENCLOSED_Vorschau.pdf (accessed June 2011).

10   Adelman, Bob and Susan Hall. 1970. *On and Off the Street*. New York: Viking.

11   Stummer, Helen M. 1994. *No Easy Walk: Newark, 1980–1993*. Temple: Temple University Press.

12   Vergara, Camilo José. 2004. *Subway Memories*. New York: Monacelli.

13   The book version is: Melbin, Murray. 1987. *Night as Frontier: Colonizing the world after dark*. New York: Free Press.

14   Schles, Ken. 1988. *Invisible City*. Pasadena, CA: Twelvetrees.

Chapter 5: Comparing societies

1   Engels, Friedrich. 1844. *The Condition of the Working Class in Manchester*. (Current edition. 2006. Penguin.)

2   Rose, Gillian. 2001. *Visual Methodologies*. London: Sage, p. 136.

3   Rose, ibid., p. 137.

4   Berger, John. 1972. *Another Way of Seeing*. London: Penguin.

5   Rose, ibid., p. 142.

6   Klett, Mark, Ellen Manchester and JoAnn Verburg. 1984. *Second View: The Rephotographic Survey Project*. Albuquerque: University of New Mexico Press, was the first contemporary rephotography project.

7   Klett, Mark, Kyle Bajakian, William Fox, Michael Marshall, Toshi Ueshina and Byron Wolfe. 2004. *Third Views, Second Sights: A rephotographic survey of the American West*. Albuquerque: Museum of New Mexico Press.

8   Rieger, Jon. 1996. Photographing Social Change. *Visual Sociology* 11 (1): 5–49; and Rieger, Jon. 2003. A Retrospective Visual Study of Social Change: The pulp-logging industry in an Upper Peninsula Michigan county. *Visual Studies* 18 (2): 157–78.

9   *Northern Lights* (1978). Produced, directed, written and edited by John Hanson and Rob Nilsson (independent production).

10   Vergara, Camilo José. 1999. *American Ruins*. New York: Monacelli.

11   Vergara, ibid., p. 83.

12   Vergara, ibid., p. 133.

13   Vergara, ibid., p. 57–58.

14   Vergara, http://www.americansuburbx.com/2009/11/theory-images-as-tool-of-discovery.html (accessed March 2011).

15   Ganzel, Bill. 1984. *Dust Bowl Descent*. Omaha: University of Nebraska Press.

16   Maharidge, Dale and Michael Williamson. 1990. *And Their Children After Them: The legacy of* Let Us Now Praise Famous Men. New York: Pantheon.

17   Rogovin, Milton. 1985. *The Forgotten Ones*. Seattle: University of Washington Press contains the nearly complete rephotography series, though some couples were photographed for a fourth time when Rogovin was in his nineties. His photographic work is fully cited in the website http://www.miltonrogovin.com/. The film *The Rich Have Their Own Photographers* (2009) and other shorter documentaries provide an overview of Rogovin's work and a portrayal of how he worked.

18   The films are called *Seven Up* (1964), *7 Plus Seven* (1970), *21 Up* (1977), *28 Up* (1985), *35 Up* (1991), *42 Up* (1998) and *49 Up* (2005). For a visual sociologist's take on the project, see Wagner, Jon. 2007. Lives in Transaction: An appreciation of Michael Apted's *UP* filmmaking project. *Visual Studies* 22 (3): 293–300.

19   Sekula, Allan. 1983. Photography Between Labour and Capital. In Buchloh, H.D. and Robert Wilkie, eds. *Mining Photographs and Other Pictures, 1948–1968: A selection from the negative archives of Shedden Studio, Glace Bay, Cape Breton*. Halifax, NS: Press of the Nova Scotia College of Art and Design. Sekula, Allan. 1986. The Body and the Archive. *October* 39: 3–64.

20   Payne, Carol. 2006. Lessons with Leah: Re-reading the photographic archive of nation in the National Film Board of Canada's Still Photographic Division. *Visual Studies* 21 (1): 4–23.

21   Payne, ibid., p. 11.

22   Margolis, Eric. 2004. Looking at Discipline, Looking at Labour: Photographic representations of Indian boarding schools. *Visual Studies* 9 (1): 73.

23   Margolis, ibid., p. 85.

24   Margolis, ibid., p. 91.

25   Norfleet, Barbara. 2001. *When We Liked Ike: Looking for postwar America*. New York: Norton.

26   Norfleet, ibid.

27   Lesy, Michael. 1973. *Wisconsin Death Trip*. New York: Pantheon. His other historical collections include:
Lesy, Michael. 1976. *Real Life: Louisville in the twenties*. New York: Random House.
Lesy, Michael. 1985. *Bearing Witness: A photographical chronicle of American Life 1860–1945*. New York: Doubleday.
Lesy, Michael. 1997. *Dreamland: America at the dawn of the twentieth century*. New York: New Press.
Lesy, Michael. 2002. *Long Time Coming: A photographic portrait of America*. New York: W.W. Norton.
Lesy, Michael. 2007. *Murder City: The bloody history of Chicago in the twenties*. New York: W.W. Norton.

28   Levine, Robert. 1989. *Images of History: Nineteenth and early twentieth century Latin American photographs as documents*. Durham: Duke University Press.

29   Harper, Douglas and Patrizia Faccioli. 2009. *The Italian Way: Food and social life*. Chicago: University of Chicago Press.

30   Harper and Faccioli, ibid., p. 171

31   Grady, John. 2007. Advertising Images as Social Indicators: Depictions of blacks in *Life* magazine, 1936–2000. *Visual Studies* 22 (3): 211–39.

32   Lutz, Catherine and Jane Collins. 1993. *Reading National Geographic*. Chicago: University of Chicago Press.

33   Suchar, Charles. 2004. Amsterdam and Chicago: Seeing the macro characteristics of gentrification. In Knowles, Caroline and Paul Sweetman, eds. *Picturing the Social Landscape*. Abingdon: Routledge, p. 149.

34   Knowles, Caroline and Douglas Harper. 2009. *Hong Kong: Migrant lives, landscapes and journeys*. Chicago: University of Chicago Press.

Chapter 6: Ethnomethodology, semiotics and the subjective

1   See Hester, Stephen and David Francis. 2003. Analyzing Visually Available Mundane Order: A walk to the supermarket. *Visual Studies* 18 (1): 36–46. Hester and Francis indicate that ". . . emphasis on talk has not been matched by a similar attention to the visual and non-verbal aspects of social interaction" p. 37.

2   Sudnow, David. 1978. *Ways of the Hand: The organization of improvised conduct*. Cambridge: Harvard University Press, p. xi.

3   Boden, Deirdre. 1990. The World as it Happens: Ethnomethodology and conversation analysis. In Ritzer, George, ed. *Social Theory: The new syntheses*. New York: Columbia University Press, p. 191.

4   Carlin, Andrew. 2003. Pro Forma Arrangements: The visual availability of textual artifacts. *Visual Studies* 18 (1): 6–20.

5   Hester and Francis, ibid.

6   The Qualitative Analysis of Visual Data, European Science Foundation Workshop on Visual Methods, 2007.

7   It may have been folklore, but I remember hearing of an ethnomethodological analysis of a two hour Ph.D. dissertation that extended for seven years.

8   Goodwin, Charles. 2001. Practices of Seeing Visual Analysis: An ethnomethodological approach. In van Leeuwen, Theo and Carey Jewitt, eds. *Handbook of Visual Analysis*. London: Sage, p. 179.

9   Their photographs and books are easily found on the Web; I recommend an initial search by name.

10   Resnick, Mason. 1988. Coffee and Workprints: A workshop with Garry Winogrand – Two weeks with a master of street photography that changed my life. http://www.photogs.com/bwworld/winogrand.html (accessed November 2010). Originally published in *Modern Photography*, 1988.

11   See Solomon-Godeau, Abigail. 1991. *Photography at the Dock: Essays on photographic history, institutions and practices*. Minneapolis: University of Minnesota Press. While this text is now several years old it remains one of the strongest arguments against documentary photography as a modernist, liberal–reformist practice. Solomon-Godeau's argument is that photographers who insist that their work is about photography per se are ignoring the fact that all photos are really about social relationships; including the question of who has the power to picture others and whose gaze will be preserved. A photographer like Cartier-Bresson is characterized as a "trophy hunter," whose "privileged subjectivity" is "at most that of a cultivated flaneur" (p. 82). The proper postmodern photographic practice deconstructs all photographic practices and sees all representation in terms of the politics they represent.

12   Burgin, Victor. 1996. *Some Cities*. Berkeley: University of California Press; and Burgin, Victor. 1986. *Between*. London: Basil Blackwell.

13   Bryson, Norman, in Burgin, ibid., 1986, unpaginated.

14   Barthes, Roland. 1972 (1957). *Mythologies*. London: Paladin.

15   The most developed analysis of the semiotics of advertising is found in the several texts and websites of Stephen Papson and Robert Goldman, discussed in more detail in Chapter 7. See their texts *Nike Culture: The sign of the swoosh*. 1998. London: Sage; and *Sign Wars: The cluttered landscapes of television advertising*. 1993. London: Guilford.

16   Goffman, Erving. 1979. *Gender Advertisements*. New York: Macmillan.

17   Harper, Douglas and Patrizia Faccioli. 2000. Small, Silly Insults, Mutual Seduction and Misogyny: The interpretation of Italian advertising signs. *Visual Sociology* 15 (1): 23–50.

18   Owens, Bill. 1972. *Suburbia*. San Francisco: Straight Arrow Books.

19   Painter, Borden. 2005. *Mussolini's Rome*. London: Palgrave.

20   This research is ongoing with Professor Francesco Mattioli of the University of Rome.

21   McLean, Alick M. 2008. *Prato: Architecture, piety, and political identity in a Tuscan city-state*. New Haven: Yale University Press.

22   Chau, Adam Yuet. 2008. An Awful Mark: Symbolic violence and urban renewal in reform-era China. *Visual Studies* 23 (3): 195–210.

23   Chau, ibid., p. 195.

24   Pauwels, Luc. 1996. Managing Impressions: On visually decoding the workplace as a symbolic environment. *Visual Sociology* 11 (2): 62–74.

25   Kalof, Linda and Amy Fitzgerald. 2003. Reading the Trophy: Exploring the display of dead animals in hunting magazines. *Visual Studies* 18 (2): 112–22.

26   Kalof and Fitzgerald, ibid., p. 112.

27   See Schama, Simon. 1988. *The Embarrassment of Riches: An interpretation of Dutch culture in the golden age*. Berkeley: University of California Press; and Alpers, Svetlana. 1983. *The Art of Describing*. Chicago: University of Chicago Press.

28   Arora, Vibha. 2009. Framing the image of Sikkim. *Visual Studies* 26 (1): 54–65.

29   Szorenyi, Anna. 2006. The Images Speak for Themselves? Reading refugee coffee-table books. *Visual Studies* 21 (1): 24–41.

30   Szorenyi, ibid., p. 29.

31   Szorenyi, ibid., p. 31.

32   There have been few broadly defined collections of cultural studies in recent years. The most important of a few years ago include:
Evans, Jessica and Stuart Hall. 1999. *Visual Studies: The reader*. London: Sage.
Mukerji, Chandra and Michael Schudson. 1991. *Rethinking Popular Culture: Contemporary perspectives in cultural studies*. Berkeley: University of California Press.
During, Simon, ed. 1993. *The Cultural Studies Reader*. London: Routledge.

33   Chaplin, Elizabeth. 1994. *Sociology and Visual Representation*. London: Sage.

34   Harper, Douglas. 1987. The Visual Ethnographic Narrative. *Visual Anthropology* 1 (1): 1–19. The ideas were further developed in several papers.

35   Nichols, Bill. 1981. *Ideology and the Image: Social representation in the cinema and other media*. Bloomington: Indiana University Press.

36   See, for example:

Quinney, Richard. 1991. *Journey to a Far Place*. Philadelphia: Temple University Press.

Quinney, Richard. 1998. *For the Time Being*. Albany: State University Press of New York.

Quinney, Richard. 2006. *Where Yet the Sweet Birds Sing*. Madison, WI: Borderland.

37   Lynch, Dorothea and Eugene Richards. 1986. *Exploding into Life*. New York: Aperture.

38   Spence, Jo. 1986. *Putting Myself in the Picture: A political, personal and photographic autobiography*. London: Camden.

39   Prosser, Jon. 2007. Visual Mediation of Critical Illness: An autobiographical account of nearly dying and nearly living. *Visual Studies* 22 (2): 185–99.

40   Personal communication.

41   Steiger, Ricabeth. 2000. En Route: An interpretation through images. *Visual Sociology* 15 (1–2): 155–60.

42   Steiger, ibid., p. 155.

43   The development of the cross-platform CD was possible because the designer of the journal, Suzan Harper, was also a multimedia expert.

The CD was widely respected and was featured in an international conference, *Beeld voor Beeld*, in Amsterdam in 2005 and a traveling exhibition. The CD form of the photo essay changed it completely, making what would be a very long article (if the images were printed individually on a page) into a brief movie that communicated the subjective dimension of the train ride better than did the photos on a page.

44   Pink, Sarah. 2006. *The Future of Visual Anthropology: Engaging the senses*. London: Routledge.

45   Pink, Sarah. 2007. Walking with Video. *Visual Studies* 22 (3): 240–52.

46   See, for example, Artieri, Giovanni Boccia, Laura Gemini and Valentina Orsucci. 2009. Visual Sociology 2.0: Imagined and travelled landscapes in Second Life. IVSA Conference, Cumbria, UK. This work has been in development for several years at the University of Umbria in Italy.

Chapter 7: Multimedia and visual sociology

1   Kickstarter is a recent development in which artists raise money for projects in a social media arrangement.

2   Lapenta, Francesco. 2011. Locative Media and the Digital Visualization of Space, Place and Information. *Visual Studies* 26 (1): 1.

3   Hagaman, Dianne. 2002. *Howie Feeds Me*. Rochester, New York: Visual Studies Workshop. (CD-ROM). The production is also available online and is adapted to modern operating systems.

4   http://www.bruno-latour.fr/virtual/paris/english/frames.html (accessed January 2011).

5   Papson, Stephen, Robert Goldman and Noah Kersey. 2007. Website Design: The precarious blend of narrative, aesthetics, and social theory. In Stanczak, Gregory C., ed. *Visual Research Methods*. Beverly Hills: Sage, pp. 307–44.

6   This is a development of what is generally called the postmodern criticism of ethnography (and anthropology in general) that began with the influential text by George Marcus and M. Fischer, cited above.

7   Papson, et al., ibid., p. 328.

8   Papson, et al., ibid.

9   Papson, et al., ibid., p. 309.

10   Papson, et al., ibid., p. 336.

11   Papson, et al., ibid., p. 337.

12   Pink, Sarah. 2001. *Doing Visual Ethnography: Images, media and representation in research*. London, Sage, pp. 158–59.

13   Papson, et al., ibid., p. 335.

14   Ricabeth Steiger's article En Route: An interpretation through images. *Visual Sociology* 15 (1–2): 155–60 included a CD where hundreds of images were blended into a movie. It is becoming common for articles to refer to websites that contain videos and other multimedia. See also Joanna Kirkpatrick's *Transports of Delight: The rickshaw arts of Bangladesh*, a CD distributed in the early 2000s by Indiana University Press.

15   Papson, et al., ibid., p. 338.

16   Meiselas, Susan. 1997. *Kurdistan: In the shadow of history*. New York: Random House. (Second edition. 2009. University of Chicago Press.)

17   In that Tufte's work is continually evolving it seems most useful to refer readers to his website: http://www.edwardtufte.com/tufte/ (accessed March 2010).

18   Swiderski, Richard M. 1995. *Eldoret: An African poetics of technology*. Tuscan: University of Arizona Press.

19   Jones, Michael Owen. 1975. *The Homemade Object and its Maker*. Berkeley: University of California Press.

20   Harper, Douglas. 1987. *Working Knowledge: Skill and community in a small shop*. Chicago: University of Chicago Press.

21   See Gould, Peter and Rodney White. 1974. *Mental Maps*. Baltimore: Penguin.
      See also: Kent, Susan. 1984. *Analyzing Activity Areas: An ethnoarchaeological study of the use of space*. Albuquerque: University of New Mexico Press.
      Kent studies how households are organized, relying on maps people draw of their home spaces, and her key idea is that memory often exaggerates or makes spaces smaller in its maps to show varying degrees of importance.

22   Psathas, George. 1979. Organizational Feature of Direction Maps. In Psathas, George, ed. *Everyday Language*. New York: Irvington, pp. 203–26.

23   Krase, Jerry. 2004. Seeing Community in a Multicultural Society: Theory and practice. In *Perspectives of Multiculturalism: Western and transitional countries*. Zagreb: Croatian Commission for UNESCO: FF Press, pp. 151–77.

24   Manovich, Lev. 2011. What is Visualization? *Visual Studies* 26 (1): 36–49.

25   http://en.wikipedia.org/wiki/Opte_Project (accessed March 2010).

Chapter 8: Photo elicitation

1   Collier, John. 1957, 856–58.

2   The CB, or citizens' band, radio was a form of communication now very likely obsolete, whereby people could be in constant contact. These were used by long distance truckers to communicate with each other, and each speaker had a nickname, or handle. Willie's was "Nighthawk One." They were also free to use, and Willie didn't have a phone. Their downside was that the radios broadcast a constant crackling sound, whether or not a person was trying to get in touch with another. I quickly discovered that this sound effectively blotted out my tape recorder.

3   Book length PE studies include:
     Barndt, Deborah. 1980. *Education and Social Change: A photographic study of Peru*. Dubuque, Iowa: Kendall, Hunt.

Barndt, Deborah. 2002. *Tangled Routes: Women, work, and globalization of the tomato trail.* Lanham, MD: Rowman & Littlefield.

Harper, Douglas, ed. 1994. *Cape Breton, 1952: The photographic vision of Timothy Asch.* University of Southern California: Ethnographics Press.

Harper, Douglas and Patrizia Faccioli. 2009. *The Italian Way: Food and social life.* Chicago: University of Chicago Press.

Schwartz, Dona. 1992. *Waucoma Twilight: Generations of the farm.* Washington: Smithsonian Institution Press.

Bunster, Ximena, Elsa Chaney and Ellan Young. 1989. *Sellers and Servants: Working women in Lima, Peru.* New York: Bergin and Garvey. And, apologies to those missed.

4 See Harper, Douglas. 1987. *Working Knowledge: Skill and community in a small shop.* Chicago: University of Chicago Press, pp. 75–91 for the full passage.

5 This is the point made by Richard Chalfen in his classic study of "home mode" photography—families made snapshots of a fairly standard list of events or scenes: marriages but not divorces; births but not deaths; holiday celebrations but not everyday dinners; graduations but not failures at school, and so forth. Furthermore, there were strong conventions that guided how these subjects were photographed. See: Chalfen, Richard. 1987. *Snapshot Versions of Life.* Bowling Green, Ohio: Bowling Green University Popular Press.

6 Colter Harper's research is summarized in his Ph.D. dissertation, The Crossroads of the World: A social and cultural history of jazz in Pittsburgh's Hill District, 1920–1970. University of Pittsburgh, 2011.

7 Payne, Carol. 2006. Lessons with Leah: Re-reading the photographic archive of nation in the National Film Board of Canada's Still Photographic Division. *Visual Studies* 21 (1): 4–23.

8 Edwards, Elizabeth. 2003. Talking Visual Histories: An introduction. In Peers, Laura and Alison K. Brown, eds. *Museums and Source Communities: A Routledge reader.* London: Routledge. Edwards is also editor and author of the definitive study of photography in the first decades of anthropology, 1992. *Anthropology and Photography 1860–1920.* London: Royal Anthropological Institute.

9 Ashevak, Mathewsie quoted in Payne, ibid., p. 16.

10 An overview of Harris's photography can be seen in:
Couch, Stanley and Deborah Willis. 2002. *One Shot Harris: The photographs of Charles "Teenie" Harris.* New York: Harry N. Abrams, Inc.

11 Van der Does, Patricia, Sonja Edelaar, Imke Gooskens, Margreet Liefting and Marije van Mierlo. 1992. Reading Images: A study of a Dutch neighborhood. *Visual Sociology* 7 (1): 4–67.

12 Ibid., p. 7.

13 Worth, Sol and John Adair. 1972. *Through Navajo Eyes.* Bloomington: Indiana University Press.

14 Van der Does et al., ibid., p. 10.

15 Suchar, Charles. 1992. Icons and Images of Gentrification: The changed material culture of an urban community. *Research in Urban Sociology* (2): 165–92.

16 Harper, Douglas. 2002. Talking About Pictures: A case for photo elicitation. *Visual Studies* 17 (1): 13–26.

17   Carlsson, Britta. 2001. Depicting Experiences. *Scandinavian Journal of Educational Research* 45 (2) June: 125–43.

18   Harper, Douglas and Patrizia Faccioli. 2009. *The Italian Way: Food and social life.* Chicago: University of Chicago Press.

19   Harper, Douglas. 1986. Meaning and Work: A study in photo elicitation. *Current Sociology* 34 (3): 24–45.

20   Wagner, Jon. 1978. Perceiving a planned community. In Wagner, Jon, ed., *Images of Information: Still photography in the social sciences.* Beverly Hills, CA: Sage Publishers, pp. 85–100.

21   *Visual Sociology* was renamed *Visual Studies* in 2002, with volume 17. In some cataloguing the earlier editions are referred to as *Visual Sociology*, and in others they are renamed *Visual Studies*. I refer to earlier issues by their original name.

22   Radley, Allan and Diane Taylor. 2003. Images of Recovery: A photo-elicitation study on the hospital ward. *Qualitative Health Research* 13 (1): 77–99. The authors seek to understand surgery and recovery in the context of Walter Benjamin's concept of mimesis.

23   Epstein, Iris, Bonnie Stevens, Patricia McKeever and Sylvain Baruchel. 2006. Photo Elicitation Interview (PEI): Using photos to elicit children's perspectives. *International Journal of Qualitative Methods* 5 (3).

24   Oliffe, L. John and Joann L. Bottorff. 2007. Further than the Eye Can See? Photo Elicitation and Research With Men. *Qualitative Health Research* 17 (6): 850–58.

25   The following are reviews of the use of photography in health research:
Riley, Robin and Elizabeth Manias. 2004. The Uses of Photography in Clinical Nursing Practice and Research: A literature review. *Journal of Advanced Nursing* 48 (4) November: 397–405.
Hurworth, Rosalind, Eileen Clark, Jenepher Martin and Steven Thomsen. 2005. The Use of Photo Interviewing: Three examples from health evaluation and research. *Evaluation Journal of Australia* 4 (1) March/April: 52–62.
Harrison, Barbara. 2002. Seeing Health and Illness Worlds—Using Visual Methodologies in a Sociology of Health and Illness: A methodological review. *Sociology of Health and Illness* 24 (6) October: 856–72.

26   Faccioli, Patrizia and Nicoletta Zuccheri. 1998. The Double Vision of Alcohol. *Visual Sociology* 13 (2): 75–90.

27   Frohmann, Lisa. 2005. The Framing Safety Project. *Violence Against Women* 11 (11): 1396–1419.

28   Frith, Hannah and Diana Harcourt. 2007. Using Photographs to Capture Women's Experiences of Chemotherapy: Reflecting on the method. *Qualitative Health Research* 17 (10): 1340–50.

29   Fleury, Julie, Colleen Keller and Adriana Perez. 2009. Exploring Resources for Physical Activity in Hispanic Women Using Photo Elicitation. *Qualitative Health Research* 19 (5): 677–86.

30   Dyches, Tina Taylor, Elizabeth Cichella, Susanne Frost Olsen and Barbara Mandleco. 2004. Snapshots of Life: Perspectives of school-aged individuals with developmental disabilities. *Research and Practice for Persons with Severe Disabilities* 29 (3): 172–82.

31   Cross, Katherine, Allison Kabel and Cathy Lysack. 2006. Images of Self and spinal cord injury: Exploring drawing as a visual method in disability research. *Visual Studies* 21 (2): 183–93.

32   Barrett, Deborah. 2004. Photo-documenting the Needle Exchange: Methods and ethics. *Visual Studies* 19 (2) October: 145–49.

33   Smith, Zoe C. and Anne-Marie Woodward. 1999. Photo-Elicitation Method Gives Voice and Reactions of Subjects. *Journalism and Mass Communication Educator* 53 (4): 31–41.

34   Johnson, Cassandra, Joseph Sharkey, Alex McIntosh and Wesley Dean. 2010. "I'm the Momma": Using photo-elicitation to understand matrilineal influence on family food choice. *BMC Women's Health* 10 (21) published online: http://www.biomedcentral.com/1472-6874/10/21/ (accessed February 2010).

35   Barnidge, Ellen, Elizabeth Baker, Freda Motton, Frank Rose and Teresa Fitzgerald. 2010. A Participatory Method to Identify Root Determinants of Health: The heart of the matter. *Progress in Community Health Partnerships: Research, Education and Action* 4 (1): 55–63.

36   Twine, France Winddance. 2006. Visual Ethnography and Racial Theory: Family photographs as archives of interracial intimacies. *Ethnic and Racial Studies* 29 (3) May: 487–511.

37   Harper, Douglas and Patrizia Faccioli. 2000. "Small, Silly Insults," Mutual Seduction and Misogyny: The interpretation of Italian advertising signs. *Visual Sociology* 15 (1): 32–55.

38   Steiger, Ricabeth. 1995. First Children and Family Dynamics. *Visual Sociology* 10 (1 & 2): 28–49.

39   Stiebling, Megan T. 1999. Practicing Gender in Youth Sports. *Visual Sociology* 14 (1): 127–44.

40   Payne, Carol. 2006. Lessons with Leah: Re-reading the photographic archive of nation in the National Film Board of Canada's Still Photographic Division. *Visual Studies* 21 (1): 4–23.

41   Hethorn, Janet and Susan Kaiser. Youth Style: Articulating cultural anxiety. *Visual Sociology* 14: 109–25.

42   Farough, Steven. 2006. Believing is Seeing: The matrix of vision and white masculinities. *Journal of Contemporary Ethnography* 35 (1) February: 51–83.

43   Vassenden, Anders and Mette Andersson. 2010. When an Image Becomes Sacred: Photo-elicitation with images of holy books. *Visual Studies* 25 (2): 149–161.

44   Thompson, Pat and Helen Gunter. 2006. Researching Bullying with Students: A lens on everyday life in an "innovative school." *International Journal of Inclusive Education* 12 (2): 185–200.

45   Rishbeth, Clare and Nissa Finney. 2005. Novelty and Nostalgia in Urban Greenspace: Refugee perspectives. *Tijdschrift voor Economische en Sociale Geografie* 97 (3): 281–95.

46   Bignante, Elisa. 2010. The Use of Photo-Elicitation in Field Research: Exploring Maasai representations and use of natural resources. *EchoGéo 11*. http://echogeo.revues.org/11622 (accessed February 2010).

47   Azzarito, Laura and Adriana Katzew. 2010. Performing Identities in Physical Education: (En)gendering fluid selves. *Research Quarterly for Exercise and Sport* 81 (1) March: 25–37.

48   Taylor, Edward W. 2002. Using Still Photography in Making Meaning of Adult Educators' Teaching Beliefs. *Studies in the Education of Adults* 34 (2) October: 123–39.

49   There are two reports from the same educational program in Manchester, UK, on studies in Africa and Indonesia:
      Kaplan, Ian, Ingrid Lewis and Paul Mumba. 2007. Picturing Global Education Inclusion? Looking and thinking across students' photographs from the UK, Zambia and Indonesia. *Journal of Research in Special Education Needs* 7 (1): 23–35.

Miles, Susie and Ian Kaplan. 2005. Using Images to Promote Reflection: An action research study in Zambia and Tanzania. *Journal of Research in Special Education Needs* 5 (2): 77–83.

50   Harrington, Charles F. and Ingrid E. Lindy. 1999–2000. The Use of Reflexive Photography in the Study of the Freshman Year Experience. *Journal of College Student Retention: Research, Theory, and Practice* 1 (1): 13–22.

51   Thomson, Pat and Helen Gunter. 2007. The Methodology of Students-as-Researchers: Valuing and using experience and expertise to develop methods. *Discourse: Studies in the Cultural Politics of Education* 28 (3) September: 327–42.

52   Cappello, Marva. 2005. Photo Interviews: Eliciting data through conversations with children. *Field Methods* 17 (2): 170–82.

53   Taylor, Edward W. 2003. Attending Graduate School in Adult Education and the Impact on Teaching Beliefs. *Journal of Transformative Education* 1 (4): 349–67.

54   Clark-Ibanez, Marisol. 2004. Framing the Social World With Photo-Elicitation Interviews. *American Behavioral Scientist* 47 (12): 1507–27.

55   See: van der Does, Patricia, Sonja Edelaar, Imke Gooskens, Margreet Liefting and Marije van Mierlo, ibid.
     Suchar, Charles S., 1988, ibid.
     Moore, Gemma, Ben Croxford, Mags Adams, Mohamed Refaee, Trevor Cox and Steve Sharples. 2008. The Photo-Survey Research Method: Capturing life in the city. *Visual Studies* 23 (1): 50–62.
     Kyle, Gerard and Garry Chick. 2007. The Social Construction of a Sense of Place. *Leisure Sciences* 29 (3) May: 209–25.

56   Schwartz, Dona. 1989. Visual Ethnography: Using photography in qualitative research. *Qualitative Sociology* 12 (2) June: 119–54.
     Stewart, Mitchell P., Derek Liebert and Kevin W. Larkin. 2003. Community identities as visions for landscape change. *Landscape and Urban Planning* 69 (2–3) July: 315–34.

57   Fitzjohn, Matthew. 2007. Viewing Places: GIS applications for examining the perception of space in the mountains of Sicily. *World Archaeology* 39 (1) March: 36–50.

58   Whitmore, Heather. 2001. Value that Marketing Cannot Manufacture: Cherished possessions as links to identity and wisdom. *Generations* 25 (3): 57–63.

59   Wust, Anna Alice. 2009. Zooming in on Home: Photo elicitation in urban planning methodology. Thesis, M.Sc in Urban Planning and Management, Aalborg University, Denmark.

60   Cannuscio, Carolyn C, Eve Weiss and David Asch. 2010. The Contribution of Urban Foodways to Health Disparities. *Journal of Urban Health* 87 (3): 381–93.

61   Kerstetter, Deborah and Kelly Bricker. 2009. Exploring Fijian's Sense of Place After Exposure to Tourism Development. *Journal of Sustainable Tourism* 17 (6): 691–708.

62   Rasmussen, Kim. 2004. Places for Children – Children's Places. *Childhood* 11 (2): 155–73.

63   Van Auken, Paul. 2010. Seeing, not Participating: Viewscape fetishism in American and Norwegian rural amenity areas. *Human Ecology* 38 (4): 521–37.

64   Rosenbaum, Mark S. 2005. The Symbolic Servicescape: Your kind is welcomed here. *Journal of Consumer Behavior* 4 (4) July: 257–67.

65   Stewart, William P. and Myron F. Floyd. 2006. Visualizing Leisure. *Journal of Leisure Research* 36 is an overview of the use of visual imagery in leisure research, and a review of the development of a model to predict visitor preferences for natural landscapes. See also:

MacKay, Kelly J. and Christine M. Couldwell. 2004. Using Visitor Employed Photography to Investigate Destination Image. *Journal of Travel Research* 42 (4): 390–96.

Cederholm, Erika Andersson. 2004. The Use of Photo-elicitation in Tourism Research – Framing the Backpacker Experience. *Scandinavian Journal of Hospitality and Tourism* 4 (3): 225–41.

66 Croghan, Rosalee, Christine Griffin, Janine Hunter and Ann Phoenix. 2008. Young People's Constructions of Self: Notes on the use and analysis of the photo-elicitation methods. *International Journal of Social Research Methodology* 11 (4): 345–56.

67 Gonzalez, Leticia, E. Newton Jackson and Robert M. Regoli. 2006. The Transmission of Racist Ideology in Sport: Using photo-elicitation to gauge success in professional baseball. *Journal of African American Studies* 10 (3) December: 1559–1646.

68 Mizen, Phil. 2005. A little "light work"? Children's images of their labor. *Visual Studies* 20 (2): 124–39.

69 Belin, Ruth. 2005. Photo-elicitation and the Agricultural Landscape: "Seeing" and "telling" about farming, community and place. *Visual Studies* 20 (1): 56–68.

70 Rieger, Jon. 2003. A Retrospective Visual Study of Social Change: The pulp-logging industry in an Upper Peninsula Michigan county. *Visual Studies* 18 (2): 157–78.

71 Warren, Samantha. 2005. Photography and Voice in Critical Qualitative Management Research. *Accounting, Auditing and Accountability Journal* 18 (6): 861–82.

72 Ketelle, Diane. 2010. The Ground They Walk On: Photography and narrative inquiry. *The Qualitative Report* 15 (3) May: 547–68.

73 Overviews and arguments for PE include:

Harper, Douglas. 2002. Talking About Pictures: A case for photo elicitation. *Visual Studies* 17 (1): 13–26.

Clark-Ibanez, Marisol. 2004. Framing the Social World With Photo-Elicitation Interviews. *American Behavioral Scientist* 47 (12): 1507–27.

Harper, Douglas. 1988. Visual Sociology: Expanding sociological vision. *The American Sociologist* 19 (1) March: 54–70.

Caulfield, Jon. 1996. Visual Sociology and Sociological Vision, Revisited. *The American Sociologist* 27 (3) September: 56–68.

Grady, John. 1996. The Scope of Visual Sociology. *Visual Studies* 11 (2): 10–24.

74 Crilly, Nathan, Alan F. Blackwell and P. John Clarkson. 2006. Graphic Elicitation: Using research diagrams as interview stimuli. *Qualitative Research* 6 (3): 341–66.

75 Samuels, Jeffrey. 2004. Breaking the Ethnographer's Frames. *American Behavioral Scientist* 47 (12): 1528–50.

76 Jenkings, K. Neil, Rachel Woodward and Trish Winter. 2008. The Emergent Production of Analysis in Photo Elicitation: Pictures of military identity. *Forum: Qualitative social research/Forum Qualitative Socialforschung* 9 (3) September: 30.

77 Robinson, David. 2002. Using Photographs to Elicit Narrative Accounts. In Horrocks, Christine, Kate Milnes, Brian Roberts and Dave Robinson, eds. *Narrative and Memory and Life Transitions.* Huddersfield: University of Huddersfield, pp. 179–87.

78 Power, Elaine. 2002. Exploring the Potential for Visual Methods in the Sociology of Food. *Journal for the Study of Food and Society* 6 (2): 9–20.

79 Carlsson, Britta. 2001. Depicting Experiences. *Scandinavian Journal of Educational Research* 45 (2) June: 125–43.

80 Woodward, Sophie. 2008. Digital Photography and Research Relationships. *Sociology* 42 (5): 857–72.

81   Van Auken, Paul, Svein Frisvoll and Susan Stewart. 2010. Visualising Community: Using participant-driven photo-elicitation for research and application. *Local Environment: The international journal of justice and sustainability* 15 (4): 373–88.

82   Stones, Michael and Marlee Bygate. 2009. Emotive Factors that Make Photographs Memorable. *Photography and Culture* 2 (2): 119–33.

83   Meo, Analia Inés. 2010. Picturing Students' Habitus: The advantages and limitations of photo-elicitation interviewing in a qualitative study in the city of Buenos Aires. *International Journal of Qualitative Methods* 9 (2), published online.

84   Lee, Raymond. 2004. Recording Technologies and the Interview in Sociology, 1920–2000. *Sociology* 38 (5): 869–89.

85   Smart, Carol. 2009. Shifting Horizons: Reflections on qualitative methods. *Feminist Theory* 10 (3): 295–308.

86   Spence, Jo. 1988. *Putting Myself in the Picture: A political, personal and photographic autobiography.* Seattle: Real Comet Press; and Richards, Eugene and Dorothea Lynch. 1986. *Exploding into Life.* New York: Aperture.

87   Chalfen's two books on the subject include
Chalfen, Richard. 1987. *Snapshot Versions of Life.* Bowling Green, Ohio: Bowling Green University Popular Press, which inaugurated the study of the home mode; and Chalfen, Richard. 1999. *Turning Leaves: The photograph collections of two Japanese American Families.* Albuquerque: University of New Mexico Press, which extended his analysis to the study of immigrants. In that family albums have given way to other forms of digital home mode, the field of study is now in a state of change.

88   Most notably Goldberg, Jim. 1985. *Rich and Poor.* New York: Random House.

Chapter 9: Photovoice

1   The book that describes this work was Worth, Sol and John Adair. 1972. *Through Navajo Eyes.* Indiana University Press (Second edition. 1997. University of New Mexico Press, revised by Richard Chalfen.)

2   Ewald, Wendy. 1985. *Portrait and Dreams: Photographs and stories by children of the Appalachians.* New York: Writers and Readers Publishing.

3   The LTP method is described in Ewald, Wendy, Katherine Hyde and Lisa Lord. 2011. *Teaching Literacy and Justice with Photography: A classroom guide.* New York: College Teacher's Press.

4   Maybe the only pre-Ewald example of this research style was anthropologist Ximena Bunster's 1978 article Talking Pictures: A study of proletarian mothers in Lima, Peru. *Studies in the Anthropology of Visual Communication* 5 (1): 37–55, which was later published as Bunster, Ximena, Elsa Chaney and Ellan Young. 1989. *Sellers and Servants: working women in Lima, Peru.* New York: Bergin & Garvey.

5   Wang, C. and M. Burris. 1997. Photovoice: Concept, methodology, and use for participatory needs assessment. *Health Education & Behavior* 24 (3): 369–87.

6   Carlson, Elizabeth, Joan Engrebretson and Robert Chamberlain. 2006. Photovoice as a Social Process of Critical Consciousness. *Qualitative Health Research* 16 (6): 836–852, p. 843.

7   Wang, C. and M. Burris. 1994. Empowerment through Photo Novella: Portraits of participation. *Health Education Quarterly* 24: 171.
Wang, C., M. Burris and Y.P. Xiang. 1996. Chinese Village Women as Visual Anthropologists: A participatory approach to reaching policymakers. *Social Science and Medicine* 42: 1391–1400.

Wang, C., W. Yi, Z. Tao and K. Carovano. 1998. Photovoice as a Participatory Health Promotion Strategy. *Health Promotion International* 13: 75–86.

8   Strack, Robert W., Cathleen Magill and Kara McDonagh. 2004. Engaging Youth through Photovoice. *Health Promotion Practice* 5 (1): 49–58.

9   Carlson, et al., ibid.

Kramer, Lelia, Pamela Schwartz, Allen Cheadle, J. Elaine Borton, Merrick Wright, Charlie Chase and Corina Lindley. 2010. Promoting Policy and Environmental Change Using Photovoice in the Kaiser Permanente Community Health Initiative. *Health Promotion Practice* 11 (3): 329–32.

10 Wilson, Nance, Stefan Dasho, Anna Martin, Nina Wallerstein, Caroline Wang and Meredith Minkler. 2007. Engaging Young Adolescents in Social Action Through Photovoice. *The Journal of Early Adolescence* 27 (2): 241–61.

11 Necheles, Jonathan, Emily Q. Chung, Jennifer Hawes-Dawson, Gery W. Ryan, La'Shield B. Williams, Heidi N. Holmes, Kenneth B. Wells, Mary E. Vaiana and Mark A. Schuster. 2007. The Teen Photovoice Project: A pilot study to promote health through advocacy. *Progress in Community Health Partnerships* 1 (3): 221–29.

12 Goodhart, Fern Walter, Joanne Hsu, Ji Baek, Adrienne Coleman, Francesca Maresca and Marilyn Miller. 2006. A View Through a Different Lens: Photovoice as a tool for student advocacy. *Journal of American College Health* 55 (1) July–August: 53–56.

13 Carnahan, Christi. 2004. Photovoice: Engaging children with autism and their teachers. *Teaching Exceptional Children* 39 (2): 44–50.

14 Wang, Caroline and Mary Ann Burris. 1997. Photovoice: Concept, methodology, and use for participatory needs assessment. *Health Education & Behavior* 24 (3): 369–87.

Wang, Caroline C. 1999. Photovoice: A participatory action research strategy applied to women's health. *Journal of Women's Health* 8 (2) March: 185–92.

Wang, Caroline. 2006. Youth Participation in Photovoice as a Strategy for Community Change. *Journal of Community Practice* 14 (1) September: 147–61.

Molloy, Jennifer. 2007. Photovoice as a Tool for Social Justice Workers. *Journal of Progressive Human Services* 18 (2) August: 39–55.

15 Ornelas, India, Jim Amell, Anh N. Tran, Michael Royster, Janelle Armstrong-Brown and Eugenia Eng. 2009. Understanding African American Men's Perceptions of Racism, Male Gender Socialization, and Social Capital Through Photovoice. *Qualitative Health Research* 19 (4): 552–65.

16 Downey, Laura H., Carol L. Ireson and F. Douglas Scutchfield. 2008. The Use of Photovoice as a Method of Facilitating Deliberation. *Health Promotion Practice Online*.

17 Schwartz, Lisa, Marjorie R. Sable, Anne Dannerbeck and James D. Campbell. 2007. Using Photovoice to Improve Family Planning Services for Immigrant Hispanics. *Journal of Health Care for the Poor and Underserved* 18 (4): 757–66.

18 Duffy, Lynne R. 2008. Hidden Heroines: Lone mothers assessing community health using Photovoice. *Health Promotion Practice Online*.

19 Fleming, John, Jane Mahoney, Elizabeth Carlson and Joan Engebretson. 2009. An Ethnographic Approach to Interpreting a Mental Illness Photovoice Exhibit. *Archives of Psychiatric Nursing* 23 (1): 16–24.

20 Vaughn, Lisa M., Janet R. Forbes and Britteny Howell. 2009. Enhancing Home Visitation Programs: Input from a participatory evaluation using photovoice. *Infants & Young Children* 22 (2): 132–45.

21   Hergenrather, Kenneth C., Scott D. Rhodes, Chris A. Cowan, Gerta Bardhoshi and Sara Pula. 2009. Photovoice as Community-Based Participatory Research: A qualitative review. *American Journal of Health Behavior* 33 (6): 686–98.

22   Baker, Tamara and Caroline C. Wang. 2006. Photovoice: Use of a participatory action research method to explore the chronic pain experience in older adults. *Qualitative Health Research* 16 (10): 1405–13.

23   Aubeeluck, Aimee and Heather Buchanan. 2006. Capturing the Huntington's Disease Spousal Carer Experience. *Dementia* 5 (1): 95–116.

24   Allen, Dawn and Thomas Hutchinson. 2009. Using PAR or Abusing Its Good Name? The Challenges and Surprises of Photovoice and Film in a Study of Chronic Illness. *International Journal of Qualitative Methods* 8 (2): 116–28.

25   Newman, Susan, Doug Maurer, Alex Jackson, Maria Saxon, Ruth Jones and Gene Reese. 2009. Gathering the Evidence: Photovoice as a tool for disability advocacy. *Progress in Community Health Partnerships* 3 (2): 139–44.

26   Lorenz, Laura. 2010. Discovering a New Identity after Brain Injury. *Sociology of Health and Illness* 32 (6): 862–79.

27   Drew, Sarah, Rony Duncan and Susan Sawyer. 2010. Visual Storytelling: A beneficial but challenging method for health research with young people. *Qualitative Health Research* 20 (12): 1677–88.

28   Lopez, Ellen D.S., Eugenia Eng, Elizabeth Randall-David and Naomi Robinson. 2005. Quality-of-Life Concerns of African American Breast Cancer Survivors Within Rural North Carolina: Blending the techniques of photovoice and grounded theory. *Qualitative Health Research* 15 (1): 99–115.

29   Brooks, Carolyn, Jennifer Poudrier and Roanne Thomas-MacLean. 2008. Creating Collaborative Visions with Aboriginal Women: A photovoice project. *Social Indicators Research Series* 34 (3): 193–211.

30   Epstein, Iris. 2007. The Perspectives and Responses of Children on the Physical and Social Environments of a Camp for Children with Cancer. Ph.D. dissertation, Nursing, University of Toronto, 2007.

31   Reynolds, Frances, Kee Hean Lim and Sarah Prior. 2008. Images of Resistance: A qualitative enquiry into the meanings of personal artwork for women living with cancer. *Creativity Research Journal* 20 (2): 211–20.

32   Hergenrather, Kenneth, Scott Rhodes and Glenn Clark. 2006. Windows to Work: Exploring employment-seeking behaviors of persons with HIV/AIDs through photovoice. *AIDs Education and Prevention* 18 (3): 243–58.

33   Mitchell, Claudia, Naydene de Lange, Relebohile Moletsane, Jean Stuart and Thabisile Buthelezi. 2005. Giving a face to HIV and AIDs: On the uses of photo-voice by teachers and community health care workers working with youth in rural South Africa. *Qualitative Research in Psychology* 2 (3): 257–70.
      Mitchell, Claudia, Jean Stuart, Relebohile Moletsane and Callistus Bheka Nkwanyana. 2006. Youth Participation Through Photo Voice in Rural Kwazulu-Natal. *McGill Journal of Education* 41 (3): 267–82.

34   Mamary, Edward, Jacqueline Mccright and Kevin Roe. 2007. Our Lives: An examination of sexual health issues using photovoice by non-gay identified African American men who have sex with men. *Culture, Health & Sexuality: An international journal for research, intervention and care* 9 (4): 359–70.

35 Schrader, S. M., E. N. Deering, D. A. Zahl and M. Wallace. 2011. Visually Storying Living with HIV: Bridging stressors and supports in accessing care. *Health Education Research*. Published online: http://her.oxfordjournals.org/content/early/2011/05/23/her.cyr023 (accessed April 2011).

36 Moletsane, Relebohile, Naydene de Lange, Claudia Mitchell, Jean Stuart, Thabisile Buthelezi and Myra Taylor. 2007. Photo-voice as a Tool for Analysis and Activism in Response to HIV and AIDs Stigmatization in a Rural KwaZulu-Natal School. *Journal of Child and Adolescent Mental Health* 19 (1): 19–28.

37 Erdner, Anette and Annabella Magnusson. 2010. Photography as a Method of Data Collection: Helping people with long-term mental illness convey their life world. *Perspectives in Psychiatric Care*. Published online: http://onlinelibrary.wiley.com/doi/10.1111/j.1744-6163.2010.00283.x/full (accessed April 2011).

38 O'Grady, Lynette. 2008. The World of Adolescence: Using photovoice to explore psychological sense of community and wellbeing in adolescence with and without an intellectual disability. Other degree thesis, Victoria University.

39 Booth, Tim and Wendy Booth. 2003. In the Frame: Photovoice and mothers with learning disabilities. *Disability and Society* 18 (4): 431–42.

40 Jurkowski, Janine M. 2007. Photovoice as Participatory Action Research Tool for Engaging People With Intellectual Disabilities in Research and Program Development. *Intellectual and Developmental Disabilities* 46 (1): 1–11.

41 Wang, Caroline C. and Jennifer L. Cash. 2000. Who Knows the Streets as Well as the Homeless? Promoting Personal and Community Action through Photovoice. *Health Promotion Practice* 1 (1): 81–89.

42 Wang, Caroline C. and Yanique A. Redwood-Jones. 2001. Photovoice Ethics: Perspectives from flint photovoice. *Health Education & Behavior* 28 (5): 560–72.

43 Wang, Caroline, Susan Morrel-Samuels, Peter M. Hutchison, Lee Bell and Robert M. Pestronk. 2004. Flint Photovoice: Community building among youths, adults, and policymakers. *American Journal of Public Health* 94 (6): 911–13.

44 Wang, C. and C.M. Killion. 2000. Linking African American Mothers Across Life Stage and Station through Photovoice. *Journal of Health Care for the Poor and Underserved* 11 (3) August: 310–25.

45 Streng, Matt, Scott Rhodes, Guadalupe Ayala, Eugenia Eng, Ramiro Arceo and Selena Phipps. 2004. Realidad Latina: Latino adolescents, their school, and a university use photovoice to examine and address the influence of immigration. *Journal of Interprofessional Care* 18 (4) November: 403–15.

46 Vollman, Ardene and Pertice Moffitt. 2004. Photovoice: Picturing the health of aboriginal women in a remote northern community. *Canadian Journal of Nursing Research* 36 (4): 189–201.

47 Wang, Caroline and Cheri Pies. 2004. Family, Maternal, and Child Health Through Photovoice. *Maternal and Child Health Journal* 8 (2): 95–102.

48 Mcintyre, Alice. 2003. Through the Eyes of Women: Photovoice and participatory research as tools for reimagining place. *Gender, Place and Culture* 10 (1): 47–66.

49 Castleden, Heather, Theresa Garvin and Huu-ay-aht First Nation. 2008. Modifying Photovoice for Community-based Participatory Indigenous Research. *Social Science & Medicine* 66 (6) March: 1393–1405.

50 Willson, Kay, Kathryn Green, Margaret Haworth-Brockman and Rachel Rapaport Beck. 2006. Looking Out: Prairie women use photovoice methods to fight poverty. *Canadian Woman Studies* 25 (3, 4).

51   Harper, Krista. 2009. Across the Bridge: Using photovoice to study environment and health in a Romani community. *The Sajó River Association for Environment and Community Development.*

52   Vaughn, Lisa M., Liliana Rojas-Guyler and Britteny Howell. 2008. Picturing Health: A photovoice pilot of Latina girls' perceptions of health. *Family and Community Health* 31 (4): 305–16.

53   Chio, Vanessa and Patricia M. Fandt. 2007. Photovoice in the Diversity Classroom: Engagement, voice, and the "eye/I" of the camera. *Journal of Management Education* 31 (4): 484–504.

54   Zenkov, Kristien and James Harmon. 2009. Picturing a Writing Process: Photovoice and teaching writing to urban youth. *Journal of Adolescent and Adult Literacy* 52 (7): 575–84.

55   Sands, Catherine, Krista Harper, Lee Ellen Reed and Maggie Shar. 2009. Snap Peas: A photovoice participatory evaluation of a school gardening program through the eyes of fifth graders. *Practicing Anthropology* 31 (4): 15–20.

56   Mitchell, Claudia, Naydene de Lange, Relebohile Moletsane, Jean Stuart and Thabisile Buthelezi. 2005. Giving a face to HIV and AIDs: On the uses of photo-voice by teachers and community health care workers working with youth in rural South Africa. *Qualitative Research in Psychology* 2 (3): 257–70.

57   Wagner, Jon. 1999. Beyond the Body in a Box: Visualizing contents of children's action. *Visual Sociology* 14: 143–60. Wagner does not use the term photovoice but his method anticipated many of its developments.

58   Wiggs, Carol, Anne Young, Beth Mastel-Smith and Peggy Mancuso. 2011. Rediscovering: The lived experience of women journeying toward aging. *Journal of Gerontological Nursing* 37 (1): 20–27.

59   Mosewich, Amber, Adrianne Vangool, Kent Kowalski and Tara McHugh. 2009. Exploring Women Track and Field Athletes' Meanings of Muscularity. *Journal of Applied Sport Psychology* 21 (1): 99–115.

60   Arendt, Jonathan. 2011. [In]Subordination: Inmate photography and narrative elicitation in a youth incarceration facility. *Cultural Studies-Critical Methodologies* May: 1–9. Published online: http://csc.sagepub.com/content/early/2011/05/19/1532708611409543.abstract (accessed April 2011).

61   Guerrero, Alba and Tessa Tinkler. 2010. Refugee and Displaced Youth Negotiating Imagined and Lived Identities in a Photography-Based Educational Project in the United States and Colombia. *Anthropology and Education Quarterly* 41 (1): 55–74.

62   Sherman, Kate, Kate Sherren, Joern Fischer, Jerome Pink, Jenny Stott, John Stein and Hwan-Jin Yoon. 2011. Australian Graziers Value Sparse Trees in Their Pastures: A viewshed analysis of photo-elicitation. *Society and Natural Resources: An international journal* 24 (4): 412–22.

63   Pierce, Janine and Jennifer McKay. 2008. On Community Capitals as We See Them through Photovoice: Cowell oyster industry in South Australia. *Australasian Journal of Environmental Management* 15 (3): 159–68.

64   Jangibeb-Abryqyagm, Gukke, 2010. Gone with the Wind?: Immigrant women and transnational everyday life in Finland. Ph.D. dissertation. University of Helsinki. https://www.doria.fi/handle/10024/59450 (accessed April 2011).

65   Burt, Steve, Ulf Johansson and Asa Thelander. 2007. Retail Image as Seen through Consumers' Eyes: Studying international retail image through consumer photographs of stores. *The International Review of Retail, Distribution and Consumer Research* 17 (5): 447–67.

66   Keller, Colleen, Julie Fleury, Adriana Perez, Barbara Ainsworth and Linda Vaughan. 2008. Using Visual Methods to Uncover Context. *Qualitative Health Research* 18 (3): 428–36.

67   Liebenberg, Linda. 2009. The Visual Image as Discussion Point: Increasing validity in boundary crossing research. *Qualitative Research* 9 (4): 441–67.

68   Cooper, Cheryl and Susan P. Yarbrough. 2010. Tell Me–Show Me: Using combined focus group and photovoice methods to gain understanding of health issues in rural Guatemala. *Qualitative Health Research* 20 (5): 644–53.

69   Guillemin, Marilys and Sarah Drew. 2010. Questions of Process in Participant-generated Visual Methodologies. *Visual Studies* 25 (2): 175–88.

70   Joanou, Jamie Patrice. 2009. The Bad and the Ugly: Ethical concerns in participatory photographic methods with children living and working on the streets of Lima, Peru. *Visual Studies* 24 (3): 214–23.

71   Martin, Noelle, Alicia Garcia and Beverly Leipert. 2010. Photovoice and its Potential Use in Nutritional and Dietetic Research. *Canadian Journal of Dietetic Practice and Research* 71 (2): 93–97.

72   Catalani, Caricia and Meridith Minkler. 2010. Photovoice: A review of the literature in health and public health. *Health Education and Behavior* 37 (3) June: 424–51.

73   Varga-Atkins, Tunde and Mark O'Brien. 2009. From Drawings to Diagrams: Maintaining researcher control during graphic elicitation in qualitative interviews. *International Journal of Research and Method in Education* 32 (1): 53–67.

74   Meyer, Franziska. 2011. Photography as a Participant Research Tool and a Means of Empowerment of Adolescents with Down Syndrome. Presented at the annual meetings of the IVSA, Vancouver, BC.

75   van Leeuwen, Theo and Carey Jewitt. 2002. *Handbook of Visual Analysis*. London: Sage.

76   Duffy, ibid., no page number; published online.

77   Baker and Wang, ibid., p. 1409.

78   Arendt, ibid., p. 6.

79   Liebenberg, ibid., p. 450.

80   Liebenberg, ibid., p. 460.

81   Cooper, ibid., p. 650

82   Varga-Atkins, ibid., pp. 53–67.

83   Crilly, N., A. Blackwell and P.J. Clarkson. 2006. Graphic Elicitation: Using research diagrams as interview stimuli. *Qualitative Research* 63: 341–66.

84   Mcintyre, ibid., p. 43.

85   van Leeuwen, Theo, ibid., p. 92.

86   Castleden, et al., ibid., p. 1401.

87   Wang, C., M. Burris and Y.P. Xiang. 1996. Chinese Village Women as Visual Anthropologists: A participatory approach to reaching policymakers. *Social Science and Medicine* 42 (10): 1392.

88   Smart, Carol. 2009. Shifting Horizons: Reflections on Qualitative Methods. *Feminist Theory* 10 (3): 295–308.

89   Wang, Caroline C. and Jennifer L. Cash. 2000. Who Knows the Streets as Well as the Homeless? Promoting Personal and Community Action through Photovoice. *Health Promotion Practice* 1 (1): 84.

Chapter 10: Teaching sociology visually

1   A version of this presentation was published as:
      Harper, Douglas. 2008. Images of Social Class. In Newman, David. *Sociology: Exploring the architecture of everyday life*. Thousand Oaks, CA: Sage, pp. 333–40.

2 The work of Davidson, Estrin, Norfleet and Owens has been previously cited.

3 Emmet, LeRoy. 1989. *Fruit Tramps: A family of migrant farmworkers*. Albuquerque: University of New Mexico Press.

4 Harper, Douglas. 2000. Reimagining Visual Methods: Galileo to neuromancer. In Denzin, Norman and Yvonna Lincoln, eds. *Handbook of Qualitative Research*, second edition. Thousand Oaks, CA: Sage, pp. 717–32.

5 *Unobtrusive Measures,* authored by Eugene Webb, Donald Campbell, Richard Schwartz and Lee Sechrest, was published in 1965 and republished in 2000 by Sage. This book introduced what amounts to an argument for a visual sociology, though it has seldom been seen as such. In the preface to the first edition, the authors note that they considered calling the book *The Bullfighter's Beard* because it was well known that the beards of bullfighters were longer on the day they fought in the ring, though there were several explanations for why that might be. In other words, the authors noted a visual phenomenon for which they offered several logics. The central argument of this book is to look at marks left by social life in order to read the meanings behind them. Visual evidence might be seen and marked on a code sheet, or photographed, or even drawn or painted.

6 For more detail on a version of this course that worked well, see:
Harper, Douglas. 1991. Visual Sociology at the University of Amsterdam: Notes and reflections. *Visual Sociology Review* 6 (1): 34–40.

7 Berger, John and Jean Mohr. 1982. *Another Way of Telling*. New York, Pantheon.

8 These include their book *A Seventh Man: Migrant Workers in Europe*. New York: Viking. 1975, which was one of the first visual books to explore a societal-level issue; an extraordinary beginning to visual sociology and a book that spoke well beyond the confines of sociology (it won the Booker Prize, among others). Their first book *A Fortunate Man: The Story of a Country Doctor*. New York: Holt, Rinehart and Winston. 1967, is a quiet and complex celebration of a doctor who serves the northern rural people of the UK.

9 Berger, 1982, ibid., p. 133.

10 Rexroth, Nancy. 1977. *Iowa*. New York: Light Impressions, p. 2.

11 Rexroth, ibid., p. 3.

12 Holdt, Jacob. 1985. *American Pictures*. Norhaven, Denmark: American Pictures Foundation.

13 Becker, Howard S. 1995. Visual Sociology, Documentary Photography, and Photojournalism: It's (almost) all a matter of context. *Visual Sociology* 10 (1–2): 5–14.

14 The film was the subject of a special issue of *Studies in the Anthropology of Visual Communication* in which several topics such as this were discussed. (6 (2), Summer 1980. Special issue on *Nanook of the North* (1922).

15 Wiseman's first film, *Titicut Follies* (1967), looked inside mental hospitals; his more than forty subsequent films have studied a vast array of issues. The films remain available and relevant to an array of sociology courses.

16 http://topdocumentaryfilms.com/ (accessed December 2010).

17 Michael Moore's most important documentaries are *Roger and Me* (1989), about the industrialization of Michigan; *Bowling for Columbine* (2002), which investigates guns and gun violence; *Fahrenheit 9/11* (2004) which studies the aftermath of 9/11 and the Bush family connections to Osama bin Laden; *Sicko* (2007), which critiques the US health

care system; and *Capitalism: A love story* (2009), which explores the financial meltdown. Several of his films won awards at Cannes and elsewhere, and their earnings are in the several hundreds of millions of dollars.

18   http://www.carnivalesquefilms.com/ (accessed December 2010).

19   Francis, Roy. 1972. Film Making in the Social Sciences. *College Student Journal* 6 (2): 51–54 is a remarkable essay about teaching filmmaking by a sociologist known for his statistical skills. Francis states: "The problem is not why those who first developed an empirical study of human life did not also pioneer film making. The problem is why today more of the currently involved [in empirical research] are not so involved." Francis suggests that the college campus "must incorporate film as part of its language system," and describes how he became proficient at filmmaking by interning at a TV station before turning to the super 8 camera in a NSF-funded course. It was cost, in the end, that mostly deterred Francis; they budgeted thirty minutes of film to each student, which produced an eight–ten minute film, but even in super 8 this became prohibitive. This little-read essay might have had an impact on sociology had it been published elsewhere, expanded and followed up. Alas, one more opportunity lost.

20   Barbash, Ilisa and Lucien Taylor. 1997. *Cross Cultural Filmmaking: A handbook for making documentary and ethnographic films and videos*. Berkeley: University of California Press is the best current text, and it works equally well for a researcher coming to the task from sociology as from anthropology.

21   Fails, Eleanor. 1988. Teaching Sociological Theory Through Video: The development of an experimental strategy. *Teaching Sociology* 16: 256–62.

22   Uncited references have been referenced in previous chapters.

23   Wang, Caroline C. 2000. The Future of Health Promotion: Talkin' technology blues. *Health Promotion Practice* 1 (1): 79.

24   Hergenrather, Kenneth, Scott Rhodes and Glenn Clark. 2006. Windows to Work: Exploring employment-seeking behaviors of persons with HIV/AIDs through photovoice. *AIDs Education and Prevention* 18 (3): 243–58.

25   Ewald, Wendy and Alexandra Lightfoot. 2001. *I Wanna Take me a Picture: Teaching photography and writing to children*. Center for Documentary Studies at Duke University: Lyndhurst Books. See also Ewald, Wendy, Katherine Hyde and Lisa Lord. 2011. *Teaching Literacy and Justice with Photography: A classroom guide*. New York: College Teacher's Press.

Chapter 11: Final words

1   And for the sociologist the cave paintings make a tantalizing case: there is visual sociology lurking, but we can't get to it. They are painted in inaccessible parts of caves; they recorded animals but not humans; and they are, to the modern eye, lyrical and beautiful. But we have no understanding, beyond that, of what role they had in their prehistoric settings. Lacking a time machine their sociological role remains unknowable.

Index

Cancian, Frank 17
Carlin, Andrew 112
Carlson, Elizabeth 191
Carnahan, Christi 191
Carnivalesque Films 233
Carter, Ovie 54–5
Cartier-Bresson, Henri 116
Castleden, Heather 203
Cederholm, Erika Andersson 184
Centre for Documentary Studies 37
Chagnon, Napoleon 145
Chalfen, Richard 148, 184, 188
Chan is Missing (film) 157
Chaplin, Charlie 235
Chaplin, Elizabeth 6, 133
Chau, Adam Yuet 128, 130
Chronicle of a Summer (film) 52
cinéma-vérité 232
city centers 86
Clark, Larry 34, 183
Clark-Ibanez, Marisol 186
Clergeau, Louis 37
coding 105, 178
Coles, Robert 21
collaborative methods in visual sociology
    155, 179–80, 237
Collier, John 8, 15, 17, 33, 56–7, 156–8,
    238
Collier, Michael 8, 15
Collins, Jane 105
community-based participatory research
    (CBPR) 192, 197
community health 192, 194
comparative method in sociology 107–10
connotative meanings 118, 130
consent forms 223
Cooper, Cheryl 200
Copeland, Alan 35
Corbis-Bettmann archive 103–4
criminology 134
Croghan, Rosalee 184
cultural studies 47, 115, 117, 132–3; use of
    photo elicitation in 182, 184–6; of
    work 182, 186–7, 193, 198–9
Cultural Studies Critical Methodologies 190
Curtis, Edward 5

Dallas 72
D'Aluisio, Faith 37
Damstraat, Amsterdam 214–15
Danforth, Loring M. 17
Davidson, Bruce 33, 208
DeMarie, Darlene 198
Devillers, Philippe 34
Diana camera 224
digital photography 9, 220
digital technologies 71, 141
Dillinger, John 28

discourse analysis 90, 98, 105–6
disposable cameras 204, 241
Divorce, Italian Style (film) 237
Documentary Educational Resources 232
documentary films 133, 159; and teaching
    of visual sociology 230–4
documentary photography 18–39, 47, 56,
    131, 203–4
La Dolce Vita (film) 237
drawings 151–2
Drew, Sarah 196
Duffy, Lynne 194
Duneier, Mitch 54–5, 98
Duquesne University 235
Durkheim, Émile 107, 150, 235
DVDs 232
Dyches, Tina Taylor 181
Dylan, Bob 36

Earhart, Amelia 28
Earle, Calvin 95
e-books 142, 149
educational research 182–3, 193, 197–8
Edwards, Elizabeth 11, 173
Emerson, P.H. 22–4, 27
Emmet, LeRoy 208
Emmison, Michael 68
empowerment 189–94, 202
Engels, Friedrich 88–90, 150
"environmental portraits" 65
Epstein, Iris 181
Ernie's Sawmill (film) 234
Estrin, Mary Lloyd 34, 208
ethical issues 242; *see also* institutional
    review boards
ethnography: autobiographic 134; visual 5,
    8–17, 22–3, 34–7, 39, 47, 51–5,
    145, 149, 168, 228
ethnomethodology (EM) 111–18; link with
    visual sociology 112–13, 118
ethnoscience 39
Evans, Walker 97
Ewald, Wendy 188–9, 201
Ewen, Michigan 92–4

Faccioli, Patrizia 6, 101, 120, 179, 184, 214
Fails, Eleanor 235
false consciousness 119
Family Portrait Sittings 52
family relationships 243
Farm Security Administration (FSA) 30–2,
    97, 209
farm systems 57–69
Farough, Steven 179, 185
fascism 27–8, 124–7, 130, 133
feature films: used in teaching of visual
    sociology 235–6; used as text
    236–7